Financial Liberalization

How Far, How Fast?

The goal of this volume is to bring a more broad-based empirical experience than has been customary to the theoretical debate on how financial systems should be managed. This is achieved not only with cross-country economic studies, but also with an account of carefully chosen and widely contrasting country cases, drawn from Europe, Latin America, Africa, East and South Asia, and the former Soviet Union. The widespread financial crises of recent years have illustrated all too dramatically the shortcomings of financial policy under liberalization. The complexity of the issues mocks any idea that a standard liberalization template will be universally effective. The evidence here described confirms that policy recommendations need to take careful account of country conditions. The volume is the outcome of a research project sponsored by the World Bank's Development Research Group.

Gerard Caprio is Director of the Financial Policy and Strategy Department in the World Bank's Financial Sector Operations Vice Presidency and Manager of Financial Sector Research in the World Bank's Development Research Group. Before joining the World Bank in 1988, he was Vice President and Head of Global Economics at J.P. Morgan, held economist positions at the Federal Reserve Board and the International Monetary Fund, and taught at George Washington University. Dr. Caprio has researched and written extensively on financial sector policy, financial reform, and monetary policy implementation, including coediting *Reforming Financial Systems: Historical Implications for Policy* and *Financial Reform: Theory and Experience* (both Cambridge University Press). His current research is on the links between financial sector regulation and supervision and the performance of financial institutions, as well as on financial crises.

Patrick Honohan is Lead Economist in the Development Research Group of the World Bank. Based in Dublin, he is also a Research Fellow of the Centre for Economic Policy Research, London. Dr. Honohan has been Economic Advisor to the Taoiseach (Irish Prime Minister), and he has spent several years as Professor at the Economic and Social Research Institute, Dublin, and at the Central Bank of Ireland. He has acted as a consultant to the European Commission, the International Monetary Fund, and the Bank for International Settlements. Dr. Honohan has published widely on macroeconomics and monetary and financial sector issues, including financial liberalization and exchange rates, and he is past President of the Irish Economic Association.

Joseph E. Stiglitz is Senior Fellow at the Brookings Institution in Washington, D.C., and is on leave as Professor of Economics from Stanford University. Dr. Stiglitz served as Senior Vice President for Development Economics and Chief Economist at the World Bank (1997–99) and served as Chairman of the U.S. Council of Economic Advisors (1995–97). Prior to holding the Council chair, he was a member of the Council and an active member of President Clinton's economic team since 1993. Dr. Stiglitz was previously a professor of economics at Princeton, Yale, and All Souls College, Oxford. In 1979, the American Economic Association awarded him its biennial John Bates Clark Award, given to the economist under 40 who has made the most significant contributions to economics. Dr. Stiglitz's work has also been recognized through his election as a Fellow of the National Academy of Sciences, the American Academy of Arts and Sciences, and the Econometric Society.

Financial Liberalization

How Far, How Fast?

Edited by

GERARD CAPRIO

The World Bank

PATRICK HONOHAN

The World Bank

JOSEPH E. STIGLITZ

The Brookings Institution and Stanford University

PUBLISHED BY THE PRESS SYNDICATE OF THE UNIVERSITY OF CAMBRIDGE
The Pitt Building, Trumpington Street, Cambridge, United Kingdom

CAMBRIDGE UNIVERSITY PRESS
The Edinburgh Building, Cambridge CB2 2RU, UK
40 West 20th Street, New York, NY 10011-4211, USA
10 Stamford Road, Oakleigh, VIC 3166, Australia
Ruiz de Alarcón 13, 28014 Madrid, Spain
Dock House, The Waterfront, Cape Town 8001, South Africa

http://www.cambridge.org

First published 2001

Printed in the United Kingdom at the University Press, Cambridge

Typeface Times New Roman 10/12 pt.   *System* QuarkXPress [BTS]

A catalog record for this book is available from the British Library.

Library of Congress Cataloging in Publication Data

Financial liberalization : how far, how fast? / edited by Gerard Caprio,
Patrick Honohan, Joseph E. Stiglitz.
p. cm.
Includes bibliographical references and index.
1. Finance. 2. Finance – Management. 3. Financial crises. 4. Monetary policy.
I. Caprio, Gerard. II. Honohan, Patrick. III. Stiglitz, Joseph E.
HG173 .F514 2001
332 – dc21   00-065151

ISBN   0 521 80369 1   hardback

Contents

Contributors

Irfan Aleem
The World Bank

Gerard Caprio
The World Bank

Yoon Je Cho
Sogang University

Fabrizio Coricelli
University of Siena, Centre for Economic Policy Research,
and Central European University

Aslı Demirgüç-Kunt
The World Bank

Enrica Detragiache
International Monetary Fund

James A. Hanson
The World Bank

Patrick Honohan
The World Bank and Centre for Economic Policy Research

Louis Kasekende
Bank of Uganda

Luis Landa
The World Bank

Fernando Montes-Negret
The World Bank

Joseph E. Stiglitz
The Brookings Institution and Stanford University

Charles Wyplosz
Graduate Institute of International Studies, Geneva, and Centre
for Economic Policy Research

Preface

The widespread financial crises of recent years have all too dramatically illustrated the shortcomings of financial policy under liberalization. The complexity of the issues mocks any idea that a standard liberalization template will be universally effective.

The goal of this volume is to bring a more broad-based empirical experience than has been customary to the theoretical debate on how financial systems should be managed. This is achieved, not only with cross-country econometrics, but also with an account of widely contrasting country cases. The evidence here described confirms that policy recommendations need to take careful account of country conditions.

The volume is the fruit of a research project sponsored by the World Bank's Development Economics Research Group.

Drafts of the chapters were discussed at a workshop at the Bank's headquarters in Washington D.C. The editors are grateful to participants in that workshop and especially to the discussants: Charles Calomiris, David C. Cole, Cevdet Denizer, Barry Johnston, Ed Kane, Don Mathieson, Huw Pill, Betty Slade, Paulo Vieira da Cunha, and John Williamson. A summary of their comments can be found at the Research Group's finance website: http://www.worldbank.org/research/interest/intrstweb.htm. Other readers who provided valuable comments, in addition to those noted in individual chapters, include Sri-Ram Aiyer, Gerard Byam, Lajos Bokros, Stijn Claessens, Jonathan Fiechter, Paul Murgatroyd, Alain Soulard, and Dimitri Vittas as well as Scott Parris and three anonymous referees of Cambridge University Press.

Thanks also to Agnes Yaptenco, whose secretarial and organizational assistance was invaluable, and to Léan Ní Chuilleanáin for editorial support.

ANALYTICS

1

Introduction and Overview: The Case for Liberalization and Some Drawbacks

Gerard Caprio, James A. Hanson, and Patrick Honohan

INTRODUCTION

Few lament the demise of financial repression. Its fate was sealed in most countries by a growing awareness of its costly distortions, together with the increasing ease with which below-market interest ceilings and other repressive measures could be bypassed.

Unfortunately, years of repression often left financial systems poorly prepared for a liberalized regime. Spectacular failures, especially in East Asia, have caused some to question the extent and speed of financial liberalization and the opening of the capital account. Could the process have been managed better, and what is the best policy structure to aim for now?

This volume provides a basis for examining these issues. Six case studies illustrate how contrasting initial conditions in liberalizing countries as well as the design and phasing of the liberalization and the effectiveness of supportive policies – especially in regulation and supervision – matter for the success of liberalization. One chapter is devoted to considering whether some countries need to employ more robust measures of financial restraint than is now conventional if they are to avoid further solvency crises. Two cross-country econometric studies document the impact of liberalization on the behavior of interest rates and on the incidence of banking crises.

This introductory chapter begins (Section 1) by describing the emergence of financial repression and the costs and distortions which it entailed. Then (Section 2) we describe the effects of liberalization, including its impact on credit rationing and the associated rents, on short-term volatility and on the incentives for corporate governance and intermediary solvency. Section 3 presents a brief chapter-by-chapter overview of the case studies, while Section 4 concludes.

Ppast as prologue / state ownership / list govt

1 FINANCIAL REPRESSION AND THE CASE
FOR LIBERALIZATION

Origins of Repression

Governments have long intervened in the financial sector to preserve financial stability and protect the public from unexpected losses, but also to limit concentrations of wealth and monopoly power, to generate fiscal resources, and to channel resources toward favored groups through the financial system rather than the more transparent instrument of public finances. Interest rate ceilings have existed – and been partially evaded – for centuries.[1] It is hard to find a country that has not had a state-owned financial institution or intervened in the sector.

Much of the twentieth century saw intensified financial repression. Governments attempted to fix interest rates well below market levels and to control the allocation of credit through directive or through ownership of the banks, especially in the years after World War II. More recently, however, a wave of financial liberalization has taken over. Most governments have relaxed or removed repressive financial controls, largely to avoid the costs discussed as follows.

The fad for financial repression was associated with the rise of populism, nationalism, and statism. Populist opinion thought of interest rate controls as a way of redistributing income. Private bank loans to large business houses or foreigners were standard populist or nationalist targets. A desire to avoid excessive concentrations of power in a few private hands, or to ensure that the domestic financial system was not controlled by foreigners who would be insensitive to long-term national goals, were familiar aspects of this type of politics. Social goals could, it was thought, be attained more easily if the activities of major financial institutions were not purely profit driven.[2] Populism also led to a slackening of debt collection, both from the state banks because of political pressures and from the legal framework as a whole.

---

[1] The discovery that interest prohibitions could be effectively bypassed through the use of forward foreign exchange contracts (bill of exchange) unleashed a great wave of financial innovation in the European Middle Ages and helps explain the historic tie between financial development and international trade (*cf.* de Roover, 1963).

[2] Lack of long-term credit was also an issue, in response to which many countries established public development finance institutions, often with multilateral assistance. With some exceptions, the experience with these institutions was poor. Generally financed either by directed credit, foreign borrowing, or – as in some oil exporting countries – the budget, many of these institutions went bankrupt, in some cases more than once. Factors in the bankruptcies were failure to collect debt service and dependence on unhedged offshore borrowing, which raised costs for either the institution or the borrowers when a devaluation occurred.

Statism may have been an even more significant factor in the increased financial repression. In midcentury, state intervention was widely regarded as a way to improve the allocation of resources and spur development. To fulfill an expanded role, the state needed more resources than could be mobilized by underdeveloped tax systems. The state also sought to expand its role in resource allocation outside the budget through interventions in the financial sector, as well as in the price system, investment decisions, and links to international markets.

Following these philosophies, the governments of many countries borrowed heavily, placed low interest ceilings on bank deposits and loans in order to reduce their borrowing costs, and directed bank credit to "priority sectors" such as agriculture, small-scale industry, and exports. The flow of resources to the budget was augmented by printing money and by imposing low-yielding reserve requirements (as much implicit taxation as tools of monetary control) on banks. Capital controls were instituted in order to curb movements of capital to countries with higher interest rates. Likewise, competition to the banking system was restricted in order to limit disintermediation.

The Costs of Repression

The economic performance of many countries deteriorated progressively under financial repression. Financial systems contracted or remained small and the efficiency of their lending (and collection) and of their operations was low, eventually leading to widespread bank insolvency. The declared distributional goals of the policies were not achieved, though the beneficiaries of the rents that were generated fostered a political constituency for their perpetuation. Growth and macroeconomic stability were impaired.

That overall development performance clearly suffered is confirmed by econometric analysis showing that countries with sharply negative real interest rates typically experienced much lower growth and allocative efficiency than those with low or positive real rates (*cf.* Caprio, Atiyas, and Hanson 1994; Levine 1998; Levine, Loayza, and Beck 1998).

Negative real interest rates predictably[3] resulted in severe disintermediation, capital flight, and a national dependence on foreign funding as domestic savers sought to preserve their capital abroad. While some repressing governments managed to keep the macroeconomy reasonably stable – albeit with shallow finance – others experienced a cyclical pattern of macroeconomic fluctuations associated with waves of intensified

---

[3] While economists initially provided little counterweight to the prevailing philosophies, by the 1970s McKinnon (1973) and Shaw (1973) had begun what became a widespread indictment of the costs of financial repression (*cf.* Fry 1995).

financial repression. Thus, emerging fiscal pressures led such governments to extract progressively more resources from the financial sector through an accelerating inflation tax and lower real interest rates, until the resulting exchange rate overvaluation and increased capital flight eventually triggered an external crisis. In extreme cases, hyperinflation reduced the ratio of financial assets (liquid liabilities) to Gross Domestic Product (GDP) to only about 4 percent in Bolivia and 7 percent in Argentina.[4]

Thus, despite being starved for loanable funds, repressed financial systems misallocated much of what they had, with credit often flowing to inefficient public enterprises and to favored (though often far-from-poor) private borrowers.

Indeed, use of below-market lending rates necessarily involves some nonmarket allocation mechanism for credit, which inevitably means that some of it goes to projects that otherwise would be unprofitable – and the low interest rate encourages the use of excessively capital-intensive techniques. At the same time, projects with higher returns are squeezed out, use self-finance, or forego efficient technology. Direction of credit, especially through state-owned banks, reduces the incentive for market-driven financial intermediaries to investigate projects and to select those most likely to have an adequate risk-adjusted return. It also reduces the motivation to recover delinquent loans and diverts official supervision from prudential considerations to verifying compliance with the credit allocation policy.[5]

The poor lending decisions and deterioration in repayment discipline came home to roost in the form of bank insolvency and large budgetary bailouts of depositors and foreign creditors.

Directed credit regimes often embodied a political dynamic that encouraged increased misallocation over time. The availability of large subsidies from eligibility for directed credit created incentives for wasteful rent-seeking behavior. The pressures for such directed credit grew as government deficits absorbed larger fractions of the available loanable funds, as "sticky" government-set rates deviated more from market interest rates and as the interest rates on remaining "free lending" inevitably increased. With credit from normal channels becoming scarcer and relatively more

---

[4] Brazil also experienced high inflation, but used indexation for much of the 1970s to maintain the real return on at least some financial assets.

[5] The operational efficiency of financial intermediaries and markets was also damaged. For example, a ceiling on deposit rates can trigger higher bank spreads which will suck excessive resources into the industry as banks employ costly nonprice means of attracting deposits. The potential profits also generate demand for bank licenses and a growth of potentially inefficient, unregulated near-bank finance. Furthermore, financial repression hinders the growth of long-term bond markets, especially when accompanied by macroeconomic instability.

expensive, would-be borrowers turned more and more to political channels thereby increasing the political pressures for nonmarket allocation
of credit.

Distributional goals were rarely helped by the financial repression
process. The wealthy and well-placed (including bank owners, management, and staff) often collected most of the rents that the ceilings created.
The ceilings also generated a potential for abuses and corruption.

Arguments for Restraint

Unfettered market-based financial intermediation does not always achieve
a socially efficient allocation of credit. Information asymmetries are pervasive inasmuch as users of funds inherently know more about their own
operations and their intended use of funds than do intermediaries (and
intermediaries know more than individual savers). Bankruptcy codes limit
bank shareholders' liability. Hence, intermediaries face both moral hazard
and adverse selection in allocating funds. As a result, they may ration
credit at less-than-market clearing prices to reduce their risks, creating a
potential case for policy action (Stiglitz 1994; Stiglitz and Weiss 1981).

Thus, while the traditional messages of demand and supply analysis
with full information remain relevant as a useful first approximation,
the full story of credit markets and their distortions cannot be assessed
without reference to information and moral hazard issues. Subtle but
important arguments suggest that well-designed government policies influencing credit allocation and risk taking may be helpful in some circumstances, a point to which we return.[6] Where problems of information and
moral hazard are especially severe – such as when bank owners have little
real capital at stake and no effective oversight – then the balance swings
in favor of significant financial restraint.

Even on the information front, market-based allocation does retain
some advantages. Although market forces do not elicit the fully optimum
amount of information discovery,[7] market-based credit allocation does

---

[6] So far as directed credit is concerned, an effective scheme would be characterized by small
size relative to total credit, small subsidies, broad base, leaving responsibility for selection
and monitoring to banks, and inclusion of a sunset provision, involving the phasing out
of the program, as it is difficult to create an argument for permanent subsidies of any activity or sector. For example, the Japanese policy based loans through the Japan Development Bank which satisfied most of these criteria, except the sunset provision, and the
program actually grew in size relative to total credit in the 1970s, after its utility likely had
passed (Vittas and Cho 1995).

[7] Individual intermediaries' and investors' benefits from information discovery will be less
than the system's benefits. Since the information, once discovered, could be shared freely,
from a systemic standpoint the amount of resources devoted to information gathering is
likely to be suboptimum.

provide more incentives for the lender to discover information about users of funds than do government-directed credit operations. This is particularly important since information is not static; bank credit in particular is often based on a continuing relationship with the borrower that calls for constant updating of information.

In sum, as explored in Chapter 2, information and other distortions highlight valid and important reasons for financial restraint, but the implied policy interventions do require careful design. Neither the motivation nor the mode of operation of such interventions should be the same as in the period of financial repression. In particular, cruder violations of the simple logic of supply and demand must still be avoided.

Evasion and Other Problems of Practical Implementation

Although, as mentioned, a regime of financial repression can have a self-sustaining political dynamic, its effectiveness tends to be undermined by the behavioral reaction of economic agents. Any hope that regulatees will remain passive in the face of a change in the rules is contradicted by experience time and again. The history of finance is dominated by the drive of private participants to create ever cheaper and more convenient substitutes for money and for bank loans not least because of the regulatory costs of banking. The more costly it is to comply with a regulation, the more likely it is to be evaded.

To be sure, some forms of regulation can be partially self-policing: Attempts by bankers to circumvent a floor on deposit interest rates by imposing minimum balance requirements or charges are likely to trigger vocal objections from the depositors (as, for example, in Rwanda during the 1980s). But, while evasion of ceilings imposed on lending rates could conceivably have the same effect, it is less likely, as it would seem dependent on the borrowers being able to procure alternative sources of credit, which (given imperfect information) may not be the case. Under-the-table payments to, or off-balance sheet contracts with, depositors make deposit interest ceilings even easier to evade, with little incentive for depositors to whistle blow (Chapter 5).

Although financial repression was not the only source of capital flight, the scale of such flight is indicative of how porous control regimes could be. By the 1980s, annual capital flight offset a sizable fraction of the annual official borrowings of many countries (Cuddington 1986; Dooley et al. 1986). Increasingly, in many high inflation countries, and not just the famous cases such as Argentina, Bolivia, and Russia in the 1990s, the U.S. dollar bill became a widely used parallel currency.

The problem of evasion of controls became progressively more severe. Four decades ago it was wholesale funds that were involved when the eurodollar market arose as a way of bypassing the U.S. Federal Reserve's Regulation Q ceiling on deposit interest rates. Now the costs of computing and communicating have fallen so far that regulatory avoidance, once the domain of money center banks, large corporations and the rich, is a middle-class pastime conducted from anywhere on the planet over cellular phones or the internet. To be effective, the regulator of today must have a lighter touch than those of earlier times when evasion was more costly.

Thus, sooner or later, market pressures induce governments to abandon onerous repression in the form of binding interest rate controls because the controls become either ineffective (bypassed) or too costly in terms of side effects. So, the real issue is not so much whether to liberalize, but whether governments will be ready for the liberalization that is forced on them, and what regulatory regime they should use to reduce financial instability.

2 CONSEQUENCES OF LIBERALIZATION

Triggers and Form

The relaxation of controls on the financial sector during the past quarter century has not proceeded in a vacuum; it has been accompanied both by a more general liberalization of the domestic economy and by an opening-up toward the outside world (Williamson and Mahar 1998). Interest rate liberalization, like other liberalization (Rodrik 1996), is seldom accomplished without the stimulus or trigger of a crisis.[8] For example, from the case studies examined in this book, it was after the crisis of 1991–92 that India began gradually to liberalize interest rates, as part of its general program of liberalization, and it was after oil revenues dropped after 1981 that Indonesia liberalized interest rates and reformed taxes (Chapter 9). The transition economies liberalized interest rates after their constitutional crises (Chapter 8). In Latin America in the mid-1980s, countries such as Ecuador, Mexico, and Uruguay liberalized interest rates to mobilize domestic resources after the debt crisis led to inflation, exploding fiscal deficits, and a cutoff of external finance (Chapter 7). In other countries, the "crisis" was the dawning realization that government intervention had

---

[8] One counterexample is Colombia in the early 1970s, where a housing finance system using indexation was created to stimulate development, as part of the Plan of the Four Strategies (Sandilands 1980). The high nominal interest rates paid by the system created pressures to raise bank deposit rates. Similarly, in Japan in the 1970s the government was able to place small amounts of debt at interest rates somewhat below market levels. However, when deficits grew as a result of higher oil prices, the banks rebelled at the larger tax and, along with foreign forces, successfully pressed for deregulation, perhaps sowing the seeds for the subsequent bubble economy. Other reform episodes are reviewed in Johnston and Sundararajan (1999).

led to grossly misallocated credit and stagnant or negative per capita GDP growth (Chapter 10).[9]

The typically turbulent initial environment and complex mix of financial and nonfinancial policy reforms that characterize the liberalization episodes combine to make it exceedingly difficult to arrive at an empirical estimate of the net economic welfare gains from financial liberalization. The hoped-for indirect responses in the form of increased financial depth were experienced in most cases, as documented in our country studies that follow. And while there was no systematic increase in overall saving (Bandiera et al. 2000), econometric studies suggest that there was an improved allocation of credit (Caprio, Atiyas, and Hanson 1994). What is clear, though, is that the process of financial liberalization itself had important effects for more than a transitory period, changing as it did the underlying conditions in which the financial sector operated. The key elements here were:

- elimination of interest rate and other price controls together with less administrative direction of credit by government agencies.[10] This meant not only a reduction in the implicit taxation of financial intermediation, and in the associated rents, but also to higher short-term volatility – at least in nominal interest rates;
- privatization of state-owned intermediaries, admission of new entrants into the financial services industry, reductions in line-of-business restrictions on financial intermediaries, and removal of legal protection for cartelized financial markets. This drastically altered the incentives for risk management and risk taking and for governance of financial intermediaries.

[9] The World Bank has actively supported financial liberalization in developing and transition economies. For reviews of its adjustment lending operations in support of such liberalization, see Gelb and Honohan (1991) and Cull (2001).

[10] Many otherwise liberalized economies still retain, as a measure of consumer protection, a fairly high overall ceiling on lending rates, to eliminate what are seen as "usurious" rates (the term was once synonymous with any interest, but gradually narrowed its meaning to the pejorative sense) imposed by monopolistic moneylenders on unfortunate or impecunious borrowers. These usury ceilings can still be of practical importance especially – though not only – where high inflation has left the legal rates out of synch with market realities. Although the modern purpose of usury laws is consumer protection, that they can in practice preclude viable and socially advantageous money-lending activities, especially among the poor, is much debated. In one environment, Aleem (1990) found that wary moneylenders built the lending relationship very slowly and were charging almost 80 percent per annum to their clients; in another, studied by Udry (1994), the existence of a stock of social capital in a tightly-knit community greatly reduced risk and interest charged.

Higher Interest Rates, Erosion of Rents, and Credit Rationing

Liberalization not only exposed poor existing portfolios, it also confronted existing credit recipients with higher costs of credit and reduced rents and altered the distribution of credit (*cf.* Agénor and Montiel 1996). Those who had secured finance under the former regime suffered from the higher, market-based price they now had to pay. The higher interest rates and loss of rent pushed some heavily indebted borrowers toward insolvency. Since the aggregate size of implicit interest rate subsidies was quite substantial even in lower inflation countries in India, this could be a significant consideration.

Although long-term borrowers would have been partly or temporarily insulated if their interest contract was a fixed one, those who had agreed to interest rates that floated with the general short-term market rate will have been hit immediately and perhaps heavily. Intermediaries could suffer under either contingency and often responded to borrowers' problems by rolling over interest as well as principal, a mechanism likely to lead to problems later but possible where supervision was weak. Of course, such rollovers depended on the intermediary being able to mobilize the corresponding resources.

Where intermediaries had funded a long-term fixed interest contract with short-term borrowing they will have immediately been squeezed. This problem was faced by many housing finance institutions, notably in Eastern Europe and Latin America (where the situation was ultimately resolved through a variety of quasifiscal devices).[11] But even if their lending had been at a floating rate, the lenders may not have been fully insulated from the rise in interest rates: Only part of the rate risk will have really been hedged, the remainder merely transformed into credit risk, as was evident in Korea and other East Asian countries during 1997.

The losers thus did include intermediaries, partly because their borrowers could not sustain the higher interest rates, and partly through loss of whatever benefit they had previously received from effective deposit rate ceilings. The net effect of liberalization on intermediary profitability varied a lot over time and between countries. A frequent experience, especially in industrial countries, was of higher apparent bank profitability in the early postliberalization years, followed eventually by a reversal as existing banks felt their way to a more aggressive stance, and as new entrants made their presence felt. Also, apparent profitability had often proved to be illusory as hidden loan losses mounted. This is well documented in the Uganda

---

[11] The same problem was, of course, the beginning of the slide of the U.S. savings and loan industry (*cf.* Kane 1989).

story (Chapter 10), where full liberalization resulted in a ballooning of quoted interest rate spreads, not yet substantially reversed. The complex evolution of Mexican interest rate spreads is documented in Chapter 7; these too remain high. As also shown by the Uganda case, higher quoted spreads do not necessarily translate into profits, but also reflect a less favorable risk-mix of the borrowers willing to pay such high borrowing rates, especially to the new entrants.

For governments that had to refinance heavy domestic borrowings at the new interest rates (or even to replace the implicit subsidies to favored borrowers with budgetary funds, as in Uganda), liberalization had an adverse impact on the budget deficit, with knock-on effects on recourse to additional taxation or borrowing, at home or abroad. This tended to increase macroeconomic fragility and uncertainty.

Nevertheless, liberalization also had the potential to impose market discipline on governments: In Europe, removal of (external) capital controls was associated with an improvement in the budget, though this was not true of domestic credit controls. Indeed, the removal of domestic credit controls worsened the budget – though not the primary deficit (Chapter 5).

On a continuing basis, the removal of interest ceilings not only shifted surplus from borrowers (including government) to lenders, but also resulted in some relaxation of rationing, so that borrowers previously crowded out of the market altogether have had a better chance to secure funds. In India it appears to have been the middle-sized firms that have stood to gain from better access to credit (Chapter 9). In Korea the middle-sized *chaebols* (conglomerates) benefited, and indeed lenders underestimated the risk which this second tier represented (Chapter 6). Increased access for these groups may prove to be highly cyclical.[12] This is especially so because of their difficulty in escaping from the remaining rationing induced by lenders' fears of adverse selection.

These effects are but one part of the wider changes in capital values that occur when structural reforms, including adjustment of real exchange rates and internal relative prices, are introduced. But the high leverage of financial intermediaries makes them unusually susceptible to unhedged interest rate changes. The initial disruption to financial and real activities from a sharp rise in real interest rates following liberalization was a costly feature of some liberalizations which might have been eased by a phased convergence of controlled interest rates toward market-clearing levels.

Volatility

Interest rate liberalization affects both the level and the dynamics of interest rates. The strength of these effects depends in part on the evolution of compe-

---

[12] As shown for the United States by Gertler and Gilchrist (1993).

tition in the financial system; this in turn depends not only on other regulatory changes[13] but is strongly influenced in turn by interest rate developments.

The process of financial liberalization was expected to increase the volatility of interest rates and asset prices, to have distributional consequences in the form of reduced or relocated rents, and to have increased competition in the financial services industry. In Chapter 3, Patrick Honohan examines the available data on money market and bank interest rates for evidence on these propositions, and shows that, as more and more countries liberalized, the level and dynamic behavior of developing country interest rates converged to industrial country norms. Liberalization did mean an increased short-term volatility in both real and nominal money market interest rates. Treasury bill rates and bank spreads were evidently the most repressed, and they showed the greatest increase as liberalization progressed: This shifted substantial rents from the public sector and from favored borrowers. While quoted bank spreads in industrial countries contracted again somewhat during the late 1990s, spreads in developing countries remained much higher, presumably reflecting both market power and the higher risks of lending in the developing world.

The liberalization process per se often contributed to macroeconomic instability with an initial surge in aggregate credit as financial institutions sought to gain market share whereas policy in the era of financial repression had often induced a cyclical macroeconomic. Consequential overheating had to be dampened down by monetary policy and/or resulted in inflation and nominal depreciation which also fed back onto nominal interest rates. The run up to the 1994 Mexican crisis provides a dramatic example.

Another potential destabilizing impact of liberalization, already mentioned above, was through the public finances in those cases where governments failed to respond to the higher interest rates by curbing deficits. When this occurred, the deficits were either monetized leading to an inflationary surge, or refinanced at ever higher interest rates in an unsustainable spiral crowding out the private borrowers and thereby feeding back onto economic growth and stability.

Some of the volatility of interest rates in the liberalized environment may represent "useless volatility," in the sense applied by Flood and Rose (1995) to exchange rates.[14] In countries where the controls were light and

---

[13] Indeed, there have been episodes of "phony" decontrol of interest rates where these other changes have been lacking. Phony decontrol can take a variety of forms, including the de facto assumption by dominant state-owned banks of the controlling role previously entrusted to the central bank.

[14] Their proposition is that fixed exchange rate regimes have not been associated with higher volatility in other variables. As such, movements in exchange rates have not acted as buffer-absorbing disturbances which would otherwise appear elsewhere in the economy in line with Samuelson's application of the le Chatelier principle.

imposed not far from market-clearing rates, the controlled rates did provide a relevant signal for the cost of funds.[15] Being stable, these controlled rates arguably anchored rate expectations and market discount rates, thereby potentially removing a source of volatility in stock market, property, and other asset prices. If so, policy could generate considerable benefits in terms of economic growth and stability, by eliminating both this "useless volatility" and the fear of such volatility contributing to the risk premium.

An independent source of uncertainty came to the fore in those transition countries where liberalization was associated with a general loss of governmental control and a consequential increase in the difficulty of enforcing contracts. As shown in Chapter 8, the combination of high nominal interest rates and low costs of default have driven much of those economies into barter.

Entry and Franchise Value: Impact on Intermediary Governance

Admission of new entrants, including foreign entrants, into the financial services industry and antitrust measures against collusive price-setting has been an important element in the liberalization of financial markets in industrial countries, and begins to be more widespread in the developing world (Claessens and Jansen 2000). However, the new entrants enter the market without the handicaps that existing banks often carry, including an overhang of nonperforming debts and costly labor contracts.[16]

Increased competition can yield straightforward efficiency gains and innovation in terms of improved range of services. These benefits are not negligible and they increase over time. But, as mentioned earlier, the new freedoms often led to an initial scramble to retain or gain market share, with banks seeking new business in unfamiliar territory whose risks they often underestimated (Honohan 1999). Even the threat of new entry could have so eroded the prospects of inefficient incumbents as to lead them into greater risk taking. Indeed, the increased macrovolatility that often accompanied liberalization implied new risks even for well-established lines of business, such as lending secured on property.

In practice, incumbents often responded to the threat of new entry with an efficiency drive and restructuring that made the task of the entrants much tougher than had been anticipated. But even if the new equilibrium saw the old players retaining much of their market share, it was now a contestable and low-margin equilibrium, without rents generated by the

---

[15] Though in repressed systems quoted rates may not have been representative of the effective (shadow) cost of funds.

[16] Overstaffing and high wages often reflect a sharing of the available rents between shareholders, management, and employees.

directed credit system. With a reduced franchise value, banks in particular now had little room for error and many succumbed to the perils of excessive risk taking, a syndrome perhaps best illustrated by the case of Mexico (Chapter 7).

In other cases, entrants opted for a less aggressive but very profitable high margin–low volume strategy, allowing high-cost incumbents, and those burdened by a nonperforming portfolio, to stay in business often with higher gross margins than before liberalization – a phenomenon well illustrated by the cases of Pakistan and Uganda (Chapter 10).

As well as having new competitors, financial intermediaries began to be allowed new scope for their activities. This included an increasing trend toward universal banking, to be applied not only to the large commercial banks, but also to formerly specialized intermediaries such as mortgage banks and savings banks. Although new freedoms brought new profit opportunities and could thereby contribute to franchise value, the breaking-down of barriers to competition between different institutions and across-the-board liberalization of restrictions on line-of-business also increased the intensity of competition for existing lines and in dimensions such as branching, often resulting in lower margins than had been anticipated.

From Liberalization to Crisis: an Inevitable Sequence?

While one form of crisis led many countries to liberalize, it has often been observed that the liberalizing countries have often encountered a more virulent form of crisis subsequently. This cycle can be explained partly by the way in which the liberalized environment laid bare the previous inefficiencies and failures in credit allocation, and partly by the poor handling of liberalization, in particular the failure to correct the weaknesses of the initial conditions in the banking sector and to develop quickly strong legal, regulatory, and supervisory frameworks.

For instance, banks have found that their existing loan portfolio was less sound in the new environment because their borrowers were no longer able to service debts, whether because of poor quality loans, higher interest costs, other parallel measures of economic liberalization that changed relative prices, or because government subsidies were cut off, or simply because implicit guarantees from government on these debts were no longer effective. In such cases (including India and Indonesia), it is more that liberalization revealed the worthlessness of the portfolio, rather than causing the losses (Honohan 2000).

Confirming this with an econometric analysis of the experience of over fifty countries during 1980–95, Asli Demirgüç-Kunt and Enrica Detragiache show in Chapter 4 that banking crises are more likely to occur in liberalized financial systems, but not where the institutional environment is strong (in terms of respect for the rule of law, a low level of corruption, and good contract enforcement).

But if liberalization does not inevitably lead to crisis, liberalized financial markets have often clearly worked to reduce the franchise value of a bank license nevertheless. That this could adversely affect bank performance has long been evident. Long before the emergence of a literature on efficiency wages – wage rates that may be set above marginal productivity to discourage shirking or quits – the desirability of having some way of bonding bank insiders to make sure they took proper care of depositors' money was well recognized in banking. Indeed, in the mid-nineteenth century it was common practice for senior bank staff to post a substantial bond which would be forfeited if they mismanaged funds (*cf.* Gibbons 1859). In more recent times, the link between lowered franchise value and increased risk of failure has been noted.[17]

Capital requirements, now commonly imposed at the – somewhat arbitrary – level of 8 percent of risk-weighted assets, represent one way of insisting on a degree of franchise value. Most banking regulators now recognize the need for early intervention to restrain bank management when capital falls below this threshold, but the difficulty of measuring the true value of capital and the fact that the incentives of insiders and other shareholders may diverge reduces the effectiveness of capital requirements, especially in an environment of diminished bank profitability (Caprio and Honohan 1999).

If financial liberalization is associated with intensified competition, banks may bid deposit rates up to the point where prudent lending practices are no longer profitable. Deposit insurance, explicit or implicit, can drive a wedge between the portfolio risk accepted by bank insiders and that perceived by depositors. This is generally thought to be an important aspect of the sorry story of the privatized Mexican banks, for example, and may also play a part in the emergence and rapid growth of a group of risk-taking Ugandan banks. Excessive risk taking is much more likely when banks are already of dubious solvency, making deregulation dangerous under such circumstances. This was seen not only in the case of the U.S. savings and loan industry, but in the case of Mexico where, it is now

---

[17] *Cf.* Caprio and Summers (1996) and Keeley (1990). It must be acknowledged, however, that protection against entry and restrictions on interest rate competition are far from being the only sources of bank franchise value in an ever-changing market. Charles Calomiris has pointed to the trend growth in the stock market value of U.S. banks in the past two decades as an illustration of the potential here. Indeed the comfortable life of the protected bank, or one governed by directed credit, can cause the other sources (appraisal skills, market intelligence, administrative efficiency) to atrophy.

thought that the fact that many of the newly privatized banks had little real capital at risk, increased risk taking there.

Deliberate risk taking and prior portfolio weaknesses are not the only sources of banking weakness in a liberalized environment. Outright managerial failure is often a significant factor (Honohan 2000). Many bankers underestimated risks in the new environment, especially as they expanded into new lines of business. Some hit problems despite believing that their bank had been in no danger of failing. The moral hazard of their behavior was often unconscious.

Sometimes the pitfalls here have been exacerbated by other aspects of poor sequencing, especially poorly considered partial decontrol, as exemplified by the case of Korea (Chapter 6). There, the order in which markets were decontrolled encouraged a spiraling of short-term claims, especially in the poorly supervised corporate paper market, and financed by short-term foreign borrowing. The latter exposed the system to the run of foreign creditors which brought down the system.

The liberalized period also usually begins with another handicap, namely with regulation, supervision, and legal systems unsuited to a market-based environment. Under financially repressed regimes and government allocation of credit, regulation of risks typically is judged unimportant and supervision is directed to enforcing directives aimed at policy goals other than that of ensuring prudence in risk taking. Legal systems typically favor debtors. Even where laws are changed as part of the deregulation, judges and courts do not become instantly skilled in their interpretation. In short, deficits in banking skills, supervisory agencies, and the legal infrastructure needed for efficient market decisions mean that liberalizations have encountered many problems (Chapter 4). But as this argument suggests, much of the blame for postreform crises lies with the prereform environment and in the pace and sequencing of financial reform. Interest rate deregulation itself is a reform that is quick, easy, and cheap to implement, while building skills, infrastructure, and incentives are time consuming, difficult, and expensive. Two decades of financial crises should suffice to convince most analysts that more of the latter is sorely needed.

In Chapter 2, Patrick Honohan and Joseph E. Stiglitz ask whether more is needed. They observe that financial liberalization brought with it a vogue for relying on an indirect approach to prudential regulation through monitoring bank capital to ensure that it remains adequate in relation to the risk being assumed. But the difficulty for regulators in a liberalized financial system of observing the true value of bank capital and the true risk of bank portfolios, means that ensuring safe and sound banking may require the imposition of more robust measures of restraint. These would be characterized by easy verification, and a presumption that banks complying with the rules will be at lower risk of failure.

Theoretical models illustrate how banking tends to respond *discontinuously* to policy, and that standard recommendations for fine-tuned regulatory policies are very model-dependent and *fragile*. These characteristics are reinforced when the normal assumption of far-sighted shareholder-controlled banks is superseded by more realistic characterizations with agency problems involving self-serving or myopic management. This supports the view that simpler, stronger, and more direct measures are not only needed to ensure that policy is not ineffective or counterproductive but also that they can offer a *quantum leap* in the degree of risk reduction.

But which rules should be tightened, and under what circumstances? By assessing the relative performance in different environments of five different types of robust regulatory restraint, bearing in mind possible side effects and implementation difficulties, Honohan and Stiglitz identify the various failure-inducing conditions for which each is likely to be effective, as well as the circumstances under which side effects are likely to be most severe. They show how different country circumstances will call for different robust measures, and that these may not be required to bite at all times.

Some of the rules considered, such as minimum accounting capital, are long-standing features of the regulator's toolkit. Others, such as interest rate ceilings, have had a long, and somewhat discredited, history as a tool of macroeconomic or development policy but may under some circumstances have a more constructive role as a prudential measure, especially if they are pitched to apply only intermittently. The policy maker needs to be able to draw on such a portfolio of robust regulatory instruments.

3 LIBERALIZATION IN PRACTICE – OVERVIEW OF THE CASES

The six case studies presented in Part 3 are chosen to illustrate the variety of liberalization experiences and to illustrate the importance of starting conditions. We begin with two studies of relatively advanced economies, Europe in the past half century and Korea in the 1990s. Then we examine liberalizations carried out in highly volatile environments – Mexico as an illustration of the high and volatile inflation that has been characteristic until recently of Latin America, and the transition economies with a special focus on Russia. Finally we turn to India, Indonesia, and Uganda, countries where continued pressures from government involvement through bank ownership and extensive directed credit have molded the financial landscape.

Liberalization in Advanced Economies (Chapters 5 and 6)

Financial liberalization started in the industrial countries. It often appeared to be a relatively smooth process, especially since gradualism was the order of the day, as interest rate distortions had been relatively mild and as financial markets were already sufficiently deep, and at least moderately competitive. Nevertheless, almost every country did experience some increase in the incidence of intermediary failure, and severe problems systemic in scale arose in Japan, Spain, the United States, and the Scandinavian countries. Most of these economies had the administrative ability and resources to cope with the failures with only moderate economic disruption (although the degree to which bank fragility has contributed to the prolonged Japanese recession of the 1990s is arguably considerable). The early liberalizations also occurred at a time when the volume and reaction speed of international capital movements was a fraction of what it is today. Perhaps the greater pace and more punishing environment can help explain the scale of collapse in the Korean economy during 1997–98.

The account of European financial liberalization provided by Charles Wyplosz in Chapter 5 starts much earlier in the aftermath of World War II. He shows intriguing parallels between institutional developments in Belgium, France, and Italy. In each case the banking system was marshalled in support of government spending or government-favored priority borrowers. Interest rates and other controls ensured a cheap flow of finance to the budget or to favored industries, regions, or firms, while also preserving the profitability of the banks. Credit to others was rationed (with credit ceilings – not always very effective – the preferred instrument of monetary control in the 1960s and 1970s), encouraging capital inflows that were indeed needed to support a balance of payments chronically in deficit. Relatively tight exchange controls, including the use of dual exchange rates, where capital receipts and payments were diverted away from the official exchange market, were employed to limit capital outflows. Nevertheless, the inflation fuelled by monetary expansion within this regime led to repeated devaluations.

Some modification and relaxation in these regimes proved necessary in the face of some leakage to nonbanks and abroad, but the main features of the regime were qualitatively in place into the 1980s. The exchange rate crisis of 1983 led to a political reassessment of the compatibility of the existing approach with exchange stability in Europe and with France's membership of the European Union. The result was a complete change of approach in France, and by the end of the decade most domestic and international financial controls had been removed. The story is echoed with some differences of detail in Belgium and Italy.

Regression analysis shows that financial repression significantly lowered the real interest rate in the sample of nine European countries over forty years. The effect is highly significant, estimated at 150–200 basis points. Thus, as it was intended to do, the repression created a rent, much of which was captured by the state. The effect on interest volatility is less clear: The choice of exchange rate regime seems to matter more than whether financial restraint is in operation – though these two policies may be jointly determined. While domestic financial controls were designed to reduce budgetary pressures, they could have encouraged a higher primary government deficit: In practice, the regression results show that this offsetting effect was not significant, and that domestic controls did lower the deficit. Governments with large primary deficits did tend to operate behind exchange controls: The direction of causality is not evident.

What of the impact on banks? Here Wyplosz notes an interesting effect. Despite a sharp fall in staff numbers in most countries, staff costs have not declined by much. He conjectures that rents have not been eliminated (heavy switching costs and brand loyalty remain strong), but have shifted from bank shareholders to bank staff. The end of financial repression saw banks move from simple, trouble-free, low, value-added activities to producing more sophisticated, high, value-added products for which they need to rely more heavily on skilled and professional staff, whose ability to capture rent is thereby enhanced.

The European experience suggests that domestic financial repression is more damaging than external capital controls. Indeed, as Wyplosz notes, all domestic financial repression entails external capital controls, while the converse is not necessarily true. As such, domestic repression adds two sources of distortions. The logic of financial repression is to direct saving toward public sector objectives, while capital controls might be required only for the correction of currency market failures. Domestic repression prevents the emergence of a competitive financial sector with the implication that capital controls cannot safely be lifted until this sector is strengthened, which may take a substantial amount of time following domestic financial liberalization. The European evidence does not provide a strong case for rapid liberalization of external capital flows.

Despite a relatively rapid rate of recovery, especially during 1999, the collapse of the Korean economy in 1997 was a severe blow. Indeed, the Korean crisis had global implications, though at the time, these were contained to a smaller scale than had appeared likely at the outset. For some, Korea's experience provided evidence that the financial liberalization on which Korea had embarked only a few years before had been a mistake, and that a continuation of the previous practice of financial repression would have been a sounder policy. Others tell the story differently, asserting that Korea's financial system had remained substantially repressed, and that a sham liberalization had not been to blame.

In Chapter 6, Yoon Je Cho shows that the true story is more subtle, though clear and strong lessons can be drawn. Korea did liberalize its financial markets substantially, but it did so in the wrong order, encouraging the development of a highly fragile financial structure both in terms of the financial instruments employed (too much reliance on short-term bills), in terms of the financial intermediaries which were unwittingly encouraged (lightly regulated trust subsidiaries of the banks, and other newly established near-bank financial intermediaries), and in terms of market infrastructure development (failure to develop the institutions of the long-term capital market).

By liberalizing short-term (but not long-term) foreign borrowing, the Korean authorities made it virtually inevitable that the larger and better-known banks and chaebols would assume heavy indebtedness in short-term foreign currency debt. Meanwhile, the second tier of large chaebols greatly increased their short-term indebtedness in the domestic financial markets (funded indirectly through foreign borrowing of the banks). The funds borrowed were being invested in overexpansion of productive capacity.

The phasing of interest rate liberalization too was misconceived, with bank deposit interest rates held well below competitive levels, driving resources off-balance sheet and away from the regulated banking sector altogether. Here Cho points out that moral suasion meant that formal deregulation did not result in completely free market determination of many interest rates.

The reasons for this pattern of deregulation include a mechanical adherence to the importance of monetary aggregates (which induced the authorities to retain controls on these, while liberalizing near-substitutes), the preoccupation with maintaining an orderly long-term capital market (which distracted them from paying attention to the emergence of a new and much more disorderly short-term corporate paper market), and the persistence of directed policy lending (which meant that interest rate spreads needed to be wide enough to allow for crosssubsidization, but at the cost of losing market share for the banks).

The quality of loan appraisal, bank regulation, and private credit rating was always in doubt; overoptimism and complacency reigned.

In the end, it was not the bursting of a property bubble that ended the Korean expansion, but the refusal of foreign creditors to roll over their loans; a refusal prompted by their increasing unease at the loss of competitiveness and heavy indebtedness of Korean corporate borrowers. Even if the main sources of the Korean crisis lay elsewhere, Cho argues that the mistaken sequencing of financial liberalization contributed to the speed and severity of the crisis both by exposing the system to roll-over risk, and by encouraging excessive indebtedness of firms.

Extreme and Turbulent Conditions (Chapters 7 and 8)

The literature on optimal sequencing and the preconditions of financial liberalization has generally agreed that macroeconomic stability should be in place before the liberalization is put into effect. But this is easier said than done, and there are many cases where the opposite has happened. For example, turbulent macroeconomic conditions aggravated by a dysfunctional financial system can create a window of opportunity conducive to political acceptance of financial liberalization, as has happened in several Latin American countries. Impatient for the benefits of reform, and believing that achievement of macroeconomic stability would be difficult or impossible, reformers have sometimes seized such opportunities. In some of the transition economies of the Former Soviet Union, the big bang of initial liberalization was partly planned, partly a collapse of control.

Chapters 7 and 8 look at cases of liberalization undertaken against a turbulent background.

Mexico's liberalization beginning in the late 1980s is representative of the experience of several other Latin American countries from the 1970s to the present in the move from repression to liberalization under conditions of macroeconomic volatility. Fiscal pressures and price- and wage-setting behavior that resulted in successive surges of high inflation have long characterized this region: Average inflation in the region fell below 50 percent only in 1995, and remains high in several key countries.

Four major turning points punctuate Mexico's rollercoaster story: 1982 (exchange rate crisis, bank nationalization, and high inflation), 1988–89 (interest liberalization and the end of high inflation), 1991–92 (bank privatization), and 1994 (Tequila crisis). Following the exchange rate crisis of 1982, prices almost doubled every year for the next six years. Although inflation was down to 20 percent by 1989, a recent history of high inflation was the backdrop when interest rates began to be liberalized as part of a wider package of reforms that proved to be successful in restraining inflation until the "Tequila" collapse at the end of 1994.

As explained by Luis Landa and Fernando Montes-Negret in Chapter 7, the other major strand of the Mexican story has been the nationalization, privatization, and renationalization of the banks. Misread at first as an unproblematic return to the pre-1982 regime, the bank privatization of 1992 was disastrously underprepared. The new owners, in effect, financed the excessive prices they paid by borrowing from the newly privatized banks themselves. Inexperience and self-dealing further weakened their financial position so that they were in no condition to absorb the 1994 shock.

But the main focus of Chapter 7 is on interest rate spreads and how they evolved during this turbulent time. Despite the difficulty of distinguishing between the effects of structural and macroeconomic changes, the findings are intriguing. Before the crisis of 1988, wholesale deposit or bill rates were usually not sufficient to compensate for exchange rate change, presumably reflecting, at least partially, effective exchange controls and the nationalization of banks. But after that crisis, excess returns on Mexican paper turned positive for five years, likely embodying a peso premium, which proved to be justified in the crisis of 1994–95. As is generally the case, the link between exchange rate uncertainty and interest rate levels is central.

Banks seem to have been able to charge wider interest spreads during episodes of high inflation. This is true both during interest spikes associated with the crises of 1988 and 1994, and on average. The pattern thus prevailed both when banks were nationalized and when they were in private ownership. Indeed, bank spreads were much higher on average during the years of nationalization, partly reflecting the banks' need to crosssubsidize directed credit programs, though it has to be borne in mind that these were also by far the years of highest inflation. A curious finding is that the use of commissions and charges associated with lending was correlated with interest rate spreads, and to a greater extent during nationalization. Looking at interest spreads alone considerably understates the true intermediation margin being applied in those years.

The intertwined strands of interest liberalization, disorderly ownership change and macroeconomic volatility make it impossible to confirm or deny for Mexico the conjecture that interest liberalization in a privately owned system may at first result in a widening of margins as incumbents exploit monopoly power, followed by a narrowing as competition deepens. But the latest postcrisis data suggests that intermediation spreads at Mexican banks – though still high – are about the same as they were before 1982.

Improvements in the legal and regulatory framework for banks lagged long behind the liberalization, whereas they should have preceded it. Though these microeconomic failures were likely decisive, the macroeconomic instability helped breed and deepen the banking crisis in Mexico – not the least of which through the high volatility of exchange rates and interest rates as well as capital flows and terms of trade shocks. There has been little financial deepening, and investors remain adverse to holding long-term financial assets.

If Latin American-style inflation and macroeconomic turbulence has posed severe problems for financial liberalization, these problems fade into insignificance when compared with the challenges faced by reformers in the transition economies. There, high and near-hyper inflation meant that the fixed interest rates at which long-established and new lines of credit from the central bank were granted to preferred enterprises were not only effectively grants rather than loans, but the financing requirements expanded the money base thereby perpetuating or exacerbating the problem. Here too, it was hard to decide what the new equilibrium exchange rates and real interest rates might be. The volatility of the real economy generated monetary and financial sector volatility, which in turn fed back onto the real economy, shrunk the financial sector, and inhibited growth.

In Chapter 8, Fabrizio Coricelli contrasts the comparative success achieved by Central and Eastern European (CEE) countries in this regard with the utter failure in Russia and some other Commonwealth of Independent States (CIS) countries.

The most striking feature of the financial landscape in all of these transition countries is the shallow penetration of the financial sector, monetary depth is well below what would be expected for the level of development, and the share of bank deposits in broad money is also very low. To be sure, inflation has been a contributory factor in this, but even with inflation slowing, financial depth has not returned in many of the CIS countries. Wide intermediation margins partly reflect inefficiency; they also are both partly caused by, and exacerbate, the heavy loan-loss experience of transition economy banks.

Coricelli documents major differences in the reform strategy. Somewhat paradoxically, it was the least well-prepared economies that exhibited unseemly haste in liberalizing at least some elements of the financial system (especially in liberalizing bank entry and the foreign exchanges). The more measured and cautious approach of the more advanced economies (in the Baltics and other parts of CEE) yielded better results in the end. Among specific contrasts are the adoption of deposit insurance in the CEE and the slower liberalization of the capital account.

But the failure of Russian finance goes deeper, despite the emergence of relatively sophisticated short-term money markets in which banks and large firms were participants. In an increasingly dichotomized Russian financial system there was also extensive use of nonmonetary payment mechanisms: barter, trade credit and bills (veksels), and accumulation of arrears. This could only happen in an environment where, through its own failure to pay its bills promptly, and by the imposition of arbitrary taxation, as well as by failing to put in place effective contract enforcement mechanisms, the government endorsed an environment of payments indiscipline, signaling to the public that the government was not committed to ensuring the protection of private financial rights.

Russia could still have avoided demonetization had it not been for the high opportunity cost of making cash payments, whether in the high nominal, low real, interest rates of the early 1990s, or the high real interest rates available on Treasury Bills in the late 1990s. Chapter 8 sketches a model of a system in which accumulation of arrears is an option which may be adopted by firms if the benefits exceed the costs. It is shown that such a model can have multiple equilibria. The Russian story can be interpreted as the emergence of the "bad" equilibrium – with low output, and possibly high inflation. Locally stable, it may be hard for an economy to escape from this bad equilibrium.

Liberal policies toward the unregulated entry of banks and the development of domestic debt markets, together with an opening of capital accounts, although not the cause of financial crises in countries like Russia or the Ukraine, sharply increased the vulnerability of these countries to crises. Furthermore, these policies contributed to create dichotomies in the system. On the one hand, rather sophisticated financial markets developed, with the participation of banks, foreign investment banks, and a few large firms; on the other hand, the bulk of the economy worked on a primitive system based on generalized default and widespread use of barter transactions.

The Russian experience, and its contrast with the performance of other transition economies, confirms that macroeconomic adjustment, especially in the fiscal area, together with further progress in developing an effective legal system, would help to improve the situation of several transition economies. But it also underlines that a necessary condition for developing well-functioning financial markets is the establishment of credible commitments on the part of the government to honor contracts.

More generally, financial liberalization against the backdrop of macroeconomic instability is a leap in the dark, and risks fanning the flames of that instability. If full liberalization can be postponed until macroeconomic imbalances and inflationary expectations have been reduced, so much the better. Meanwhile regulations can be rationalized to eliminate the worst distortions (and there should be no delay in strengthening the institutions that will be needed to support the liberalized regime).

Government Ownership and Control (Chapters 9 and 10)

Directed credit and direct government control over bank behavior through ownership have been key elements of the era of financial repression. The way in which these pressures have been removed or reduced has often determined the character and success of the liberalization. Our final two case studies focus in particular on these aspects which have dominated the scene in the countries studied.

Many other countries, even when not operating a socialist system, have relied heavily on directed credit, resulting in highly leveraged firms that had become heavily dependent on a continued reliable flow of financing at low interest rates. The removal of these financing assurances has revealed a structural financial weakness in the corporate sector and presented those economies too with a problem of transition. Indeed, like the transition economies, countries that relied on directed credit and heavy financial repression have inherited a skills deficit in both risk management and prudential supervision.

In Chapter 9, James A. Hanson points out that it was populist political ideology that led both India and Indonesia to repress interest rates and directly allocate much of available credit from the early 1970s, albeit in different ways. In Indonesia, tight bank-by-bank credit ceilings and repressed deposit rates resulted in stagnation of financial intermediation; in India an expansion of bank branches, and less severe interest rate repression allowed financial depth to increase. In both countries the public sector was a major beneficiary, along with agriculture. Priority nongovernment borrowers received a cross subsidy amounting to about 1 percent of GDP in India, but the indications are that little development gains resulted, though capital intensity of production increased. It was middle-size firms that found their access to credit most curtailed. In addition, the allocation mechanism succumbed to political interference and weakened the banking system, which was dominated by public banks. Regulators became embroiled in the minutiae of loan documentation without concern for the return on capital of public banks.

In both countries interest rate and financial liberalization formed part of wider economic reform programs. India liberalized interest rates gradually from 1992–98, along with reserve requirements and liquidity requirements, while priority sector lending was only partially reformed in that interest rates were increased and additional types of credit were made eligible. Regulation and supervision were tightened at the same time. Indonesia freed bank interest rates overnight in mid-1983, and about one-half of directed credit was made ineligible for renewal, although in practice the central bank continued to expand directed credit until 1990. There was little concern for prudential regulation or supervision, although, to be fair, Indonesia was not in that respect an outlier at the time.

Deposit mobilization grew rapidly in both countries following deregulation and credit allocation changed, but not always in the ways that fit the theory of financial liberalization. In Indonesia, despite the announcement that directed credit would be cut, low cost liquidity credits continued until 1989, maintaining the old beneficiaries of directed credit. However, the growth in bank credit and the growth of the private banks led to increased access to credit for a much wider group of borrowers who used capital more efficiently. In India, despite the drop in the liquidity requirement, banks continued to invest nearly the same percentage of their portfolio in public sector debt – the only drop in government liabilities held by the system was in the cash reserve requirement. However, nonbank financial corporations, stock market liberalization, and external resources provided funding for the private sector expansion and new types of credit.

Although growth picked up in both countries after interest liberalization, and there is some indication that investment productivity increased, Hanson argues that it is hard to separate the impact of financial liberalization here from the other elements of reform, especially in India. The relation between the financial liberalization process and financial distress seems fairly tenuous in both countries. The banking problems suffered by Indonesia in the early 1990s and especially in 1997 came between eight and fourteen years after interest liberalization (though the era of free banking ushered in by the later reforms of 1988 did result in a toleration of weak banking).

Poor economies have relied heavily on just a few, often state-owned, banks and on subsidized credit. Although this has meant that full liberalization has had the potential to result in very substantial shifts in the direction of credit and in the allocation of rents, change has often been slow. Liberalization has often been a partial and protracted process notably because of the substitution of implicit controls through shareholder direction of the state-owned banks. It is often found that elite groups captured the benefits of the old regime. The small number of financial firms has often meant that liberalization has not been accompanied in these countries by any great increase in competition. The resulting cartelized environment has meant that the benefit of the change is largely captured by financial sector insiders – a group often overlapping with the elite that benefited from the rents implicit in the old regime.

The case of Uganda, described in Chapter 10 by Irfan Aleem and Louis Kasekende, illustrates a phased liberalization behind capital controls. Though some of the gains in growth were easily won in the early years of stability after a devastating civil war, the sustained growth for a decade, accompanied by strong financial deepening, reflects the success of the policy stance, including the pattern of financial liberalization. In particular, a strong long-term impact of higher real interest rates on financial deepening is documented. Indeed, causality tests suggest that financial variables led growth, and not the reverse.

Although nominal interest rates fell sharply with the initial liberalization, real interest rates have tended to be higher than before. Furthermore, the completion of the interest rate liberalization program has been marked by a substantial widening of quoted spreads. Though the sector was opened to new entrants, competition in banking has been marked by a continued dominance of the traditional banks (state-owned and foreign-owned), albeit with their combined market share falling rapidly from well over 90 percent in 1988–92 to less than 70 percent in 1996–98. The main beneficiary of this shift in market shares is a group of aggressive banks that bid aggressively for deposits in the early years, but ran into serious loan recovery problems, despite (or because of) much higher spreads, and which had to be intervened and restructured. The continued presence of the state-owned banks, still carrying a heavy, though declining, deadweight of nonperforming loans, helped the more conservatively run banks to make substantial profits. This pattern of market segmentation is documented with interest rate and market share data for the different classes of bank. Analysis of the profit-and-loss accounts of banks suggests that intermediation spreads widened after liberalization, even after adjusting for nonperforming loans. This fragile evolution with limited and problematic de facto competition and high spreads suggests that Uganda has yet to enjoy the full gains from liberalization.

Aleem and Kasekende's analysis of explicit and implicit subsidies going to a sample of state-owned enterprises indicates that overall these have successfully resisted the loss of subsidy that might have been expected from financial liberalization.

4   CONCLUDING REMARKS

Having a substantially liberalized financial system is clearly the only viable way forward for any country that wants to participate fully in the benefits of economic growth.

As it worked out in practice, financial liberalization was far from a smooth transition to an equilibrium, competitive interest rate. Indeed, the static shifts in rents from previously subsidized borrowers may often have been the least important element of the regime change – and have in some cases been partially substituted by explicit budgetary subsidies. Instead, especially where capital account was opened early, and especially where fiscal and other sources of macroeconomic instability were prominent, interest rate volatility contributed to banking fragility. In extreme cases of the Former Soviet Union (FSU) countries, liberalization unsupported by contract enforcement led to an implosion of the monetary economy itself. In most countries, interest rate spreads widened to levels that suggest a remaining lack of competition in practice, despite free entry. Indeed, banking authorities seemed often ill-equipped to apply necessary prudential restraints on entry, and to intervene to ensure exit of insolvent institutions or unsound management.

If we could turn the clock back, it would (of course) not be to restore repression, but to adopt a more measured and nuanced approach to liberalization. Eliminating the most severe interest rate distortions did not necessitate complete and immediate removal of interest rate controls, especially in the presence of insolvent or fragile banks. Removal of controls on foreign capital (especially as affecting short-term flows) could have been phased in late rather than early. Free entry should have been interpreted as qualified by adequate capitalization and personal and professional suitability of management. A longer lead-in would have allowed more thorough training and professional preparation of regulatory personnel, though their effectiveness might still have been limited by political interference.

There are still many countries who have not yet progressed very far down the road of financial liberalization. For them, these lessons of sequencing will be relevant.

For others, turning the clock back is not a practical option. They will have to push forward on the lengthy agenda of institutional strengthening now widely accepted as being the prerequisite of a successful liberalized financial sector. Meanwhile, they may be able to enhance the effectiveness of regulatory restraint by exploring some novel approaches to regulation.

REFERENCES

Agénor, P.-R. and P.J. Montiel. 1996. *Development Macroeconomics*. Princeton, NJ: Princeton University Press.

Aleem, I. 1990. "Imperfect Information, Screening and the Costs of Informal Lending: A Study of a Rural Credit Market in Pakistan." *World Bank Economic Review* 4(3):329–49.

Bandiera, O., G. Caprio, P. Honohan, and F. Schiantarelli. 2000. "Does Financial Reform Increase or Reduce Savings?" *Review of Economics and Statistics* 82(2):239–63.

Caprio, G., I. Atiyas, and J.A. Hanson. 1994. *Financial Reform: Theory and Experience*. New York, London: Cambridge University Press.

Caprio, G. and P. Honohan. 1999. "Restoring Banking Stability: Beyond Supervised Capital Requirements." *Journal of Economic Perspectives* 13(4):43–64.

Caprio, G. and L.H. Summers. 1996. "Financial Reform: Beyond Laissez Faire." In D. Papadimitriou (ed.), *Financing Prosperity into the 21ˢᵗ Century*, pp. 400–421. New York: Macmillan.

Claessens, S. and M. Jansen, eds. 2000. *The Internationalization of Financial Services – Issues and Lessons for Developing Countries*. Dordrecht: Kluwer.

Cuddington, J. 1986. "Capital Flight: Estimates, Issues, and Explanation." *Princeton Studies in International Finance* No. 58.

Cull, R. 2001. "Financial Reform: What Works and What Doesn't." *Economic Development and Cultural Change* 49.

de Roover, R. 1963. *The Rise and Decline of the Medici Bank*. New York: Cambridge University Press.

Dooley, M., W. Helkie, R. Tyron, and J. Underwood. 1986. "An Analysis of External Debt Positions of Eight Countries Through 1990." *Journal of Development Economics* 21(2):283–318.

Flood, R.P. and A.K. Rose. 1995. "Fixing Exchange Rates: A Virtual Quest for Fundamentals." *Journal of Monetary Economics* 36(1):3–37.

Fry, M. 1995. *Money, Interest, and Banking in Economic Development*. Baltimore, MD: The Johns Hopkins University Press.

Gelb, A. and P. Honohan. 1991. "Financial Sector Reforms in Adjustment Programs." In V. Thomas, A.J. Chhibber, M. Dailami, and J. de Melo (eds.), *Restructuring Economies in Distress*, pp. 76–100. London: Oxford University Press.

Gertler, M. and S. Gilchrist. 1993. "The Cyclical Behavior of Short-term Business
Lending: Implications for Financial Propagation Mechanisms." *European Economic Review* 37:623–31.

Gibbons, J.S. 1859. *The Banks of New York, Their Dealers, the Clearing House and
the Panic of 1857*. New York: Appleton.

Honohan, P. 1999. "A Model of Bank Contagion Through Lending." *International
Review of Economics and Finance* 8(2):147–63.

Honohan, P. 2000. "Banking System Failures in Developing and Transition
Countries: Diagnosis and Prediction." *Economic Notes* 29(1):83–109.

Johnston, R.B. and V. Sundararajan. 1999. *Sequencing Financial Sector Reforms*.
Washington DC: International Monetary Fund.

Kane, E.J. 1989. *The S&L Insurance Mess: How Did It Happen?* Washington, DC:
The Urban Institute Press.

Keeley M.C. 1990. "Deposit Insurance, Risk and Market Power." *American Economic Review* 80:1183–200.

Levine, R. 1998. "Financial Development and Economic Growth: Views and
Agenda." *Journal of Economic Literature* 35(2):688–726.

Levine, R., N. Loayza, and T. Beck. 2000. "Financial Intermediation and Growth:
Causality and Causes." *Journal of Monetary Economics* 46(1):31–77.

McKinnon, R. 1973. *Money and Capital in Economic Development*. Washington,
DC: The Brookings Institution.

Rodrik, D. 1996. "Understanding Economic Policy Reform." *Journal of Economic
Literature* 34(4):9–41.

Sandilands, R. 1980. *Monetary Correction, and Housing Finance in Colombia,
Brazil and Chile*. Westmead, England: Gower Publishing.

Shaw, E.S. 1973. *Financial Deepening in Economic Development*. New York: Oxford
University Press.

Stiglitz, J.E. 1994. "The Role of the State in Financial Markets." In M. Bruno
and B. Pleskovic (eds.), *Proceedings of the World Bank Annual Conference on
Development Economics, 1993*, pp. 19–52. Washington, DC: The World Bank.

Stiglitz, J.E. and A.A. Weiss. 1981. "Credit Rationing in Markets with Imperfect
Information." *American Economic Review* 71:393–410.

Udry, C. 1994. "Risk, Insurance and Default in a Rural Credit Market: An
Empirical Investigation in Northern Nigeria." *Review of Economic Studies*
61(3):495–526.

Vittas, D. and Y.J. Cho. 1995. "Credit Policies: Lessons from East Asia." *World
Bank Policy Research Working Paper 1458*.

Williamson, J. and M. Mahar. 1998. "A Survey of Financial Liberalization."
Princeton Essays in International Finance No. 211.

2

Robust Financial Restraint

Patrick Honohan and Joseph E. Stiglitz

INTRODUCTION

Few advocates of financial liberalization ever envisaged a complete dismantling of prudential regulation of financial intermediaries. Many of the banking regulations that were liberalized had been directed to economic or sectoral objectives other than prudence. Besides, many had become ineffective or dysfunctional, often outflanked by technological change or subverted by special interests. Furthermore, the old regime often masked endemic banking insolvency, notably where government had diverted banking resources for quasifiscal purposes. But, by mechanically limiting the scope of banking activities and by conveying valuable franchises, many of the old rules had incidentally served to reduce the incidence of crashes.

In response, international efforts have focused on codifying accounting rules and harmonized capital requirements, and there has been stepped-up supervision at the national level. But parallel financial innovation has complicated the traditional work of the regulator, and enforcement has, in practice, been weak. The fashionable response – a minimalist retreat into indirect prudential regulation relying largely on assessing intermediaries' risk control procedures and requiring only a moderate risk-adjusted minimum of accounting capital – seems dangerously complacent for developing countries. For example, it neglects just how imperfectly bank capital is measured and the fact that bank management may have an incentive to increase the measurement difficulties. It overrates the accuracy of the risk adjustments, potentially encouraging banks to increase their assumption of underpriced risk. Finally, it overemphasizes accounting measures of capital, neglecting the economically relevant aspects of franchise value.

By contrast, this chapter considers the economic case for a more robust approach to financial restraint. By robustness in policy we imply both the ability to cope with a variety of failure-inducing circumstances and behavior and a deliberate lack of subtlety in method. Both features are

31

desirable because of the need to deal with information and enforceability constraints, as well as agency problems at a number of levels and problems of time consistency. Not only are violations of robust policy rules easier to detect but sanctions can also be enforced more easily.

Policy that is too subtle neglects the possibility of achieving a discontinuous or quantum improvement in risk reduction. In addition, many proposed policies based on a fine tuning of incentives require the regulator to have a degree of information which is wholly unrealistic, especially in developing countries. Besides, such policy prescriptions are often based on what may be the wrong models of behavior. As such, they could, in practice, actually contribute to risk and thus be worse than ineffective.

The chapter is organized as follows: Section 1 highlights the various levels at which agency problems have contributed to financial failure in developing countries, and explains the goal of achieving a regime shift from failure proneness toward safety. Section 2 draws on the theoretical literature on bank regulation to show the potential of robust policies in achieving a quantum reduction in risk, as well as the danger of relying on overly subtle or fine-tuned policies. Section 3 discusses the relative strengths in practice of different types of robust policy measures and suggests a ranking of measures matched to country circumstances. Section 4 concludes.

1 USING ROBUST POLICY TO RESTORE SAFE BANKING

Characteristics of Bank Failure

Although each new crash comes as a surprise to some, the long history of financial fragility reveals a consistent pattern. Research on the sources of bank crashes in developing countries (Caprio and Klingebiel 1997; Honohan 2000) clearly points to a limited range of recurrent characteristics of banks that failed. Aside from those whose problems have derived more or less directly from obtrusive government intervention in the operations of the banks, and aside from those – fewer than might be supposed – whose failures are attributable primarily to bad luck, we see some characteristic weaknesses of bank management or decision making. Whether or not the failure is associated with a macroeconomic boom-and-bust cycle, one of three general elements is usually present. In brief these are deliberate gambling, overoptimism, or self-dealing.

If the regulatory regime is designed with a view to eliminating just one of these elements, the system may remain vulnerable to the others. In particular, measures designed to strengthen the incentives for risk avoidance will tend to be ineffective against incompetence and overconfidence, or indeed against looting.

Of course, the liberalization of recent years has had a dynamic which militated against effective regulation. To begin with, there was the changed incentive structure which was sure to lead to mistakes and a shakeout of previously protected institutions. The inexperience extended to regulators as well as bankers, and the regulatory agencies' job was often hampered by having their best agents poached by the private financial system. Enforcement has also been problematic against newly privatized banks often owned by politically powerful interests. But it would be naïve to suppose that the failures are just teething trouble. There are good reasons from agency and information theory to believe that the task of regulator will continue to be structurally more demanding than many have allowed (Stiglitz 1998).

Agency and Information Problems in Developing Countries Argue for Robust Policy

At the root of many problems is the familiar fact that in finance, to a more significant extent than in other fields, almost every participant is acting as an agent for others. Managers of banks act as agents of the shareholders, financial regulators act as agents of government and so on. Although depositors act as principals, they may believe themselves – and may actually be – insured from loss, thereby also creating a moral hazard. Policy design that ignores this agency structure is likely to miss its target. Regulations that are seen as incentive compatible may not be so if they compel the agent under the false assumption that the agent is a principal. For financial agency is very imperfectly monitored and the agents have much leeway to pursue their own private goals. Here we have a complex collection of interacting agency problems.

High Marginal Value of Information

The central agency relationship in the present context is between the regulator as principal and the bank as an agent whose behavior the regulator wishes to influence. But the information available to the regulator as principal is very imperfect.

For example, the true economic value of a loan portfolio and the risk of future losses are both especially difficult to assess in developing countries whose economies are volatile and undiversified. The lack of diversification means that risk pooling is less effective than in more stable and diversified economies, and that risk-reducing measures such as the taking of collateral are of more limited value because of the correlation of collateral value with loan value.[1] Information that does become available to

---

[1] Collateral is typically valued as if the item were to be sold in normal market conditions; in practice, a bank is faced with having collateral to sell just when all other lenders are in the same position and the market price is depressed.

some market participants is less likely to be shared because of the absence of institutions that can do so directly or indirectly.

At a general level, then, the marginal value of information is higher in developing countries, because of weaknesses in informational infrastructure and the higher level of exogenous risk. Regulatory strategies that require high quality information are thus to be avoided. (Furthermore, measures that stifle the private incentive to acquire information could be especially costly.)

At the same time, attempts to build self-selection into the regulatory design in order to circumvent information problems are complicated by uncertainty about the nature of the decision-making process and motivation of bank decisionmakers. Private domestically owned banks are a new or relatively new phenomenon in many parts of the world. The absence of a long track record makes it difficult to judge what model of bank behavior is most realistic. As we have seen from the history of failures, it is not only that the bank may be adopting a reckless strategy with a view to walking away from losses; the regulator must also provide for overoptimistic or incompetent bank decisionmakers, or indeed of self-dealing, looting, and fraud. It will be evident that the problem of regulatory design is greatly exacerbated when the regulator does not know which of recklessness, overoptimism, or fraud it is most likely to be dealing with.

Managerial Agency

Intertwined here is another agency problem, namely the fact that managers of financial intermediaries act as imperfectly monitored agents of shareholders. Institutional weaknesses in developing countries heightens the likelihood that banks may be managed to the benefit of managers rather than (as is customarily assumed) for shareholders. If shareholders' control is weak, this managerial autonomy greatly weakens, for example, the effectiveness of accounting capital requirements, the cornerstone of most modern bank regulation, in limiting bank risk taking. For example, managers whose tenure is unsure, or who have stock options, may benefit more from bank profits than they suffer from bank losses. Indeed, as we will see, unless backed-up by other regulatory measures, this managerial agency problem could make accounting capital requirements counterproductive, serving to increase risk taking to a socially destructive extent.

Or it may be that bank insiders intend to loot the bank, diverting as much of its total assets to their own use at the expense of depositors and other claimholders. Long-term profitability of the bank is of no concern to looters.

Corruption and Concentrations of Power

At a further level, the consideration that regulators can act as imperfect agents of government is behind the concern that giving the regulators too much discretion in regard to such matters as forbearance on accounting capital adequacy could simply be transmitted into special favors for well-connected bankers.[2] (Hence the introduction, first in the United States and being imitated elsewhere, of the requirement of mandatory "prompt corrective action.") More generally, the quality of governance may also be suspect in many economies. Agents who implement regulations may become corrupted. The concentrations of economic power which are characteristic of many developing countries likely contribute to such difficulties. One needs to be especially wary of exacerbating such problems through regulatory design.

Limited Credibility of Governments

As the final level of this pyramid of agency, the government too can be seen as an imperfect agent of the public good. That public good includes maintenance of a stable financial environment, as well as the protection of small depositors for whom it is impractical to monitor the soundness of banks.[3] In developing countries, the commitment and ability of government to implement stated policies is less certain than in most industrial countries. In bad times, a government may not be believed when it promises to protect certain depositors, making it helpless to reduce uncertainty. On the other hand, in good times, government promises on exchange rate and fiscal stability may be given unwarranted credence, leading to excessive risk taking. Attention must therefore be given to avoiding reliance on what will be seen as incredible policies.

Absent agency problems, and in the presence of excellent and low-cost information, the task of the regulator could be relatively simple. But these provisos are not satisfied in developing countries, and that must influence policy design. This is one important reason why one has to reach for robust policy instruments.

---

[2] It has also been suggested that the opposite risk can also be present: Sufficient legal protections must be in place to ensure that the liquidation of a failed bank is conducted in a proper manner maximizing the recovery for the benefit of the creditors of the remaining assets of the failed entities.

[3] The high social cost of the public funds which are used in rescuing depositors in developing countries implies that the government must monitor and regulate intermediaries to reduce the risk of costly failures. In general, we take the commonsense view that the prudential regulator has two main practical goals, which are interrelated, namely first, to limit these fiscal losses (whether arising from explicit or implicit insurance of depositors) and second, to limit the disruption and deadweight losses that result from disorderly bank failure. Both of these goals are substantially achieved in a safe-and-sound banking environment. Of course, isolated failures will never be wholly eliminated, nor would it be efficient to seek to do so, but an environment in which bankers have a greatly reduced risk tolerance does seem attainable.

Seeking a Quantum-leap from the Failure-prone to the Safe-and-sound

With so many banking failures in recent years, one might be forgiven for assuming that it is the normal state of bank management to be in reckless or foolhardy search of high-risk investment and lending opportunities on which to gamble the funds provided for depositors – that is, when it is not engaged in self-dealing and looting of the bank's assets. There are many examples of such behavior, and many theoretical models that rationalize it. It might seem to follow that financial crashes can be limited only by reliance on constant supervision of the portfolio and procedures of each bank, and on the imposition of detailed binding constraints on its conduct. Given the practical obstacles, this prospect is not an encouraging one.

But this ignores the fact that banks, large and small, can and have functioned profitably for decades without any evidence of undue risk taking and without going close to failure. Such banks have not been on the brink of disaster; thus, for example, the consideration that a depositor safety net may help underpin their sources of funding has not been part even of their contingency planning. Such banks are in business for the long haul. They function profitably without having to assume undue risks. Their loan portfolios are diversified and secured by independently valuable collateral; they know their customers and have reason to be confident of repayment. The investment of such banks in market portfolios is designed chiefly to hedge rather than assume risks. Safe-and-sound banking is conceivable. It is just not as common as it was.

Clearly, financial liberalization has played a part in the decline of safe-and-sound banking. But financial liberalization has itself been driven by forces stronger than ideology. Reestablishing the full panoply of controls of the 1950s would be impossible in view of the computing and communications revolution that make evasion so easy.

But the goal of restoring safe-and-sound banking as the norm rather than the exception is worth seeking. The distinction between a safe and a failure-prone banking system is better seen as a dichotomy than as a continuum. From this perspective, policy can aim to make a decisive shift in the incentives of bankers out of the failure-prone into the safe zone, without strangling the social contribution which banks can make to the financing of economic growth.

This dichotomous view is borne out by theoretical models. Indeed, as we will see, many models of bank behavior display discontinuities, whether at the level of the individual bank, or of the system as a whole, whereby small changes in exogenous factors can switch equilibrium behavior into a different regime in which the risk of failure is materially higher. The introduction of regulatory policy measures represent one type of exogenous change that needs to be taken into account.

Theoretical models also alert us to the fact that policy actions can have counterintuitive equilibrium effects. For example, several models predict that, under some circumstances, a small increase in capital adequacy requirements could actually increase the risk of bank failure. Although not a general rule, this finding does point to the risks of tinkering: Regulation that is fine tuned to a model that imperfectly captures the real world may miss its mark or at worst contribute to a crash.

To restore a regime of safe banking may thus require a more aggressive use of policy instruments than has recently been fashionable, especially in developing country financial systems, which may be less responsive and less capable of a degree of self-regulation.

Minimal regulation may not be enough to move the system into a zone of safe-and-sound banking. *Subtle* regulation based on a precise model of bank and financial system behavior could prove counterproductive if the model does not correspond to reality.

At the same time, banks do create value through their intermediation activity. Regulations that restrict their activities will result in losses of potential social value. When we have reached the safety zone, these trade-offs assume importance. In other words, we must seek to use only those measures that achieve the plateau of safety with the least side effects. Safety and soundness is not the only objective of financial policy!

The regulator attempting to avoid an institutional or systemic crash can be likened to a hillwalker in poorly mapped and foggy mountainous terrain. Although contouring at low elevations saves energy, it can lead one too close to the edge. Following sheep tracks may lower the risk of falling, as may the use of an ice ax and crampons. But with the chance of encountering precipitous cliffs or crevasses it is better to stay well away from the steep parts even if it means an exhausting climb to a high plateau.

Against this background, the goals and the main features of regulatory policy design need to be clear and simple. This allows market participants and the policy community alike to work within a clear regime of assignment of responsibilities. The purpose of each measure should be clearly understood within the overall policy design. Enforcement of and compliance with measures should, as far as possible, be easily verified. That means in practice that the regulations must apply to outcomes as well as to incentives, as purely incentive-based systems can miss their mark where so many actors are agents not principals. Of course incentive design can make a positive contribution, and indeed there have been some very promising initiatives designed to provide incentives for monitoring to a wider range of participants, including large depositors or holders of subordinated debt. The point here is that these may not be enough.

2 LEARNING FROM THEORETICAL MODELS

Observation of the behavior of banks in a liberalized environment has clearly exposed the inadequacy of first-generation models of bank regulation which took risk as exogenous, assumed that banks always invested in value-enhancing projects, and saw capital as an observable quantity. First generation models assumed that placing a floor on capital as measured would be sufficient to keep banks safe.

A second generation of models has introduced a bewildering array of agency problems associated with asymmetric information. Risk has come to be seen as a choice variable of the bank decisionmakers (Calomiris 1998). For example, even though a tier of shareholder capital can help provide a buffer against loan losses, requiring some minimum capital amount can sometimes even encourage the bank to choose riskier loans.

The bank in these models is pursuing goals other than the choice of value-increasing projects: Indeed, bank decisionmakers may not even be maximizing shareholder value. Because of the hard-to-measure risk that bank assets embody, the true value of bank assets and hence bank capital is increasingly seen as an opaque quantity, especially to regulators and shareholders. And the degree of opaqueness may also be a choice variable of the banks' managers.[4]

As the literature has fragmented into a multiplicity of specific models, each emphasizing one aspect of the complexity of incentive structures and behavior of banks and other financial intermediaries, apparently conflicting policy recommendations emerge, thereby weakening the impact of the literature on actual policy design. The recommendations differ as to what should be controlled[5] and how it should be controlled.[6]

In this section we review a selection of models that focus on different aspects of the regulatory problem. We have selected these particular models not only to display the variety of modelling approaches that are in play, but also because they illustrate rather well two key features that frequently emerge in models of bank regulation. First, we show how theory has undermined the view that moderate and carefully calibrated policy instruments would be sufficient. We also show how nonconvexities frequently arise in these models, leading to the conclusion that a discon-

---

[4] As shown, in a different context, by Edlin and Stiglitz (1995).

[5] The principal can propose incentives or constraints (nonlinear incentives) on the agent's output, inputs, or the processes employed by the agent. The verification costs typically increase as we move from outputs to inputs to processes, but so also do the benefits of the control.

[6] The distinction between an incentive scheme and a constraint (a form of nonlinear incentive) is relevant, as is the question of how to ensure that rules are effectively enforced.

tinuous quantum change in behavior or equilibrium can result from policy action.[7] These two keynotes: The *fragility* of earlier policy conclusions and the potential for *discontinuities* in policy response help underpin our advocacy of robust policies.[8]

Stopping Banks Bidding for Deposits to Gamble

The major focus of the theoretical literature has been on reducing the risk that is assumed by banks in pursuit of their managerial or shareholder goals. Since the wave of financial liberalization, the main policy instrument actually used in practice to reduce risk in most countries has been minimum capital adequacy. But this may be insufficient to achieve a low-risk outcome in an efficient manner.

This has been shown most clearly in a recent model (Hellman, Murdock, and Stiglitz 2000) in which banks bid for insured deposits in an imperfectly competitive deposit market, and decide whether to choose a risky or safe portfolio. The bankers are seen as maximizing expected future profits, recognizing that they will forgo the franchise value of staying in operation if the gamble fails. If the deposit market is too competitive, the continuing franchise is not worth much, and it is shown that the banks will, in an uncontrolled equilibrium, choose to gamble, even though the risky asset has lower expected value than the safe one.

In this model by construction all risky lending is socially bad, and so one seeks policies that can eliminate it.[9] A ceiling on deposit interest rates can increase the bank's franchise to the point where it prefers the safe asset.

The market equilibrium may involve a *discontinuous* response to policy here. Thus, starting from a safe equilibrium supported by a sufficiently high capital requirement, deposit interest rate control, even when imposed at the same level, allows the capital requirements to be lowered discretely without triggering risky lending even if deposits are insured. (This is because the interest rate ceiling prevents a lightly capitalized bank from trying to bid up the deposit rate with a view to gambling, thereby destabilizing the whole market – see Appendix 1.)

A corollary is that, if accumulating capital is socially costly, then control of deposit interest rates may dominate a policy of capital adequacy alone (a *fragility* result in the sense discussed above).

---

[7] Nonconvexities lead to corner solutions where small policy changes will be wholly ineffective, but robust policies can swing the equilibrium to another, preferred corner. This contrasts with the situation in a convex world where moderate policies yield moderate gains.

[8] That complex modern financial systems may respond to policy in hard-to-predict ways is the theme of Honohan and Vittas (1997).

[9] The bank's decision as between safe and risky cannot be directly observed by depositors, shareholders, or regulators.

If deposits are not insured, then the banks will not so easily be able to mobilize deposits for gambling. Hellman, Murdock, and Stiglitz show that, in the uninsured case, the gambling equilibrium may be displaced by a safe equilibrium in which each bank holds enough capital to convince depositors that it does not intend to gamble. However, this will not happen if the extra burden of holding this signaling capital is too great; in that event the gambling equilibrium will still prevail.

Once again a ceiling on what are now uninsured deposit rates can eliminate the gambling equilibrium, by preventing banks from paying more than can be afforded from a safe portfolio. Although capital requirements alone might equally eliminate the gambling equilibrium, introduction of interest ceilings can economize on capital, albeit now at the cost of shrinking the total volume of deposits mobilized and thereby losing some of the (depositors') consumer surplus.[10]

Reducing Banks' Appetite for Risk in Lending Decisions

Imperfect Competition in the Market for Risky Loans

The Hellman, Murdock, and Stiglitz model previously discussed is focused on strategic behavior in the market for deposits, with banks behaving as pricetakers in the market for loans.[11] But the characteristics we have identified can also arise when the market power of banks arises on the lending side.

Suppose then that banks are pricetakers in the deposit market (and thus implicitly that the deposits are insured, explicitly or implicitly). A model of capital and risky lending in such an environment has been proposed by Milne and Whalley (1999). In their model, banks can choose the riskiness of their loan portfolio, making capital endogenous over time. The bank risks losing the franchise value of future profits if it happens to be inspected when its accounting capital is below the regulatory threshold. As a result, the bank is virtually risk neutral when its capital is comfortably high, becomes more risk averse as its capital declines toward the regulatory threshold, but switches discontinuously to risk preference when capital is so low that closure is inevitable.[12]

---

[10] Early formal models of banking implied that deposit-interest ceilings would have no impact on bank lending behavior (Klein 1971; Monti 1972). That was because they assumed that banks would have certain access to money-market liquidity; the introduction of liquidity risk has the effect of linking deposit and lending behavior (Prisman, Slovin, and Sushka 1986; Freixas and Rochet 1997).

[11] Indeed, in this model an interest ceiling on lending, pitched at the risk-free return, would also ensure prudence without any capital requirements, and would yield a higher deposit rate, at the cost of lower bank profits.

[12] In a somewhat similar model leading to similar conclusions Honohan (1999) uses the assumption of bounded risk (used in a related context by Stiglitz 1975) to describe the equilibrium in an imperfectly competitive banking system with capital requirements, where the

Policies of restraint can reduce the incidence of banks falling into the risk-loving region in this type of model especially if they help to increase bank franchise value.

Capital requirements may be enough to ensure that banks are operating in a zone where the risk of failure is zero, even though they are investing in risky assets. But this kind of model shows that new entry and other increases in loan market competition can switch the regime into one where the same banks now accept and exploit a risk of failure. The capital requirements that were once adequate are no longer so, and need to be increased or supplemented by other controls that prevent excessive risk, perhaps here including administrative ceilings on the quantity held of identifiable classes of high-risk assets.

Taking Account of Banks' Private Lending Opportunities

To an important extent, banks' most profitable lending opportunities are based on private information acquired by the bank. Kupiec and O'Brien (1998) present a relevant model of portfolio choice that focuses on this aspect of the opportunity set of an individual bank, thus including a collection of profitable (i.e., not just breakeven) lending opportunities as well as a riskless bond and a high-risk market instrument.[13] Because of the lack of competition from other lenders for these private lending opportunities, they may present risk and return opportunities which violate the usual assumption that risk is a concave function of expected return. Thus an interior solution for the bank's portfolio decision is not guaranteed. Instead, Kupiec and O'Brien show that to find the bank's best strategy it must calculate and compare the best portfolios from three distinct strategies: (1) deposits fully invested in the risk-free asset, with loans financed by equity; (2) no equity and deposits all invested in the risky security; or (3) a mixture of some loans and the remainder in the risky security. (By using deposits, the bank can exploit the deposit put, but it must pay the deposit insurance premium.) Evidently (1) is free of failure risk, while (2) carries the greatest risk of failure. A change in the regulatory environment can qualitatively alter the level of social risk by swinging the equilibrium from one of these three distinct strategies to another – another instance of discontinuous response (see Appendix 2).

Where private lending opportunities exist, it is hard to see how a regulator can fine tune such instruments as the schedule of deposit

banks are not at risk of failure, despite holding risky assets and incurring administrative expenses. But as exogenous risk or competition for loans increases, the bank may switch out of this safe region. Around the switchpoint, behavior can be discontinuous as the presence of failure risk affects not only the shareholders' expected payoff from the risky loan but also the payoff from the risk-free loan, as this too will be lost if the bank fails.

[13] In their model the return on individual assets is modeled as log-normal – hence 100 percent loss is possible for all of the risky assets. They also assume that deposit taking is always strictly profitable with a fixed percentage margin.

insurance premia. Kupiec and O'Brien indeed provide a numerical example to show that no separating insurance premium schedule exists (i.e., one which would be accepted only by safe banks) – another instance of the *fragility* of standard policy prescriptions.

Possible Perverse Results from Fine-tuning of Incentives

If, as shown by these examples, the equilibrium of the banking system can be very sensitive to small changes in the way risk presents itself to bank decisionmakers and their ability to take steps that alter the risk they face, it follows that attempts to fine-tune the incentives faced by bank decisionmakers may be ineffective. Additionally, they can even lead to perverse results, if based on inaccurate information.

Capital Requirements

Although it is natural to suppose that increased capital should normally serve to bond the decisionmakers, as well as directly increasing the cushion against loan losses and other risks, this may not always be so.[14] Where the bank can choose the extent of risk in its portfolio along a continuum, increased nominal capital requirements normally will result in the bank choosing an offsetting increase in portfolio risk which could, under some circumstances, actually increase the probability of bank failure, even if it improves the ex ante position of the shareholders.[15] This is a further illustration of *fragility*, although this problem could in principle be overcome by appropriate adjustment of capital requirements for the risk assumed.

Deposit Insurance Premia

The possible incompatibility of private information with correctly priced deposit insurance premia has already been mentioned. Yet many authors have proposed contexts in which deposit insurance premia might be

---

[14] For instance, in the Hellman, Murdock, and Stiglitz model discussed previously, higher capital requirements may under some circumstances so damage the banker's franchise value as to actually increase the propensity to gamble. Note that in that model the bank's decisionmakers are concerned only with excess profits (over the required return, and they ignore losses of that required return in the event of failure). If shareholders' value were being maximized, the likelihood of the perverse case would be reduced.

[15] This type of result has been extensively discussed, beginning with Kahane (1977) and Koehn and Santomero (1980), but the simple mean-variance treatment of risk in these early studies vitiated their conclusions: see Keeley and Furlong (1990) for a technical critique. A more rigorous approach is attributed to Gennotte and Pyle (1991), who stress the importance in this context of recognizing that the portfolio investments of banks do not have zero ex ante net present value but can yield net profits. As such, it seems that the perverse result here too derives from a loss of franchise value. Note that no corresponding result can be obtained in the private information model of Kupiec and O'Brien (1998), discussed previously.

fine-tuned to the risk assumed by the bank in what amounts to a form of corrective taxation or subsidies. For example, in a leading contribution, Giammarino, Lewis, and Sappington (1993) note the incentive for bank decisionmakers to underspend on measures to reduce risk. If the authorities can observe only the actual ex ante portfolio risk and not the risk-reduction efforts made by banks, (Giammarino, Lewis, and Sappington argue that) they might still influence behavior by proposing a schedule of risk-related deposit insurance premia and capital to assets requirements. One of the main results of that article is the claim that the optimum schedule of deposit insurance premia will be calibrated to induce a level of risk that is above the first-best optimum. The reason for targeting a higher level of risk is that aiming any lower would result in too little revenue being raised from deposit insurance premia, essentially because rewarding a good measured quality of portfolio will subsidize those banks that can more cheaply achieve it.

But what if the regulator cannot observe the quality of the loan portfolio as accurately as he or she thinks? Perhaps banks have, unknown to the policymaker, a way of making the ex ante risk of their portfolio seem lower to the regulator than it actually is. Then the true social cost of adopting a less demanding target for measured risk may be much higher than intended, as banks exploit their ability to masquerade this level of portfolio quality resulting in a much higher incidence of subsequent failures. In that case (as a simple example shows, see Appendix 3) the refined policy may work out to be much worse than a cruder policy which ignored the subtleties of maximizing deposit insurance premium income introduced by Giammarino, Lewis, and Sappington and instead chose the premia to aim at much lower risk, even at the cost of appearing to provide a modest subsidy to the better-placed banks. This *fragility* result would appear to be a good example of the best being potentially the enemy of the good, and one of particular application where the human capital resources available to the regulator are very limited, as in many developing countries.[16,17]

---

[16] The degree to which regulators can measure bank capital is a crucial element. Another example of the sensitivity of fine-tuning measures to availability of information is in Fries, Mella-Barral, and Perraudin (1997), who derive a nonlinear schedule of optimal deposit insurance premia from assumptions on the stochastic process of the bank's capital value. They assume that capital can be accurately measured; indeed, because of the way in which the premia vary close to the optimal point, the schedule is highly sensitive both to the measurement of capital, and to the parameters of the stochastic process.

[17] Though many models take the structure of information available to regulators as given, others model costly information acquisition either in the form of ex ante screening (e.g., Thakor 1996) or ex post auditing, perhaps on a stochastic basis (Townsend 1979). Park (1997) models regulators as deciding whether to exclude a bank from deposit insurance on the basis of a probabilistic audit of its risk and its capital adequacy. A conclusion of the model is that banks with high charter value may assume higher risk.

Limiting Agency Problems, Errors, and Overoptimism

The shortcomings of this fiscal fine-tuning approach to bank regulation are even more evident when it comes to dealing with the problems of overoptimism, insider dealing, and exogenous shocks and fraud. Clearly, a policy designed to induce socially optimal outcomes on the assumption of rational behavior on the part of a well-informed principal may be wholly inadequate and potentially counterproductive if the bank decisionmaker is swayed by false expectations, is not pursuing the goals of the principal, or is vulnerable to large and unanticipated shocks.

One interesting illustration of this type of agency problem generating more risk than would be preferred by shareholders is described by Gorton and Rosen (1995). They observe that low-ability managers whose incompetence in choosing safe assets are more readily evident to shareholders may opt to gamble excessively on risk assets whose disappointing returns can more easily be put down to bad luck (Boot and Greenbaum 1993; *cf.* Edlin and Stiglitz 1995; Rey and Stiglitz 1993). Just like the case of overoptimism, regulatory policies designed to modify the incentives of the shareholders will be wide of the mark in this kind of environment where managers are not pursuing the goals of the shareholders. Here too are instances of *fragility* suggesting that more direct action may again be needed.

3   TYPES OF PRUDENTIAL POLICY IN PRACTICE

Five main types of restraining measure have been used in relatively recent times to achieve prudential goals (among other purposes). These can be classified into the following categories: restrictions on entry; on the composition of liabilities (especially, but not only, minimum capital requirements); maximum interest rates; on the composition of assets, and on the overall size of the risk portfolio.

Restraints on *entry* can take the form of moratoria on new licenses, restrictions on foreign-owned banks, or on their ability to compete in local branches or in retail operations generally. Rules limiting the size of any one shareholder's portion may have a similar effect.

The most common restraint on the *composition of liabilities* is, of course, minimum capital requirements, whether in terms of a percentage of assets, weighted or unweighted for risk characteristics, or in terms of an absolute minimum amount (which has the effect of generating a minimum practical scale). Another interesting liability-side restraint is to require a minimum issue of subordinated debt to parties unrelated to the shareholders (Calomiris 1998).[18] This brings a new pair of watchful eyes

---

[18] Such a mechanism is in effect in Argentina, where the holders of the subdebt must be reputable international banks.

into play. The yield on such debt may provide an early warning system to the authorities regarding the market's perception of a bank's risk, especially if a ceiling is imposed on the yield if the debt is to meet the regulatory requirement.

Interest rate ceilings are often used in a wider context. Though often imposed on lending rates, a ceiling on deposit interest rates may be more directly effective in limiting reckless competition while allowing for differential remuneration of different risks.

As to the *composition of assets*, a number of restraints have been employed. The most extreme is the "narrow bank" proposal, which would limit the banks to investing in absolutely safe assets such as Treasury Bills. Other restraints could be imposed on lending sectors perceived as risky, such as real estate, or on foreign currency denominated assets, or to borrowers who were themselves exposed to foreign currency risk. In addition, a range of maturity and currency matching requirements can be seen as falling into this category.

Restraints on the overall size or *growth* of the loan portfolio, or generally on risk assets have often been imposed on an annual basis. A variety of particular interest is speed limits: Always in effect, but pitched at such a high level that they are only binding in times of boom.

In designing a robust policy, is there a best or dominant type of measure, or do some measures have natural spheres of application?[19]

Effectiveness

In terms of limiting risk of costly failures, all of these measures are intended either to provide a financial cushion against unforeseen losses, or to shift the incentives of the bank's decisionmakers in a risk-reducing direction; sometimes both. Any one of the measures listed can be effective at least partially in this effort, though each is thought of as working in a slightly different way.

From limited *entry*, banks gain considerable franchise value, and those controlling this value will be more anxious to ensure that they retain the flow of benefits that comes from this.[20] The merits of high-yielding, but risky, assets will have to be weighed against the risk that they could trigger insolvency and thus the loss of franchise. Likewise, looting by insiders of

---

[19] Other measures, such as the precise design of deposit insurance (including such aspects as the schedule of premiums), rules and procedures for intervening in banks, and for bank closure; and line-of-business restrictions, fall outside the scope of the this chapter.

[20] To be sure, a competitive banking system can also retain franchise values if the range of managerial ability and other sources of X-efficiency is sufficiently wide. Measures of financial restraint should not be so constraining that they eliminate franchise value coming from such sources.

parts of the existing balance sheet may be much less valuable than the continued flow of franchise benefits that such looting will compromise.

Capital adequacy requirements directly insulate depositors (and the deposit protection agency) by providing a first line of reserve to absorb losses. They can also provide a bonding effect on shareholders, thereby partly substituting for franchise value. The shareholder's future flow of dividends – even if no higher than the required return on equity capital – will be threatened by insolvency or loss of the license, and they will be concerned to control the behavior of their managers to preserve this flow. While varying small capital requirements can conceivably lead to counterproductive behavioral responses, the bonding and cushioning effects become dominant at higher levels of required capital. Modifications of limited liability, increasing the obligation of shareholders in the event of failure, represent an alternative, more common in the distant past, but attracting renewed attention.

A variant is the requirement, recently introduced in Argentina, of a supplementary tier of subordinated and uninsured debt, subscribed by independent financial institutions of substance. Not only does this add an additional cushion to absorb losses before they hit depositors' funds, but it also adds an extra pair of watchful eyes monitoring the behavior of the banks' decisionmakers and on guard not only against behavior that might enrich the managers at the expense of the shareholder, but against behavior that favors shareholders while putting other claimants at risk.

Ceilings on *deposit interest* are a robust policy that can give banks market power in the deposit market, at least to the extent that there are no perfect substitutes outside the scope of the ceilings. As such, they will provide a franchise value. They may also serve to limit the scale on which banking can be conducted (as would-be depositors look elsewhere for higher-yielding assets), and this may also mean a portfolio with lower average risk, depending on the range of loan opportunities available to banks.

A ceiling on the proportion or absolute amount of *risk assets* acquired by banks naturally reduces the risk of the portfolio by definition. Specific restrictions such as a ceiling on loans to real estate property, or on foreign currency denominated loans (and deposits) have been employed. In addition to limiting identified risky assets, overall portfolio risk can be reduced on the asset side requiring relatively large holdings of safe, liquid assets. These help insulate against liquidity shocks as well as providing insulation against losses elsewhere in the portfolio (Chang and Velasco 1998).

Ceilings on overall loan *portfolio size* may reduce the intensity of competition, thereby increasing franchise value. It may also reduce average portfolio risk, as discussed previously.

Although, as we have seen in Section 3, attempts to fine-tune these measures can be ineffective or even counterproductive, it can be recognized that more aggressive use (higher capital, tighter risk asset ceilings, etc.) will generally increase effectiveness, albeit perhaps at the risk of side effects in dimensions other than risk reduction.

In order to judge the overall relative merits of adopting these various measures, whether used separately or in combination, we need to look beyond their theoretical effectiveness in achieving their goals when perfectly implemented. They vary to the degree in which they are prone to implementation problems, and they can have strong side effects, favorable or unfavorable. The intensity of these side effects will depend on country conditions.

Side Effects and Implementation Problems

The heightened information and agency problems highlighted in Section 2 can create considerable implementation problems. These, together with side effects in dimensions other than risk reduction, should influence one's decision as to the optimal design of the policy package so that it will be not only robust, but have the least side effects of any effective policy. The following list of implementation problems or side effects is by no means exhaustive:

First, there are the *information* or *monitoring problems*. It is all very well to assume that a ceiling has been imposed on risk assets, but how is this to be achieved in practice? Can the regulator distinguish between high- and low-risk assets in an adequate manner, or are the information requirements for this kind of measure simply too great?

Second is the *agency problem of bank managers*. A measure such as capital adequacy requirements will lose much of its force if the bank's behavior is not truly being driven by the objective of the shareholders' interest, but instead by some combination of managerial and shareholder goals.[21] The managerial behavior could include the assumption of excessive risk resulting from the use of out-of-the-money options as management inducements; excessive administrative costs benefiting the managers, possibly including overexpansion of activity; and looting, defined as the diversion of part of the bank's assets to the managers or other insiders at the expense of the shareholders' interests defined as dividends plus bank's capital value. Lack of robustness of the measures to this agency problem is a central issue for several types of measure.

---

[21] Weakness of shareholders relative to managers can also reflect fragmented ownership, inadequate legal protections for outside shareholders or state ownership.

**Table 2.1. Suggested Ranking of Each Measure in Potential
to Avoid Adverse Side Effects**

Side effect	Measure				
	Entry	Capital & sub debt	Deposit interest	Risk ceiling	Total assets
Monitoring costs	1	4	2	5	3
Managers' agency	4	5	3	1	2
Information processing	5	1	3	2	4
Cost reduction	5	1	3	2	4
Rent seeking	5	3	1	4	2
Disintermediation	2	1	5	3	4

Note: For each side effect, the measures are ranked from best (1) to worst (5) in their potential to be designed in such a way as to avoid that side effect.

The key economic function of banks in society is an *information processing* one, particularly in risk and creditworthiness assessment, and in monitoring by borrowers. This is a familiar aspect of "finance as the brain of the economy." Some measures of restraint can have the side effect of dulling the incentive to carry out such activities.

Measures that inhibit competition for market share will tend to have a depressing effect on the pressures for *cost-reduction* and technological innovation by banks.

With all discretionary regulations there is the potential of capture of the regulators by the regulated. *Rent-seeking* behavior induced by the existence of regulations can greatly distort behavior and impose welfare costs.

Regulations are always limited in the institutions and activities to which they apply. Competition from unregulated institutions or products can imply a high elasticity of demand for the controlled product. The resulting *disintermediation* reduces the effectiveness of all regulations and, to the extent that it favors the expansion of unregulated domestic intermediaries, can also increase the incidence of failure in the unregulated sector.

Ranking Different Measures as to Side Effects or Costs

On an intuitive level, it seems possible to pencil in indicative rankings of the different types of measure in accordance with their likely ability to avoid the above-mentioned side effects (Table 2.1). The basis on which the table is constructed is given below.

Monitoring Costs

Information and *monitoring costs* seem likely to be highest for any attempt to control the amount of risk asset investment directly. Information requirements are particularly severe here: The regulator effectively has to make a detailed audit of each loan to verify its degree of risk; any simple rule of thumb is likely to be very inadequate. Monitoring is equally difficult for such risk ceilings. For example if a ceiling is imposed on lending for real estate development, it will often be found that the bank will surreptitiously book such lending under a different sectoral heading, and the cost of ensuring that such a loan does not in fact contribute to real estate finance will be high.

Capital adequacy is also a matter that requires rather sophisticated accounting, if it is to be done properly. Indeed, measuring capital is one of the most challenging normal tasks for the bank accountant in that it represents the residual of the balance sheet and accordingly embodies all of the errors and uncertainties of the other items, including the appropriate level of provisions for loan-loss. Mechanical provisioning rules based on the degree to which loan servicing is current do not provide a very accurate measure of the underlying expected value of a loan portfolio. If the capital requirement is risk adjusted, then the information requirements are even more severe (unless the risk adjustments are pre-specified in a mechanical way, in which case their adequacy can be questioned).

At the other end of the scale, monitoring entry seems simpler, and verifying that a deposit interest ceiling is being broadly complied with is only somewhat more difficult. Compliance with interest ceilings does not involve any difficult conceptual problems in accounting. Subsidized (often free) transaction charges and other in-kind side payments may be somewhat concealed and hard to legislate with any precision. But by the same token, they are likely to be only a partial evasion.

Managers' Agency

Treating the bank as a homogeneous entity operated on behalf of its shareholders gives a more straightforward set of policy prescriptions than if the managers pursue their own objectives, whether driven by the perquisites obtainable from asset size, from stock options (the maximization of whose expected value is not equivalent to the maximization of the expected value of the stock), or from looting. Information issues aside, placing ceilings on risk assets is likely to provide especially good insulation against these problems, followed by ceilings on overall asset size. Much less effective in this context are capital requirements (which influence the incentives of shareholders much more than those of managers), and entry restrictions, which may simply reduce the market pressures on managers to deliver good returns to shareholders.

Information Processing

When it comes to incentives for information processing, measures such as capital adequacy requirements and deposit interest controls score well in that they preserve all or most of the incentives for banks to employ information to the maximum. In contrast, risk-asset ceilings tend to reduce the need for banks to conduct their own risk assessments and may prevent them from seeking out and funding the more creditworthy of apparently risky ventures. The same will be true, though to a lesser extent, if total asset size is restricted.

Cost Reduction

Neither capital adequacy requirements nor risk-asset ceilings will blunt the incentive for cost reduction to maintain market share and increase profitability of the noninformation aspects of banking, whereas entry restrictions and limitations on total asset size will have precisely that effect. A point to be borne in mind here is that where restrictions on entry apply particularly to foreign banks an important potential for technology transfer is lost.

Rent Seeking

Rent-seeking behavior is likely to be strongest where the degree of discretion in regulations is high. Entry restrictions and risk-asset ceilings are the most problematic of the measures we have discussed in this regard,[22] whereas deposit-interest ceilings and total-asset size are more transparent and less likely to be implemented in a discretionary manner on a case-by-case basis.

Disintermediation

Finally, when it comes to disintermediation it is evident that large deposits are particularly prone to having close substitutes outside the scope of controls, perhaps in offshore banks. Ceilings on total asset size will also mean that lower-risk assets will be financed almost as easily without the assistance of the regulated intermediaries. On the other hand, entry restrictions, and minimum capital requirements will be less likely to induce strong disintermediation.

---

[22] All too often, a discretionary regime of entry restrictions ends up with the licenses going to those with friends in high places.

Table 2.2. Suggested Importance of Side Effects for Different Country Conditions

	Condition					
Side effect	Weak governance	Structural change	Recent liberalization	Complex system	International openness	Low per capita GDP
Monitoring costs	X	X	X			
Managers' agency	X		X			
Information processing		X				
Cost reduction				X		X
Rent seeking	X					
Disintermediation				X	X	

Matching the Policy Package to Country Circumstances

The likely severity of implementation difficulties and side effects will vary depending on country circumstances. As a result, each type of financial restraint measure has its sphere of comparative advantage depending on country circumstances. After all, vulnerability to the side effects discussed previously will depend on circumstances such as quality of governance, extent of recent structural change, sophistication and complexity of financial system, openness of economy, and level of per capita income. The entries in Table 2.2 are suggested by the following discussion.

Quality of governance means both the dimensions of competence and of probity. Evidently these are qualities needed to reduce the problems of monitoring costs and rent seeking mentioned above. They will also be needed to come to grips with the problems of managerial agency. Absent good governance, deposit-interest ceilings and ceilings on total assets may be the most appropriate and robust policies.

Rapid structural change in the economy at large, including transition to market and other structural adjustments (whether policy induced or exogenous) greatly increase the difficulty for the regulator monitoring bank risk, but on the other hand increase the potential value added of banks making their own risk assessments. These considerations point to both interest ceilings and tough capital requirements as being the most effective tools.

A *recently liberalized financial system* is especially prone to the managerial agency problems that we have referred to (the Mexican privatizations of the early 1990s are a good example) as well as presenting exceptional difficulties to the regulator in attempting to monitor the behavior of banks because of the lack of a track record. Not surprisingly the very traditional tools of interest ceilings, entry limitations, and ceilings on total asset accumulation have the best marginal effect here – recognizing that removal of these very instruments may have been an important part of the recent liberalization.

There is a difference between regulating a narrow core segment of a simple financial system and tackling *complex financial systems* with a variety of different types of financial intermediary and instrument. Attempts to escape regulation by moving offshore or adopting any of a variety of legal avoidance procedures are likely to be effective in such environments. Furthermore, the fact that these restraints can inhibit the positive contribution of intermediaries to development and risk pooling becomes arguably more important if they are applied more widely in the financial system: The more complex the system, the more potential is being lost here. Capital adequacy (and its variant – subordinated debt) requirements come into their own here, and the effectiveness of limitations on investment in certain identified risky assets may also be relatively high.

International openness of the economy makes it very susceptible to disintermediation, which tends to mean that capital adequacy and entry restrictions may be the best option.

Finally, a low level of per capita GDP, to the extent that it is not correlated with other conditions discussed, places a premium on avoiding excessive operational costs, and this points in the direction of capital adequacy rules and limits on identified risk assets.

Intertemporal Aspects: Adapting to the Cycle and Responding to Evasion

It is not only to country circumstances that the regulatory regime needs to be adapted. Attention also needs to be given to the changing circumstances of any given country over the business cycle. While, for example, capital standards need to be high on average over the cycle, a case can certainly be made for procyclical requirements. Rigid capital standards could destabilize the economy by squeezing lending just when it is needed to restore the economy to its potential path. And the economywide influences on bank capital imply that procyclical capital adequacy rules can generate better microeconomic incentives (Dewatripont and Tirole 1994).

Speed bumps – constraints that bind only when the bank is expanding above a safe normal speed – also have similar procyclical character. Naturally, the danger is that too much tinkering in the direction of cyclical adjustment could reintroduce the problems of fine-tuning to which we have referred.

Adapting the design of regulation to meet the evasive actions that will inevitably be adopted by regulated entities is a never-ending task. Obvious analogies with the evolutionary battle of antibiotics and bacterial diseases can be drawn. Here again there is much to be said for speed bumps and other controls that bind only intermittently. These have the merit of not presenting a constant target for evasion, and as such may be more effective and easy to police. They are not in effect long enough to make the development of evasive measures cost effective, or to make it easy to refine such measures through practice.

4 CONCLUDING REMARKS

Discouraged by the declining effectiveness of the old regulations, and driven too by an idealized and – as is now evident – not wholly applicable model of perfectly competitive financial systems, the progress of financial liberalization has discarded some instruments of potential value. The current vogue favoring exclusive regulatory reliance on institutional risk-management capacity (together with risk-related capital adequacy requirements and perhaps deposit insurance premia) requires a threshold of information processing capacity that goes far beyond the current and prospective capacity of most regulatory administrations in developing economies. Further, depending on subtle evaluations as they do, these sophisticated systems depend on policy independence of the regulators, if their regulatory judgments are not to be second-guessed.

All in all, therefore, exclusive reliance on the sophisticated indirect model of control is only appropriate for environments where the regulatory capacity is strong, where even-handed enforcement can be relied upon, and where a complex and deep financial structure makes the effectiveness of cruder instruments problematic.

Other countries may need to draw on a portfolio of robust policy instruments that does not exclude the direct as well as the indirect, and even some price (interest rate) controls. Some of these instruments have in the past been used to achieve (other) economic rather than prudential goals. Their use in the present context is not, however, one of repression, quasitaxation or bending the functioning of finance toward detailed goals of economic planning. Nor should such measures be so constraining as to limit the scope for franchise values based on innovation and particular sources of "X-efficiency." Rather their purpose is to recognize the externalities involved in bad banking, and the informational limitations of regulation. They are intended to restrain financial practitioners from generating the type of severe economic damage that has recently been all too evident in inadequately regulated financial systems.

APPENDIX

Bank Capitalization and Deposit Interest Rates

In the model of Hellman, Murdock, and Stiglitz (2000) banks bid for deposits, then choose between a risky and a safe portfolio. The higher their capitalization, the less they will be willing to bid high for deposits; the

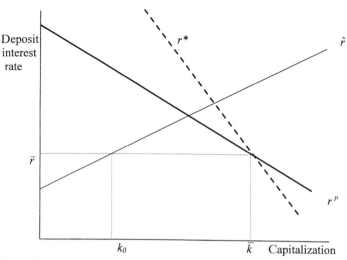

Figure 2.1. Discontinuity illustrated: imposition of deposit interest ceiling allows capital requirement to be reduced discretely without triggering risky lending.

lower the interest rate, the more likely they will be to choose a safe asset, especially if highly capitalized. Figure 2.1 shows combinations of deposit interest rate and bank leverage as derived in the Hellman, Murdock, and Stiglitz model. There are thus three key loci: upward-sloping $\hat{r}(k)$ is the maximum rate consistent with the bank choosing a safe portfolio; downward-sloping $r^p(k)$ would be the equilibrium rate of interest if the risky asset were not available; also downward-sloping, and more steeply, $r^*(k)$ is the lowest common rate of interest from which no bank will choose to deviate by bidding up. The intersection $r^p(\bar{k}) = r^*(\bar{k})$ then defines the lowest capital requirement $\bar{k}$ sufficient to ensure that the banks will not bid up interest rates so high that they end up investing in the risky asset.

Here we note that, if the corresponding interest rate $\bar{r}$ is imposed as a ceiling, then the same investment decision and deposit interest rate can be achieved at the much lower capital level k_0.

Pricing the Deposit Put in a Nonconvex Model

Figure 2.2 is a much simplified schematic representation of the model considered by Kupiec and O'Brien (1998). The bank gets value from investing in profitable private lending opportunities, and/or by assuming risk to exploit deposit insurance. Each star (✳) represents a possible choice of its portfolio. The bank's investment strategy depends *discontinuously* on the relative price (dashed line) of these two sources of value, a price which can be influenced by such policies as deposit insurance premia, capital require-

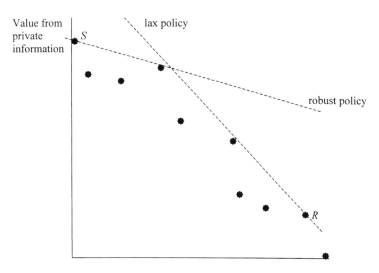

Figure 2.2. Illustrates discontinuous response of risk profile to policy change.

ments, and deposit-interest ceilings enhancing the franchise value of future activities. By adjusting this relative price, policy can lower or eliminate the social costs of bank failure, e.g., shifting the bank's preferred portfolio from the risky R to the safe S. The opportunity set of the bank is a set of discrete points rather than a smooth and concave curve because the bank has a collection of profitable private lending opportunities (whose risk need not bear any particular relation to expected yield).

Gaming an Over Subtle Deposit Insurance Pricing Scheme

Figure 2.3 displays the fragility of the policy recommendations drawn from models such as that of Giammarino, Lewis, and Sappington (1993). Because of the value of the deposit put, bank value net of insurance premium is a diminishing function of portfolio quality q. The deposit insurance premium is a diminishing function of *apparent* portfolio quality r. The honest bank chooses quality level q_0, and pays insurance premium p_0. But if at cost $F(r,q)$ a bank with true quality q can appear to have quality r, then exploiting this, the bank can, while retaining apparent quality $r = q_0$ and thus without increasing its insurance premium, increase its net return by lowering true quality to q_1. The optimum position of the bank will be to reach an intermediate level of quality q_2 and a higher level of apparent quality $r > q_0$. The result for social welfare is increased losses for the deposit insurance fund not only because of lower premium income,

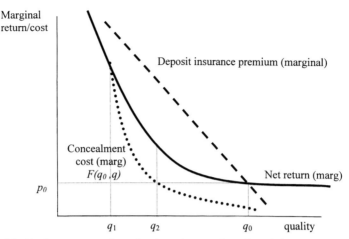

Figure 2.3. Bank exaggerates its safety in order to reduce deposit insurance premium.

but also because of increased cost of the deposit put because of lower bank portfolio quality.

The shape of the marginal net value curve is based on a simplified version of the Giammarino, Lewis, and Sappington model in which the deposit insurer's net value is

$$S(z) = P(z) + A(z), \quad A(z) = (1+b)\int_{-\infty}^{-a} x\,dG(x, z)$$

where P is the insurance premium and A is the expected social value of the claims on the insurance fund. The distribution of the bank's future return x is G depending on the quality of the portfolio z. The bank's breakeven return is $-a$ below which the bank fails and the insurer absorbs the negative returns.

The bank's net value is:

$$B(q) - C(q) - P(r) - F(r, q), \quad B(q) = \int_{-a}^{\infty} x\,dG(x, q)$$

where B is the expected value to the bank of the portfolio return, C is the cost of achieving portfolio quality q and F is the cost of masquerading as apparent quality r when true quality is q. We assume $F_r(z,z) = 0$, and F convex. Note that: $A(z)/(1 + b) + B(z) = 0$.

If G is uniformly distributed on $[-1/z, 1/z]$, then we can deduce:

$$A(z) = \frac{1+b}{4z}(a^2z^2 - 1) \quad A'(z) = \frac{1+b}{4z^2}(a^2z^2 - 1)$$

$$B(z) = \frac{1}{4z}(1 - a^2z^2) \quad B'(z) = \frac{1}{4z^2}(1 - a^2z^2)$$

which yields the shapes of Figure 2.3.

Exploiting its ability to masquerade, the bank's optimum apparent quality r^* satisfies:

$$F_1(r^*, q^*) = P'(r^*)$$

which implicitly defines $r^*(q^*)$. The first order condition for the optimum actual quality q^* is then:

$$B'(q^*) - C'(q^*) = F_1(r^*(q^*), q^*)\frac{\partial r^*}{\partial q^*} + F_2(r^*(q^*), q^*).$$

REFERENCES

Akerlof, G. and P. Romer. 1993. "Looting: The Economic Underworld of Bankruptcy for Profit." *Brookings Papers on Economic Activity* 1993(2):1–73.

Berger, A.N. and R. de Young. 1997. "Problem Loans and Cost Efficiencies in Commercial Banks." *Journal of Banking and Finance* 21:849–70.

Bhattacharya, S., A. Boot, and A. Thakor. 1998. "The Economics of Bank Regulation." *Journal of Money Credit and Banking* 30:745–70.

Boot, A.W. and S.I. Greenbaum. 1993. "Bank Regulation, Reputation and Rents: Theory and Policy Implications." In C. Mayer and X. Vives (eds.), *Capital Markets and Financial Intermediation*, pp. 262–85. New York: Cambridge University Press.

Calomiris, C. 1998. *The Post-modern Safety Net.* Washington, DC: American Enterprise Institute.

Caprio, G. and P. Honohan. 1999. "Restoring Banking Stability: Beyond Supervised Capital Requirements." *Journal of Economic Perspectives* 13(4): 43–64.

Caprio, G. and D. Klingebiel. 1997. "Bank Insolvency: Bad Luck, Bad Policy or Bad Banking?" In M. Bruno and B. Pleskovic (eds.), *Proceedings of the World Bank Annual Conference on Development Economics, 1996*, pp. 79–104. Washington, DC: The World Bank.

Chang, R. and A. Velasco. 1998. "Financial Crises in Emerging Markets: A Canonical Model." *NBER Working Paper* 6606.

Dewatripont, M. and J. Tirole. 1994. *The Prudential Regulation of Banks.* Cambridge, MA: MIT Press.

Edlin, A.S. and J.E. Stiglitz. 1995. "Discouraging Rivals: Managerial Rent-Seeking and Economic Inefficiencies." *American Economic Review* 85:1301–12.

Flannery, M.J. 1998. "Using Market Information in Prudential Bank Supervision: A Review of the US Empirical Evidence." *Journal of Money, Credit and Banking* 30:273–305.

Freixas, X. and J.-C. Rochet. 1997. *Microeconomics of Banking.* Cambridge, MA: MIT Press.

Fries, S., P. Mella-Barral, and W. Perraudin. 1997. "Optimal Bank Reorganization and the Fair Pricing of Deposit Insurance." *Journal of Banking and Finance* 21:441–68.

Gennotte, G. and D. Pyle. 1991. "Capital Controls and Bank Risk." *Journal of Banking and Finance* 15:805–24.

Giammarino, R.M., T.R. Lewis, and D. Sappington. 1993. "An Incentive Approach to Banking Regulation." *Journal of Finance* 48:1523–42.

Gorton, G. and R. Rosen. 1995. "Corporate Control, Portfolio Choice and the Decline of Banking." *Journal of Finance* 50:1377–420.

Guttentag, J.M. and R.J. Herring. 1996. "Disaster Myopia in International Banking." *Princeton Essays in International Finance* 164.

Hellman, T., K. Murdock, and J. Stiglitz. 2000. "Liberalization, Moral Hazard in Banking and Prudential Regulation: Are Capital Requirements Enough?" *American Economic Review* 90(1):147–65.

Honohan, P. 2000. "Banking System Failures in Developing and Transition Countries: Diagnosis and Prediction." *Economic Notes* 29(1):83–109.

Honohan, P. 1999. "A Model of Bank Contagion through Lending." *International Review of Economic and Finance* 8(2):147–63.

Honohan, P. and D. Vittas. 1997. "Financial Networks and Banking Policy." In H. Wolf (ed.), *Macroeconomic Policy and Financial Systems*. London: Macmillan.

Kahane, Y. 1977. "Capital Adequacy and the Regulation of Financial Intermediaries." *Journal of Banking and Finance* 1:207–18.

Kane, E.J. 1998. "Capital Movements, Asset Values and Banking Policy in Globalized Markets." *NBER Working Paper* 6633.

Keeley, M.C. and F.T. Furlong. 1990. "A Re-examination of Mean-Variance Analysis of Bank Capital Regulation." *Journal of Banking and Finance* 14:69–84.

Klein, M. 1971. "A Theory of the Banking Firm." *Journal of Money, Credit and Banking* 3:205–18.

Koehn, M. and A. Santomero. 1980. "Regulation of Bank Capital and Portfolio Risk." *Journal of Finance* 35:1235–44.

Kupiec, P.H. and J.M. O'Brien. 1998. "Deposit Insurance, Bank Incentives, and the Design of Regulatory Policy." *Federal Reserve Board, FEDS Working Paper* 98-10.

McKinnon, R. and H. Pill. 1998. "International Overborrowing: A Decomposition of Currency and Credit Risks." *World Development* 26(7):1267–82.

Milne, A. and A.E. Whalley. 1999. "Bank Capital and Risk-Taking." *Bank of England Working Paper* 90.

Monti, M. 1972. "Deposit, Credit, and Interest Rate Determination under Alternative Bank Objectives." In G.P. Szegö and K. Shell (eds.), *Mathematical Methods in Investment and Finance*. Amsterdam: North Holland.

Park, S. 1997. "Risk-taking of Banks under Regulation." *Journal of Banking and Finance* 21:491–507.

Prisman, E., M. Slovin, and M.E. Sushka. 1986. "A General Theory of the Banking Firm Under Conditions of Monopoly, Uncertainty and Recourse." *Journal of Monetary Economics* 17:293–304.

Rey, P. and J. Stiglitz. 1993. "Short-term Contracts as a Monitoring Device." *NBER Working Paper* 4514.

Stiglitz, J.E. 1975. "Incentives, Risk and Information: Notes Towards a Theory of Hierarchy." *Bell Journal of Economics* 6:552–79.

Stiglitz, J.E. 1994. "The Role of the State in Financial Markets." In M. Bruno and B. Pleskovic (eds.), *Proceedings of the World Bank Annual Conference on Development Economics, 1993*, pp. 19–52. Washington, DC: World Bank.

Stiglitz, J.E. 1998. "The East Asian Crisis and Its Implications for India." *http://www.worldbank.org/html/extdr/extme/js-051998*.

Thakor, A.V. 1996. "Capital Requirements, Monetary Policy, Aggregate Bank Lending: Theory and Empirical Evidence." *Journal of Finance* 51:279–324.

Townsend, R. 1979. "Optimal Contracts and Competitive Markets with Costly State Verification." *Journal of Economic Theory* 21:265–93.

CROSS-COUNTRY EVIDENCE

3

How Interest Rates Changed under Liberalization: A Statistical Review

Patrick Honohan[1]

INTRODUCTION

The process of financial liberalization was expected to increase the volatility of interest rates and asset prices, to have distributional consequences in the form of reduced or relocated rents, and to have increased competition in the financial services industry. In this chapter we examine the available data on money market and bank interest rates for evidence of these propositions.

We show that, as more and more countries liberalized, the level and dynamic behavior of developing country interest rates converged to industrial country norms. Liberalization did mean an increased short-term volatility in both real and nominal money market interest rates. Treasury Bill rates and bank spreads were evidently the most repressed, and they showed the greatest increase as liberalization progressed: This shifted substantial rents from the public sector and from favored borrowers. Whereas quoted bank spreads in industrial countries contracted again somewhat during the late 1990s, spreads in developing countries remained much higher, presumably reflecting both market power and the higher risks of lending in the developing world.

Sections 1 and 2 review the global pattern of long-term and short-term dynamics in interest rate levels and spreads. Section 3 proposes an approach to judging when the de facto liberalization of wholesale rates occurred, and Section 4 measures the speed of adjustment of developing country interest rates to external interest rate shocks before and after these dates. Section 5 examines the way changes in wholesale rates pass through to bank lending and deposit rates. Using the date of de facto wholesale interest rate liberalization, Section 6 compares overall

[1] Thanks to Aslı Demirgüç-Kunt, Aart Kraay, and Philip Lane for helpful comments and suggestions and to Anqing Shi for painstaking research assistance.

Table 3.1. Median World Real Interest Rates, 1960–99

	Money market	Deposit rate	Lending less deposit
1960	1.3	2.4	3.6
1965	−0.5	0.5	3.5
1970	−0.7	0.8	2.9
1975	−5.8	−3.5	3.5
1980	−6.1	0.0	3.7
1985	2.0	5.0	4.2
1990	0.4	5.1	5.5
1995	2.2	3.4	5.9
1999	1.8	2.7	5.9

Note: In this table deflation is by current inflation, i.e., these are ex ante real rates with stationary expectations.

economic performance before and after. Section 7 contains concluding remarks.

1   GLOBAL TRENDS IN INTEREST RATE LEVELS AND SPREADS

Global Trends since 1960

Broad trends in global interest rates since 1960 are summarized by the world medians shown in Table 3.1.[2] There appears to have been a general upward trend in the level of world median real interest rates, but the most striking feature is a pronounced secular swing in real rates over the past forty years, with a sharp dip into negative rates in the 1970s followed by a recovery to higher than previous levels in the 1980s and 1990s, and the beginnings of a reduction again more recently. The swing is evident in both money market and deposit rates.

From a theoretical point of view, variations over time in the general level of unregulated wholesale ex post real interest rates can be explained by deviations of actual from expected inflation, and because of cyclical or trend changes in the productivity of capital and the propensity to save and perceptions of risk. Changes in the degree to which these interest rates are administratively controlled will also be a factor.

---

[2] In this section, unless otherwise stated, "real" rate data shown are computed as ex post real interest rates simply adjusted for consumer price inflation (see Data Appendix). In Table 3.1, for each year, the median is formed from all of the countries for which IFS data exists for that year.

The causes of the secular swing in world interest rates since the 1960s, a well-known feature of industrial country data, have been debated in the literature at length.[3] Was there a downturn in the marginal efficiency of capital (possibly associated with the surge in petroleum and other primary product prices); or was there a transitory increase in the propensity to save? These are probably the leading explanations. In a fully integrated world capital market, these real factors would be transmitted fully across all markets, and would not retain any national features. Nominal, currency-specific factors such as shifts in the relation between actual and expected inflation are of greater interest in the present context, where we are looking at differences in the behavior of interest rates from country to country. Thus, a fairly plausible and parsimonious (albeit somewhat underrated) interpretation attributes part of the U-shaped evolution to a long lag in the formation of inflation expectations. In this account the relatively high inflation of the 1970s in most industrial countries was unexpected and its persistence continued to be underestimated for most of that decade.[4] Furthermore, even where the market did revise its inflation expectations upward, interest rate controls inhibited the response of some markets to the expected inflation. In contrast, although inflation began to come under control in most industrial countries by the mid-1980s, by that time inflation expectations were high and remained stubbornly so, placing upward pressure on nominal market interest rates. By then also, many interest rate controls had been dismantled, so that actual rates more closely reflected market forces. A subsequent decline in real rates by the mid-1990s is explained in this account by the gradual decline in inflation expectations in recent years. In addition to these effects of the "great inflation" of the 1970s, the stance of countercyclical monetary policy has also been a factor.

The degree to which developing country rates have tracked the long swing is an indication of the degree to which elements of global financial integration were already in effect by 1960.

The median quoted intermediation spread between deposit and lending rates remained broadly constant during 1960–80 but has risen rather sharply since then. A number of interpretations are possible. For example, there could have been an increase in the market power of banks, possibly

---

[3] An important early analysis of the episode is Blanchard and Summers (1984). Jenkinson (1996) presents a useful overview of empirical work explaining long trends in real interest rates in the industrial countries.

[4] That is not to say that inflation was underestimated in each quarter. Agents' continued willingness to hold low-yielding monetary instruments (despite predictable short-term capital losses) during the early burst of high inflation in the 1970s may be attributable to the set-up costs and risks that would then have been involved in investing in alternatives that could offer both liquidity and an inflation hedge. Incurring such set-up costs could only have been justified if one expected inflationary conditions to persist.

Table 3.2. Median ex post real world interest rates: 1970s to 1990s

%	Money market		Treasury bill		Deposit		Loan less deposit	
	Industrial	Developing	Industrial	Developing	Industrial	Developing	Industrial	Developing
1977–79	0.0	−1.4	−0.4	−4.6	−2.2	−4.3	3.1	4.8
1982–84	4.3	3.1	3.7	0.0	1.0	−0.5	4.2	4.7
1987–89	4.6	3.6	4.3	−0.1	2.5	0.7	4.3	5.3
1992–94	6.5	5.4	5.5	3.8	3.3	2.6	4.5	6.8
1997–99	2.6	6.4	3.2	5.0	1.6	3.6	3.7	8.2

Note: Based on annual average data. The table shows the mean over three years of the median across countries. Here (and in Figure 3.1), in contrast to Table 3.1, the deflation is by actual inflation over the subsequent year.

associated with the relaxation of interest rate controls. Another factor could be the deterioration in loan-loss experience in the latter part of the sample: Equilibrium spreads should have widened to take account of the credit risk. Finally, the degree to which the quoted rates are representative will have varied over time, with large depositors and first-rate borrowers beginning to have new nonbank opportunities.

The Developing Countries Catch Up: Annual Data from 1975

Data for the early years in Table 3.1 are sparse: The early years included very few observations. Only from about 1980 on is there data for at least several dozen countries in each case. Table 3.2 and Figures 3.1 and 3.2 provide more detail for the period since 1977, distinguishing between industrial and developing countries. These show mean and percentile figures in addition to the median on an annual basis. Along with money market and Treasury Bill rates, we show bank deposit rates and the quoted intermediation spread, i.e., the difference between quoted deposit rates and quoted lending rates, for as many countries as have sufficient annual observations included in *International Financial Statistics*.[5] The general trend is summarized by three-yearly averages of the medians shown in Table 3.2.

This annual data reveals some similarities and some contrasts between developing and industrial country interest rates.

---

[5] These figures and data are based on countries for which annual data is available for at least twelve years from 1980–93. It is not a balanced pool: The number of countries varies somewhat from year to year, but more according to the series, from a mean of thirty-five for money market and thirty-six for Treasury Bill rates to fifty-nine for intermediation spreads and sixty-two for deposit rates. This sample selection strategy represents a compromise between the desirability of including as many countries as possible with the risks of too unbalanced a pool.

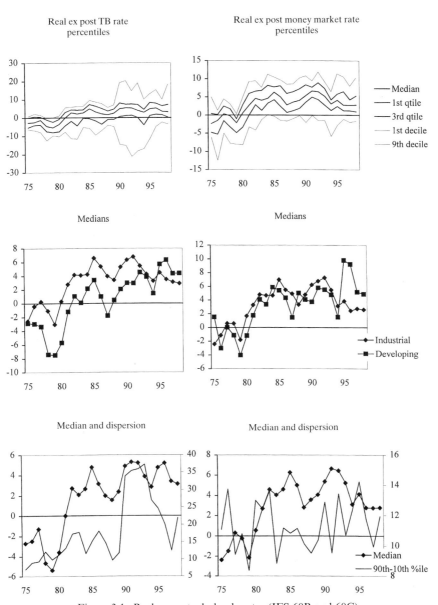

Figure 3.1. Real ex post wholesale rates (IFS 60B and 60C).

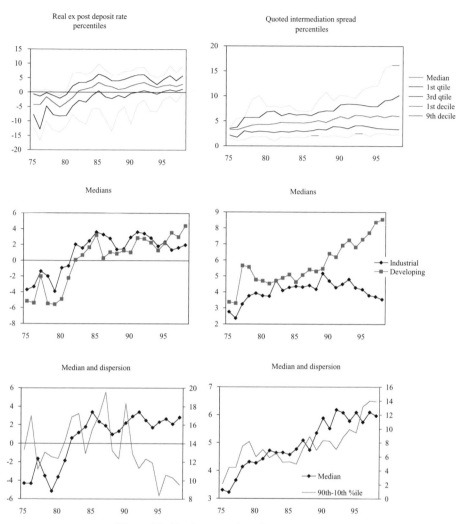

Figure 3.2. Real ex post deposit rates (IFS 60L).

Developing Country Real Interest Rates on an Upward Trend

The real interest rates shown begin at predominantly negative levels, with even the third quartile generally negative or close to zero in the late 1970s. Developing country rates were, on average, even lower than those in industrial countries up to the mid-1980s; but thereafter developing country rates increased and passed the industrial countries to end the period higher. The reduction in industrial country rates from the mid-1990s was not systematically followed in the developing world.

Market Reranks Different Interest Rates

Market forces can be expected to push deposit rates below, and lending rates above, wholesale money market rates, reflecting costs and risks. Assuming that quoted interbank money market rates relate to lending that is highly liquid and virtually free of credit risk, Treasury Bill rates at the same maturity should be very close to money market rates. In the data, median deposit rates[6] were generally lower than money market rates, but not always lower than Treasury Bill rates. Until the 1990s, Treasury Bill rates fell below money market rates in developing countries, probably reflecting controls, taxes, or other administrative requirements (including compulsory take-up rules) more than a market assessment of differential risk. The fact (not illustrated) that official discount rates switch from being lower than money market rates to being higher may reflect changing mechanisms of central bank liquidity support to the market as more central banks shifted away from a subsidized and rationed facility to a penalty rate facility as their main off-market method of intervening.

International Dispersion of Real Interest Rates Does Not Fall

Evidence on trends in the international dispersion of real interest rates is ambiguous. All standard measures of dispersion increase from the 1960s to the 1970s, though the small number of countries included in the early years may affect this. Subsequently the interquartile range and the gap between top and bottom decile show little clear trend,[7] but the standard deviation and range increase, at least until the 1990s, reflect more extreme outliers.[8] This finding is, perhaps, slightly surprising: Had the data been drawn from countries with and without interest controls we might have expected an increase in dispersion in the 1980s when real interest rates increased in the uncontrolled countries, followed by a narrowing as more

---

[6] Note that, of course, in general a different country will be the median for each rate, and for each year.

[7] For example, the estimated least-squares (LS) time trend for the interquartile range of money market rates is −5.8 basis points per annum – small relative to a mean range of 459 basis points – with a standard error of 2.7, just significant at the 5 percent level. The steepest shrinkage of interquartile is for the deposit rate, with an estimated annual trend of −15.8 basis points, highly significant with a standard error of 4.4. (Note in contrast that the interquartile range for the intermediation spread does show a statistically significant widening over time.)

[8] Especially negative outliers – in several years the distribution across countries has a highly negative skew.

and more countries decontrolled. Increased volatility of inflation is one source of the increased range of ex post interest rates. It also alerts us to the possibility that interest rate controls may not have been fully effective in the early years, at least for these countries. Bear in mind, however, that the sample of countries may suffer from selection bias to the extent that reporting of statistics to International Financial Statistics (IFS) may be correlated with degree of regime liberalization.

Bank Spreads Increase

Bank quoted gross intermediation spreads (as measured by subtracting quoted deposit from quoted lending rates) increase sharply with the general increase in rates during the 1980s. In industrial countries the increase is from 2.8 percent in the mid-1970s to 5.2 percent in the early 1990s. In the developing countries the spreads are wider: increasing from 4.1 percent to 6.8 percent. During the 1990s, these spreads continue to increase in developing countries, whereas they decline in the industrial countries.[9] The median quoted rates for the developing countries are almost always higher than for the industrial countries. The gap becomes quite wide by the late 1990s. Once again, this result cannot be extrapolated to an increase in bank profitability for a variety of reasons. For one thing, the single rates used do not purport to be average rates, but quoted rates for instruments of standard quality. Furthermore, the risk profile of borrowers and the extent to which quoted rates bundle the cost of other banking services to customers may have changed systematically over time.

2 SHORT-RUN DYNAMICS OF WHOLESALE RATES – OVERVIEW

We have nearly complete monthly data since 1980 on wholesale[10] interest rates and inflation for some twenty-eight significant[11] developing countries. In later sections we will have something to say about nominal rates, but here the focus is on rates adjusted for exchange rate change and expected inflation. We find that both forms of adjusted rates have displayed extremes of high and low – both spikes and on a sustained basis.

---

[9] To what extent this recent reversal in industrial countries reflects disintermediation from banking is not clear: It is widely believed that industrial country banks have lost some market power in the past decade, which would have narrowed spreads. But although it is their most creditworthy customers that they have lost to securities markets, the shifting composition of their loan portfolio toward lower quality is unlikely to influence the *quoted* spreads, which are usually for standard borrower categories.

[10] We use the term to imply either money market or Treasury Bill rates.

[11] The total would be forty-three before excluding microstates and multiple members of currency unions (see Data Appendix).

Expected or ex ante Real Interest Rates in Developing Countries

Our approximation for expected, or ex ante real exchange rates, is to subtract a smoothed rate of inflation (Hodrick-Prescott filter – see Data Appendix) from actual nominal rates. This simple procedure has the advantage of eliminating the volatile month-to-month noise in the inflation data. Because of the high smoothing parameter used, short-run changes in the real interest series thus derived are largely attributable to interest rate changes rather than expected inflation (and this is true of all spikes). When plotted, the resulting real rates are characterized by gentle fluctuations with a period of a few years punctuated by intervals of sometimes violent fluctuations on a month-to-month basis.[12] So, in contrast to what is predicted by simple models of market efficiency, rational expectations and static preferences, real interest rates in developing countries have had a considerable degree of persistence, as well as being subject to short-term reversible shocks.

Developing Country Interest Rates Have Been High

Some of these countries have experienced extended periods of very high real interest rates. Of the seventeen Treasury Bill countries in our data set, eight have had mean real interest rates in double digits continuously for at least three years. Guyana had the highest three-year mean real interest rate at over 26 percent. Much higher real interest rates have been sustained for periods as long as one year: five of the countries had one-year means of over 20 percent: one (Sierra Leone) with 45 percent and another (Mexico) with 33 percent.

. . . And Volatile

But there have also been very low real interest rate observations in developing countries, and, despite a low (negative) mean value, the mean of twenty-five developing country monthly standard deviations (excluding Argentina and Brazil) in our sample is 877 basis points, compared with just 187 basis points for the eight control industrial countries. And this is not just due to some outliers: The smallest of developing country standard deviations is 221 basis points for Singapore.

Negatively Skewed Distribution of US Dollar-adjusted Rates

Volatility and extreme values are also evident in Table 3.3, which compares the 1980–97 average statistics of monthly wholesale returns for

---

[12] Unit root tests can reject nonstationarity of at least half of the country series at the 5 percent level, suggesting that these apparent slow oscillations are not just an optical illusion.

Table 3.3. Ex post Dollar-adjusted Money Market Rates, Monthly Data: 1980–97

% per annum[a]	26 Developing countries	12 Industrial countries
Mean over countries of:		
Mean (standard error)	0.5 (9.4)	7.3 (1.1)
Median	3.1	7.6
Maximum month	192.4	136.8
Minimum month	−99.3	−61.3
Standard deviation	70.4	33.5
Skewness	−3.9	−0.1
Median over countries of:		
Median	6.9	6.1
Standard deviation	42.2	38.4

Note: 26 large developing countries not including Argentina or Brazil.
[a] Annualized logarithmically.

developing and industrial countries adjusted for actual change in exchange rates against the U.S. dollar. Although the mean of developing country dollar-adjusted money market rates was on average much lower than for industrial countries, this mainly reflected the wider variation over time of exchange-rate adjusted interest rates for developing countries, and in particular, the negative skewness (influence of extreme negative observations). In other words, occasional sharp devaluations were not fully compensated for by a sufficient excess return or peso premia in developing country interest rates in normal times.

3 THE TIMING OF LIBERALIZATION: WHOLESALE RATES

For the purpose of describing liberalization, we should distinguish between at least three main types of control: First, external capital (exchange) controls which drive a wedge between domestic and foreign wholesale rates but need not involve any administrative control of domestic rates. Second, administrative control of domestic wholesale rates (this is unlikely to be very effective in the absence of exchange controls). Third, control of retail bank deposit and lending rates. Note that even in a liberalized environment, the authorities can also influence wholesale interest rates by use of monetary policy instruments, but such action is to be distinguished from "control."

Because relaxation of these three controls is rarely simultaneous, it is not normally possible to define a single date on which liberalization occurred. Worse, multiplicity of different interest rates in any country and the varied array of administrative controls[13] that have been employed make it impossible in most cases to define a single liberalization date even for one of the three types of control. Besides, not infrequently, there have been partial reversals of prior liberalizations.[14] Finally, all observers concur that the timing in practice of particular relaxations often does not coincide with the formal relaxation: Sometimes the control has become a dead letter long before formally removed; in other instances formal control has been replaced by informal administrative suasion, or de facto control exercised by the government through its ownership of dominant banks.

By the mid-1990s the process of liberalization has proceeded in many countries to full or almost full abolition of all three types of control; but the process has been a protracted one with many stages varying in importance. This clearly points to the need for detailed country-by-country analysis.[15] But it is also an obstacle to econometric estimation of the impact of liberalization on a cross-country basis, as knowledge of the timing is all but indispensable.

An alternative is to try to infer the timing of key aspects of liberaliza-tion from the statistical properties of the interest rate data themselves.[16] Two classic approaches to measuring the degree of external capital account liberalization by looking at interest rate and other macroeconomic time series have been proposed by Edwards (1985) and Edwards and Khan (1985), where interest rate data is available, and by Haque and Montiel (1991) where interest rate data is not available. Each of these approaches assumes that the effective interest rate is a weighted average of that which would prevail in fully controlled and uncontrolled regimes respectively; the estimated weight then becomes an indicator variable representing the *degree* to which the domestic money market is open and uncontrolled. They could be adapted to allow some time variation in the indicator, and hence

---

[13] For example, foreign exchange controls may be relaxed for certain classes of investors; or ceilings on capital exports may be increased. Controls on Treasury Bill rates may be retained, along with compulsory investment requirements from banks and other institu-tions, while other wholesale rates are freed. Controls on lending rates may be relaxed for certain sectors of borrowers, or for certain categories of bank or near-bank. Controls on bank deposit rates may be relaxed for certain size categories, or maturities, or for accounts attracting a particular class of income tax treatment.

[14] Thus it is not surprising to find, for example, that a recent study's table presenting just twenty-seven liberalization dates had to be accompanied by two-and-a-half pages of qualifying notes (Galbis 1993).

[15] As is also illustrated in Chapters 5, 6, and 7.

[16] If there is data for unregulated curb market differences between the curb and formal market interest rates that can be used as a measure of the degree to which the controls bite. This approach has been used for domestic curb markets by Reisen and Yechès (1993), and extensively for off-shore "euro"-markets, *cf.* Chapter 5.

in principle to identify a liberalization date. While both approaches thus offer elegant solutions to the problem at hand, they have the important shortcoming that each assumes that uncovered interest parity (UIP) prevails in an uncontrolled market. The well-known fact, that UIP is empirically questionable even for countries without any form of foreign exchange control, mars the use of this as an identifying assumption. There are also difficulties with the specification of equilibrium in the controlled market.[17]

A simpler approach that does not rely on UIP depends instead on the assumption that the short-run dynamic behavior of interest rates changes with liberalization.

For administratively controlled interest rates this assumption seems readily acceptable. If rates that were held absolutely constant for extended periods are suddenly found to change from month to month, there has to be a presumption that controls have been relaxed. We find (see the following) that simple filters designed to detect shifts of this type from administratively fixed rates to variable identify plausible regime shift dates for many developing country bank nominal wholesale rates.

Where rates are market-determined but behind effective exchange controls, they are exposed to fluctuations in money supply, but may be partly insulated from the pressures of speculation related to changing exchange rate expectations. If the second form of disturbance is likely to be higher than the first, liberalization of capital controls will be marked by an increase in short-run interest rate volatility. A sharp increase in short-run wholesale interest rate volatility during the period known to be one of liberalization may then indicate a critical effective date of liberalization. We will see in what follows that a filter of this type based on recursive residuals of a simple dynamic model of wholesale interest rate unambiguously identifies regime shift dates for many developing countries, plausibly marking significant shifts toward elimination of capital controls.

Regime Shift of Type A – Relaxation of Nominal Rate Controls

Several countries begin the period with a pattern of only occasional nonzero changes in nominal money market rates, and then make a tran-

---

[17] Characterizing the controlled regime as one of internal monetary equilibrium, as these approaches do, is not enough to distinguish it from a liberalized regime, because internal monetary equilibrium is not incompatible with UIP. So to find that a certain interest rate is halfway between the UIP value and that of internal monetary equilibrium should not allow us to conclude that it is halfway between the controlled and fully-free values. Furthermore, Haque and Montiel's device of subtracting actual capital flows from the money stock in an attempt to construct a counterfactual money supply series that might prevail if the capital account were totally closed likely induces serious measurement bias – and results in an explanatory variable which is perilously close to being defined as the dependent variable plus noise. These points are amplified in the working paper version of this chapter (World Bank Policy Research Working Paper 2313).

sition into frequent changes. To identify key dates for relaxation (or reimposition) of fixed rate administrative control we applied a filter which triggers "control off" whenever the number of changes in the following seven months is four or more, and subsequently triggers "control on" if there is a period of more than twelve months without any change. "Control off" periods are identified as such in Table 3.4.

Regime Shift of Type B – Marked Increases in Real Interest Volatility

In order to identify shifts of this type, we estimated an econometric model of each country's ex ante real interest rate and looked for large forecast errors. Specifically, we fitted a simple error-correction model for each country's real interest rate, assuming that it could be modeled as a function of changes in the world interest rate,[18] of the gap between the world and the local interest rate, and by some autoregressive dynamics.[19] The estimates were by recursive least squares, and we tested the fitted equations for break points indicated by systematic failure of one-month ahead recursive forecasts.[20] Examples of the procedure are shown in Figures 3.3 (a) and (b) for India and Kenya. The recursive residuals from the dynamic interest rate model are shown, bracketed by 5 percent confidence intervals. In the lower panel is plotted the probability level at which the hypothesis of no structural change can be rejected in each period. For the Indian data, March 1990 is identified as the break point, and for Kenya, March 1993.

As the method identifies regime change events with short-term increases in volatility, the subsequent finding that volatility remained high after the change is not an inevitable and tautological consequence of the identification method, but represents an independent observation. (Indeed, to verify this, we also computed postevent volatility removing a six-month window after the event.)

Repeating the exercise for all of the countries we found a plausible pattern of breaks (Table 3.4). For fifteen of the seventeen developing country treasury bill (TB) rates, there was a single break during the sample period.[21] Following the break, the residual standard error was much higher – the median ratio of the before and after residual standard errors was

---

[18] We used the first principal component of the eight large industrial country real Treasury Bill rates as a proxy for the world rate.

[19] The model employed is equivalent to that of equation (1′) in the next section below, with $k = 1$.

[20] The criterion for a break was three forecast errors in four consecutive months each statistically significant at least at the 1 percent level. (A single data outlier in the level of interest rates could have triggered a break if the criterion had required only two significant forecast errors). Note that this method cannot detect a gradual increase in volatility.

[21] Two breaks for Trinidad and Tobago.

Table 3.4. Estimated Dates of De facto Liberalization of
Wholesale Interest Rates

Approach:	"Control off" Date *A*	Marked volatility increase 1980–97	
		Date *B*	Volatility ratio
60C Treasury bill			
Fiji	82:08	85:06	4.7
Ghana	84:08–84:11; 87:10	91:10	2.1
Guyana	87:03–88:07; 89:10	89:10	5.5
Jamaica	80:08	91:03	4.3
Kenya	pre-80	93:03	4.2
Sri Lanka	85:09	88:03	1.6
Mexico	pre-80	83:11	2.6
Malawi	92:06	92:06	5.3
Nepal	89:08	89:10	32.5
Philippines	pre-80	84:06	3.8
Papua New Guinea	80:07	86:01	1.1
Swaziland	82:12	None	
Trinidad & Tobago	80:02	84:07; 94:11	6.7
Sierra Leone	91:12	87:08	4.9
Uganda	92:03	81:10	135.0
South Africa		None	
Zimbabwe	pre-80	92:04	2.4
60B Money market			
India	pre-80	90:03	4.6
Korea	pre-80	None	
Malaysia	pre-80	None	
Pakistan	pre-80–86:12; 89:12	92:03	3.7
Singapore	pre-80	None	
Thailand	pre-80	90:03	2.1
Cote d'Ivoire	82:07–90:05	None	
Mauritius	85:02	None	
Industrial countries			
Australia	pre-80	82:02	2.3
New Zealand	85:02	83:08	7.9
Spain	84:01	83:01	21.3
Portugal	83:01	82:06	90.5

Notes: Industrial countries included are those for which regime changes of type (B) were identified post-1980. Volatility ratio is the ratio of the standard error of estimate of dynamic regression model in the postliberalization period to that in the preliberalization period.

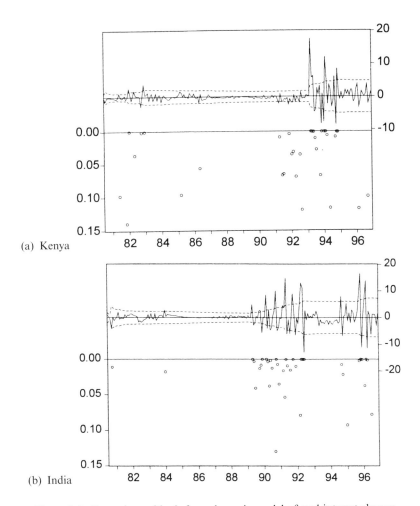

Figure 3.3. Recursive residuals from dynamic model of real interest change.

4.3.[22] Thus we find not only an episode of increased volatility as estimated by the recursive prediction failure, but also that subsequent volatility is higher on a sustained basis.

The filter flags sudden increases in volatility, but, based as it is on recursive (backward-looking) regressions, it does not imply a sustained

---

[22] The calculation was also made after deleting six observations at the break in order to verify that the increase in variance was peristent and not solely driven by a few months around the date of the break.

increase in volatility after the liberalization date. Our finding that volatility did stay high after the liberalization date does, therefore, represent an independent finding.

The coefficients of the error-correction process are not all well determined, but sometimes there is also an indication of a stronger impact of world interest rates after the break. All in all, the empirical patterns detected seem to confirm the a priori belief that this method would capture a significant date in the liberalization of wholesale interest rates.[23]

The same approach was extended to eight of the ten money market rates (Argentina and Brazil excluded because of the difficulty of defining a satisfactory smoothed inflation series). Here a further three break points were detected as shown in Table 3.4, again with high volatility ratios. The indications were that most of the remaining countries may have crossed that threshold before 1980.[24]

The liberalization dates identifed in Table 3.4 are shown again in Table 3.10 alongside those provided for the same countries by other recent studies. The differences between the dates reflect differences in the concept of liberalization date being used. They should thus be considered as complementary to the dates obtained by approaches (A) and (B) here. The Galbis (1993) study uses dates at which preferential lending rates, or controls on key bank deposit or lending rates were removed. Demirgüç-Kunt and Detragiache (Chapter 4) use deregulation of bank interest rates as the observable policy change to date liberalization. Williamson and Mahar (1998) are looking at a wider concept of financial liberalization and provide two dates: "start of liberalization" and "largely liberalized."

4 CONVERGENCE OF INTEREST RATES

What does liberalization mean for global integration of world financial markets? Some indication can be found by modeling the dynamic behavior of real interest rates. We arrive at two main conclusions.

First, real ex ante wholesale interest rates in developing countries are quite strongly influenced by world real interest rate movements. Furthermore, if we distinguish between before- and after-the-liberalization

---

[23] We also carried out the same exercise for the thirteen industrial countries. Break points within the sample period were also found for four of these. (An unusual situation arose for one country, Ireland, where a break existed, but the postbreak residual variance was lower than the prebreak. In fact the identified break was in this instance related to the EMS crisis of 1992–93 rather than to liberalization.)

[24] Liberalization is not irreversible; the data from Malaysia (late 1981), and to a lesser extent India (early 1984) and Pakistan (late 1985) provide some indications of a reversal to a narrower range of fluctuation.

events (type B) reported in Table 3.4,[25] we find that the impact of world interest rates and the speed of convergence both increase following liberalization.

Second, nominal wholesale interest rates help predict subsequent exchange rate movements to a larger extent than is the case in the industrial countries. Following liberalization, their predictive power is no better than before.

The textbook model of an efficient and frictionless expectations-driven financial market without risk aversion (and with sufficient goods-market integration to ensure purchasing-power parity) implies that real interest rates will be equalized across countries and that nominal interest rates differentials will represent unbiased predictions of inflation and exchange rate change. Imperfectly integrated and partially efficient financial markets will still tend to be influenced by world interest rates and by expectations, though perhaps partially and with a lag. This section provides a quantification of the imperfection, and how it evolves with liberalization.

Dynamic Error-correction Model

For our real ex ante wholesale interest rates, we estimated a dynamic error-correction model in which the change in the interest rate is influenced by current world interest rates changes, and by the lagged gap between domestic and world (real) interest rates, together, perhaps with the lagged dependent variable.

Thus, if the real world interest rate at time t is denoted r_t^w and the real interest rate for country i is denoted r_t^i then the convergence model can be written:

$$\Delta r_t^i = a_i + b_i \Delta r_t^w + c_i \left(r_{t-1}^w - r_{t-1}^i \right) + d \Delta r_{t-1}^i + u_t^i \tag{1}$$

or,

$$\Delta r_t^i = a_i + b_i \Delta r_t^w + c_i \left(r_{t-1}^w - r_{t-1}^i \right) + u_t^i \tag{1'}$$

with (in 1′) $u_t^i = \Sigma_{j=1}^k \rho_j u_{t-j1}^i + \varepsilon_t$.

Here the coefficient a_i indicates an average deviation between country i's real interest rate and that of the "world," b_i measures the impact effect of a change in world interest rates on those in i and the "catch-up effect" c_i indicates the speed with which deviations from the mean relationship with the world interest rate are closed. Provided $d < 1$ (or that the autoregressive dynamics of the residual are stable), a positive value of c_i implies

---

[25] In respect of the countries for which no liberalization events of type B are detected, we treat the wholesale rates as liberalized throughout the sample.

that the impact of any transitory shock Σr_t^w or ε_t on r^i is eventually completely damped.[26] The coefficient d, or the autocorrelation coefficient ρ, capture the remainder of the dynamics (Equation (1′) is also the model used in Approach (*B*) above to identify a liberalization date.)

For a country whose financial system has not been liberalized and integrated into the world economy, one would expect smaller values of b and c, together with possibly larger values of a. (Indeed, if the domestic financial system was not at all linked to the rest of the world, even indirectly, the coefficients b and c would be zero.)

Pooled cross-section time series estimation was employed. Although the restriction that coefficients were the same across countries (i.e., for all i) could be statistically rejected, it was discovered that the rejection was at lower levels of significance if the autoregressive coefficients were unrestricted, while the impact of world rates was restricted. The point estimates obtained from such a model indicate that, even *before* the identified dates of liberalization, world interest rates did have an impact on developing countries. The point estimate of the catch-up term is estimated to be twice as high after liberalization than before. Table 3.5 provides a representative selection of estimates.[27]

The typical speed of adjustment of these developing country interest rates to a shock in world interest rates is also estimated to be faster *after* liberalization. If dynamics are the same across all countries, then the simulated[28] response of developing country rates to a hike in world rates from 10 to 15 percent is as shown in the left hand panel of Figure 3.4. While the impact effect in the first few quarters is much faster after liberalization, the subsequent convergence to the new equilibrium is slow in both (though the precision of the estimate of long-term adjustment is naturally weak). Using estimates based on long (eighteen-month) country-specific autoregressive disturbance dynamics accentuates the simulated difference between before and after (right-hand panel of Figure 3.4, based on the Regression F of Table 3.5).

Interest Differentials as Predictors of Exchange Rate Change

A topic of extensive previous research for industrial countries is the degree to which uncovered interest parity prevails. Most research shows that it

---

[26] Note that a statistical test here requires cointegration techniques, on which a large literature exists, *cf.* Wu and Zhang (1996); O'Connell (1998).

[27] Accepted zero restrictions on common parameters are imposed. Although the restriction that country coefficients are common is not accepted, we report country-specific coefficients only for the variable that gives the largest increase in log-likelihood.

[28] Using point estimates from Regression C of Table 5. Note that the 95 percent confidence intervals do overlap.

Table 3.5. Estimate of Dynamic Model of Wholesale Interest Rate Convergence – Equation (1)

	A Constrained		B Country-specific dynamics		C Effect of liberalization		D Common dynamics		E Liberalization changes dynamics		F Country-specific autocorrelation	
	Coeff.	(t-stat)	Coeff.	(t-stat)	Coeff.	(t-stat)	Coeff.	(t-stat)	Coeff.	(t-stat)	Coeff.	(t-stat)
a	0.079	(8.3)	0.042	(6.1)	0.046	(6.5)	0.040	(3.3)	0.044	(5.9)	0.054	(3.9)
b	0.135	(3.3)	0.071	(3.0)							-0.014	(5.4)
c	0.017	(10.4)	0.011	(9.0)	0.008	(5.5)	0.009	(4.6)	0.007	(5.0)	0.010	(3.9)
d	0.320	(24.6)	varies		varies		0.683	(28.5)			0.759	(17.1)
$dum*a$							0.063	(3.5)			0.141	(5.4)
$dum*b$					0.102	(2.9)	0.148	(2.8)	0.093	(2.5)	0.077	(3.1)
$dum*c$					0.009	(4.1)	0.011	(3.8)	0.008	(3.7)	0.035	(5.8)
$dum*d$							-0.449	(16.5)	-0.207	(6.5)	-0.211	(6.2)
Sample	26 developing 80:03–96:12		26 developing 80:03–96:12		26 developing 80:03–96:12		26 developing 80:03–96:12		26 developing 80:03–96:12		26 developing 80:03–96:12	
Method	SUR		SUR		SUR		SUR		SUR		SUR; 18 AR	
RSQ/DW	0.097	2.06	0.157	2.02	0.161	2.03	0.103	2.03	0.164	2.03	0.332	1.98

Notes: "Country" means country-specific coefficients estimated (not reported); Method: SUR is seemingly unrelated regressions system estimate of pool coefficients; 18 AR = 18th order autocorrelation.

81

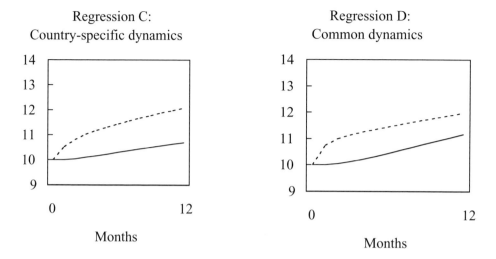

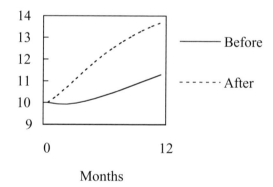

Figure 3.4. Speed of adjustment of developing country real interest rates before and after liberalization.

Table 3.6. Uncovered Interest Parity

	A Industrial		B Developing	
	Coeff.	(t-stat)	Coeff.	(t-stat)
f	3.43	(3.2)	9.96	(6.1)
g	−0.22	(1.1)	0.59	(5.9)
ρ	0.34	(18.5)	0.20	(3.0)
Sample	12 industrial countries 80:01–97:12		25 developing countries 80:01–97:12	
Method	Pooled LS		Pooled LS	
RSQ/DW	0.097	2.06	0.157	2.02

Note: Dependent variable: log-change in US$ exchange rate – Equation 3. St. Lucia is omitted, because there is no variation in the exchange rate.

does not,[29] using some variant of a regression of the exchange rate change (Δe) on interest differentials, i.e.,

$$\Delta e_{t+1} = f + g(r_t^i - r_t^{us}) + u_t$$

and finding that the intercept f is nonzero and the slope g not unity.

Although subtle econometric issues arise, a simple pooled regression on monthly data for twelve industrial countries in our sample (differentials against the U.S. dollar) is not out of line with standard findings: The estimated intercept at 3.4 percent is significantly different from zero, the estimated slope is −0.21 (wrong sign) and significantly different from plus unity. (Also the autoregressive parameter is significantly different from zero, contrary to the uncovered parity and rational expectations hypothesis.) The same pooled regression for twenty-five developing countries has an even larger intercept, but now the slope is positive at 0.59, though it is still significantly different from unity (Table 3.6).

Because of the empirical failure of this theory for industrial countries, and the absence of an accepted theory to explain this,[30] it would be unwise to draw strong conclusions from the fact that developing country interest

---

[29] But weaker tests of the theory can hold: Deviations from UIP are generally found to be stationary and may have mean insignificantly different from zero. See Tanner (1998), whose decomposition of UIP deviations highlights the relatively more important role in developing countries of inflation and real interest rate fluctuations. However, in our data (which excludes Argentina and Brazil), a zero global mean of UIP deviations is strongly rejected (i.e., in the cross-section time-series pool).

[30] Most of the explanations advanced invoke some form of expectations formation error or lag, perhaps combined with an activist monetary policy which makes the interest differential endogenous (e.g., Froot and Frankel 1990; Kaminsky 1993; McCallum 1994). There are also acute small sample econometric problems (Beckaert et al. 1997).

rates are correlated with subsequent exchange rate movements. A plausible interpretation is that future exchange rate change in high inflation developing countries contains a more predictable component which is absent from exchange rate change in the industrial countries over this time period.[31]

Interestingly, the inclusion of postliberalization dummies did not improve the fit of these interest parity regressions.

Levine (1991) found for five industrial countries that forecast changes in the real exchange rate $(\Delta q = \Delta e_{t+1} - \pi_t^i + \pi_t^{us})_t$ were also a best forecast of deviations $(uip = \Delta e_{t+1} - r_t^i + r_t^{us})_t$ from UIP, pointing to a dominant role of anticipated real exchange rate fluctuations in causing the failure of UIP. This result does not appear to carry over to the pool of developing countries. Although forecast values of Δq do help forecast UIP, these forecasts can be improved upon.

The models of Edwards and Khan and Haque and Montiel, discussed earlier, rely on the idea that the domestic interest rate is a weighted average of the rate that would prevail if UIP were valid and a rate determined by domestic considerations. Adapting that idea, we calculated the predicted exchange rate change on the basis of available data for each country, and use that prediction as an explanatory variable in a regression of the interest rate. The domestic explanatory variables should not enter separately in the equation. Interestingly, we found that the coefficient on the predicted exchange rate change was insignificantly different from zero for preliberalization periods, but highly significant, and with a coefficient of about 0.37 for postliberalization. However, though free of some other problems mentioned earlier in connection with these models, this approach has the drawback of relying on the UIP framework.

5   DYNAMIC BEHAVIOR OF BANK RATES AND INTERMEDIATION SPREADS

Severely repressed financial systems often display inversions of interest rate structures, with bank lending rates, at least for some categories of borrower, being controlled below the wholesale rates that might otherwise be considered as representing the marginal cost of funds. This is not the case in the countries with subannual data which we have been considering in the previous sections. Instead, we find that bank interest rates in these countries do respond to movements in wholesale rates quite quickly. Typically, deposit rates respond first, with the result that an increase in rates widens intermediation spreads at first. Spreads then narrow, as lending rates gradually adjust, but the catch-up is estimated to be incomplete, so

---

[31] This meshes with the finding of Mishkin (1992) that the Fisher effect applies only where there is a stochastic trend in inflation.

that a positive long-term equilibrium relationship is estimated to exist between intermediation spreads and the level of interest rates.

Here again our main approach was to use a simple error-correction formulation in a pooled cross-section and time series. An error-correction model explaining movements in lending rates by those in deposit rates in thirty-two countries estimated on quarterly data 1980–97 suggests a rapid pass through: over 81 percent of any change in deposit rates being picked up in lending rates in the same quarter, and over 93 percent by the second quarter. However, such a relationship can hardly be considered causal, as both bank rates are likely to be influenced by the same exogenous factors.

Instead, therefore, we modeled the determination of both deposit and lending rates as being jointly influenced by wholesale rates, using the model:

$$\Delta r_t^l = a^l + \sum\nolimits_{j=1}^{k} b_j^l \Delta r_{t-j+1}^m + c^l \left(r_{t-1}^l - r_{t-1}^m \right) + d^l \left(r_{t-1}^p - r_{t-1}^l \right) + u_t^l \qquad (2)$$

$$\Delta r_t^p = a^p + \sum\nolimits_{j=1}^{k} b_j^p \Delta r_{t-j+1}^m + c^p \left(r_{t-1}^p - r_{t-1}^m \right) + d^p \left(r_{t-1}^l - r_{t-1}^p \right) + u_t^p \qquad (2')$$

where superscripts l, m, and p denote deposit, wholesale and lending rates respectively. (Country identifier has been suppressed.)

Estimating these equations in a pooled cross-section and time series with twenty-one developing countries and nineteen industrial countries shows that the speed of adjustment is quite similar for deposit rates as between developing and industrial countries (Regressions A and B of Table 3.7). Relaxation of the constraint that the catch-up coefficient c^l is the same for all of the developing countries provides a very substantial improvement in fit (Regression C of Table 3.7). The estimated contemporaneous response of the deposit interest rate to wholesale rates from this equation varies widely from between about 75 and 85 percent for Guyana and four African countries (Mauritius, Morocco, Uganda, and Zimbabwe) to only 4 percent for Fiji (Table 3.8), suggesting a ranking of the degree to which these countries have a competitive and unrestricted banking market.

Adjustment of the lending rate p follows a somewhat similar pattern, though it appears that gradual adjustment to any deviation from the mean gap that has opened up between deposit and lending rates takes place through adjustment in the lending rate rather than the deposit rate. Thus the deposit rate can be seen as a faster-adjusting variable than the lending rate (Regression D of Table 3.7).

The impact of liberalization is indicated by the second panel of Table 3.7, which contains estimates in which the parameters are allowed to shift with the liberalization (dates as before, augmented by Table 3.10 where necessary). Although the parameter values change, there is little overall impact on the speed of adjustment, as illustrated in Figure 3.5 (showing

Table 3.7(a). Estimate of Dynamic Model of Bank Interest Rate Convergence: Full Period

	Deposit rate A: Eqn. 2		Deposit rate B: Eqn. 2		Deposit rate C: Eqn. 2		Lending rate D: Eqn. 2′		Spread E: Eqn. 3	
	Coeff.	(t-stat)	Coeff.	(t-stat)	Coeff.	(t-stat)	Coeff.	(t-stat)	Coeff.	(t-stat)
a	0.018	(0.5)	−0.081	(2.9)	−0.044	(1.9)	0.254	(5.5)	varies	
b_1	0.361	(30.7)	0.402	(33.3)	varies		0.361	(29.2)	0.032	(6.2)
b_2	0.140	(10.4)	0.086	(7.4)	0.079	(9.7)	0.104	(8.0)	varies	
b_3	0.027	(24.6)	0.037	(3.3)	0.019	(2.5)	0.028	(2.2)		
c	−0.006	(1.0)	−0.010	(1.7)	0.002	(0.4)	−0.033	(3.5)	0.095	(10.1)
d	−0.042	(4.6)	−0.049	(6.5)	−0.031	(4.3)	−0.013	(1.6)	0.216	(12.8)
Sample	21 developing 80:Q4–98:Q2		19 industrial 80:Q4–98:Q2		21 developing 80:Q4–98:Q2		21 developing 80:Q4–98:Q2		21 developing 80:Q2–98:Q2	
Method	SUR		SUR		SUR		SUR		SUR; AR(1)S	
RSQ/DW	0.530	1.96	0.451	2.09	0.660	1.84	0.481	2.03	0.241	1.96

Table 3.7(b). Estimate of Dynamic Model of Bank Interest Rate Convergence: Effect of Liberalization

	Deposit rate F: Eqn. 2		Deposit rate G: Eqn. 2		Deposit rate H: Eqn. 2		Lending rate J: Eqn. 2′		Spread K: Eqn. 3	
	Coeff.	(t-stat)	Coeff.	(t-stat)	Coeff.	(t-stat)	Coeff.	(t-stat)	Coeff.	(t-stat)
a	−0.069	(1.7)	−0.040	(1.2)	−0.078	(3.0)	0.109	(3.1)	varies	
b_1	0.504	(16.3)	0.543	(17.9)	varies		0.246	(9.5)	0.024	(2.8)
b_2	0.040	(1.2)	0.023	(0.7)	0.045	(2.1)	0.036	(1.3)	varies	
b_3	0.034	(1.0)	0.031	(1.0)	0.003	(0.1)	0.068	(2.4)		
c	0.007	(1.0)					−0.024	(2.0)	0.088	(6.6)
d	−0.056	(3.8)	−0.056	(3.9)	−0.068	(5.3)	0.011	(1.1)	0.216	(10.7)
$dum*a$	0.094	(1.3)	−0.104	(2.1)	0.031	(0.1)	0.298	(4.0)	0.578	(3.1)
$dum*b_1$	−0.154	(4.7)	−0.678	(2.1)	−0.063	(2.0)	0.144	(5.0)	0.099	(2.9)
$dum*b_2$	0.111	(3.1)	0.101	(3.0)	0.028	(1.2)	0.061	(2.0)		
$dum*b_3$	−0.012	(0.3)	−0.005	(0.1)	0.040	(1.7)	−0.052	(1.7)	−0.000	(0.0)
$dum*c$	−0.023	(1.8)					−0.004	(0.2)	0.004	(0.2)
$dum*d$	0.010	(0.5)	−0.013	(0.7)	0.042	(2.9)	−0.056	(3.5)	0.050	(2.6)
Sample	21 developing 80:Q4–98:Q2		21 developing 80:Q4–98:Q2		21 developing 80:Q4–98:Q2		21 developing 80:Q4–98:Q2		21 developing 80:Q2–98:Q2	
Method	SUR		SUR		SUR		SUR		SUR; AR(1)S	
RSQ/DW	0.530	1.96	0.582	2.21	0.780	1.98	0.489	2.01	0.252	2.00

Notes: Equations (2), (2′), and (3). Dependent variables are first differences in the interest rates and spread as indicated; "Varies" means country-specific coefficients estimated (not reported but see Table 3.8); Method: SUR is seemingly unrelated regressions system estimate of pool coefficients; cross-sections with missing data deleted. "AR(1)S" means country-specific first order autocorrelation coefficient estimated.

87

Table 3.8. Estimated Catch-up Term (From Regression C of Table 3.7)

	c^l	(t-stat)		c^l	(t-stat)
Fiji	0.041	(2.9)	Philippines	0.527	(14.0)
Sri Lanka	0.082	(6.2)	St. Lucia	0.551	(0.6)
Indonesia	0.124	(3.5)	Papua NG	0.552	(10.6)
Cote d'Ivoire	0.181	(3.0)	South Africa	0.618	(10.6)
Sierra Leone	0.191	(3.6)	Zimbabwe	0.745	(11.9)
Trinidad	0.264	(1.6)	Mauritius	0.760	(8.2)
Korea	0.374	(5.7)	Uganda	0.775	(12.8)
Malawi	0.452	(7.5)	Swaziland	0.788	(9.5)
Zambia	0.458	(20.1)	Morocco	0.800	(16.1)
Jamaica	0.492	(11.6)	Guyana	0.863	(23.4)
Singapore	0.506	(10.4)			

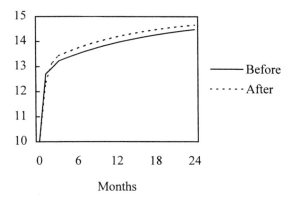

Figure 3.5. Speed of adjustment of developing country deposit interest rates before and after liberalization.

response to a 500 basis point increase in money market rates, based on Regression G of Table 3.7). Ten months after the shock, the liberalized deposit rate is within 100 basis points of the new equilibrium.

Dynamics of the Spread

The dynamic pattern of movements in the intermediation spread is summarized by a similar error-correction equation, with the change in the spread as dependent variable:

$$\Delta r_t^p - \Delta r_t^l = a^s + b_1^s r_t^m + b_2^s \Delta r_t^m + c^s \left(r_{t-1}^p - r_{t-1}^m \right) + d^s \left(r_{t-1}^l - r_{t-1}^p \right) + u_t^s \qquad (3)$$

Table 3.9. Macroeconomic Performance Before and After Interest Liberalization

	Before	After	Before	After	Difference
	liberalization		(rel. control group)		(t-stat)
Inflation (CPI growth %)	27.7	21.8	+19.9	+18.5	−1.4 (0.2)
Liquidity ratio (M2/GDP %)	35.3	37.0	−23.9	−27.2	−3.4 (0.5)
GNP growth (%)	2.3	2.6	+0.6	+0.2	−0.4 (0.6)

Notes: Annual data 1975–97. The liquidity ratio takes the ratio of end-year M2 to the mean GDP of same and following year. Nineteen liberalizing countries including Portugal as in Table 3.1. Control group: The United States, the United Kingdom, Germany, Italy, Sweden, Switzerland, and Canada. Date of liberalization is method *B* above.
Source: *International Financial Statistics*.

(Regression E of Table 3.7). This reveals that the spread does widen in response to an increase in money market rates, converging gradually to an equilibrium relationship, and that the equilibrium spread is positively related to the general level of interest rates, as indicated by the significant coefficient on the lagged wholesale rate (equivalent results are obtained when the deposit rate is substituted for the wholesale rate). Inclusion of liberalization dummies suggests that the long-term equilibrium relation between spread and level of rates is primarily a postliberalization phenomenon.

6   ECONOMIC PERFORMANCE BEFORE AND AFTER LIBERALIZATION

How did aggregate economic performance change following liberalization? A simple before-and-after experiment can be no more than suggestive (and even the most sophisticated cross-country regression can be unconvincing in this context). Still, it is interesting to find that there is no clearcut change in mean rates of inflation, monetary depth, or GDP growth after liberalization. If anything there is a small average improvement in inflation, but a disimprovement in monetary depth and economic growth, relative to industrial country trends. Table 3.9 shows mean pre- and postliberalization mean values of these variables for the set of countries for which liberalization dates for the Treasury Bill rate have been identified above. The data are also shown normalized as the difference between the subject countries and the mean for seven large industrial countries taken as a control group. Inflation – much higher than in the control group – fell somewhat more after liberalization, but the difference of 1.4 percent is not statistically significant. The modest increase in monetary depth (liquidity ratio and in annual GNP growth) is in both cases less than that

Table 3.10. Liberalization Dates (as reported in various studies)

| | Statistical (wholesale) | | Expert datings | | | |
| | | | | | W&M | |
Method:	"Control off" (a)	Volatility jump (b)	Galbis	D&D	Start	Largely
Argentina			77:6		77; 87	82; 93
Australia	pre-80	82:2		81		
Bangladesh					89	–
Bolivia			85:8			
Brazil			75:3		89	–
Cameroon			90:10			
Chile			75:4	pre-80	74	85
Colombia			80:1	pre-80	80	95
Costa Rica			86:8			
Cote d'Ive	82:7–90:5	–	89:10			
Ecuador				86–87; 92		
Egypt				91	91	–
El Salvador				91		
Fiji	82:8	85:6				
Ghana	84:8–11; 87:10	91:10				
Guatemala				89		
Guyana	87:3–88:7; 89:10	89:10		91		
Honduras				90		
China-HK					78	73
Hungary			91:1			
India	pre-80	90:3		91	92	–
Indonesia				83	83	89
Israel				90	87	91
Jamaica	80:08	91:3	85:10	91		
Jordan				88		
Kenya	pre-80	93:3		91		
Korea	pre-80	–	Not lib	84–88; 91	83	–
Malawi	92:6	92:6				
Malaysia	pre-80	–	78:10	pre-80	78	92
Mauritius	85:2	–	81:11			
Mexico	pre-80	83:11	85:3	89	74; 89	92
Morocco					91	96
Nepal	89:8	89:10	86:5		89	–
New Zealand	85:2	83:8		pre-80; 84		
Nigeria			87:7	90		
Pakistan	pre-80	92:3				
Papua New Guinea	80:7	86:1		pre-80		
Paraguay				90		
Peru					91	93

Table 3.10.

Method:	Statistical (wholesale)		Expert datings			
	"Control off" (a)	Volatility jump (b)	Galbis	D&D	W&M Start	Largely
Philippines	pre-80	84:6	82:12	81	81	94
Poland			90:1			
Portugal	83:1	82:6		94		
Romania			91:4			
Sra Leone	91:12	87:8				
Singapore	pre-80	–			78	73
S. Africa	pre-80	–			80	84
Spain	84:1	83:1	87:3			
Sri Lanka	85:9	88:3		80	78	–
Swaziland	82:12	–				
Taiwan					89	–
Tanzania			91:7	93		
Thailand	pre-80	90:3	90:3	89	mid-80s	92
Togo				93		
Trinidad & Tobago	80:2	84:7; 94:11				
Turkey			80:7; 87:7	80–82; 84	80; 88	90
Uganda	92:3	81:10	88:7			
Uruguay			79:9	pre-80		
Venezuela			81:8; 89:2	89	91	–
Zaire				pre-80		
Zambia				92		
Zimbabwe	pre-80	92:4				

Note: Other studies (based on expert assessments of administrative changes): Demirgüç-Kunt and Detragiache 1998; Galbis 1983; Williamson and Mahar 1998 – start of liberalization and "largely liberalized" dates (see text).

which occurred simultaneously in the control group, though again the difference is insignificant.

The increase in interest rates and their volatility have not been the only factors influencing economic development over the past two decades. Furthermore, financial liberalization has normally been a complex, long, drawn out, and sometimes reversed process. It would be surprising if a before-and-after comparison based on our data identifying a single – albeit key – date were to show a significant impact.[32]

---

[32] The econometrics of these issues are addressed in the context of financial development and growth by King and Levine (1993a,b), Levine, Loayza, and Beck (2000), and *cf.* Nausser and Kugler (1998).

7 CONCLUDING REMARKS

Even an analysis confined to the countries for which data is available provides unmistakable evidence for an increase in the general level of real interest rates as financial liberalization progressed, and this increase was more pronounced than the contemporaneous increase in industrial country rates. The volatility in wholesale rates also jumped in most liberalizing countries, the regime change in this respect often being quite marked.

Though evidence of an increase in global integration of interest rates is also noted, the indications here are more muted than might have been expected, probably reflecting the fact that pressures of globalization often persisted through the preliberalization period, and were certainly present before 1980.

Changes in the relative position of different interest rates also have had a distributional effect and an effect on incentives. As well as the implicit redistributions associated with changes in the level of wholesale rates. That the increase in Treasury Bill rates is closer to other wholesale rates is one important aspect here, as is the widening of bank interest spreads, and the tendency for such spreads to be correlated in the long run with the level of wholesale rates.

DATA APPENDIX

The interest rates data used is from *International Financial Statistics* (*IFS*). Five interest rate categories are used: Official rates (*60*) represent rates at which the central banks lend to financial institutions. Money market rates (*60B*) – representing interbank lending – and Treasury Bill rates (*60C*) are the two wholesale rates, while bank deposit (*60L*) and lending (*60P*) rates are described as retail rates, though the data collected does typically refer to rather large transactions. IFS also contains some long-term government bond interest rates which we have not examined in this paper.

Up to the mid-1970s interest rate data other than official rates was only available for a handful of countries. Country coverage of the interest rate series in *IFS* improved rapidly in the late 1970s so that from 1980 on fairly comprehensive coverage exists for the wholesale interest rates of over fifty countries, and the official and retail rates for over seventy countries.

For the monthly time series analysis of wholesale rates, we confined our analysis to countries for which complete or nearly[33] complete data was available over the period 1980–97. Treasury Bill rates (*60C*) are available

---

[33] In a few cases short stretches of missing data were filled by interpolating available quarterly figures, or by using regression relationships with available data.

for some forty countries, of which twenty-seven are developing countries.[34] As it happens, five of these countries are all tiny members of the East Caribbean Central Bank (ECCB), with a common interest rate and exchange rate policy. A further five have populations of under 0.5 million. Therefore most of our analysis concentrates on the remaining seventeen larger developing countries, together with one representative for the ECCB. In addition we find a further seventeen developing countries for which substantially complete monthly data on money market rates (*60B*) is available, of which seven share a common rate in the West African Monetary Union (UMOA). Excluding all but one of the latter, this gives a total of twenty-eight developing countries for which complete data on the movements in wholesale rates can be analyzed. These countries are: Argentina, Brazil, Côte d'Ivoire, Fiji, Ghana, Guyana, India, Jamaica, Kenya, Korea, Malaysia, India, Sri Lanka, Mexico, Malawi, Mauritius, Nepal, Pakistan, Papua New Guinea, Philippines, St. Lucia, Sierra Leone, Singapore, Swaziland, Thailand, Trinidad and Tobago, Uganda, South Africa, and Zimbabwe. Although a microstate, St. Lucia is included as a representative of the ECCB. Côte d'Ivoire represents the UMOA. The following twelve industrial countries, for which monthly data on *60C* exist, were included as controls: Australia, Belgium, Canada, Germany, Ireland, Italy, New Zealand, Portugal, Spain, Sweden, Switzerland, the United Kingdom, and the United States.

For the expected or ex ante real interest rates, a Hodrick-Prescott filter with parameter 1600 was applied to the log change in each country's consumer price index (CPI), and the result subtracted from the nominal exchange rate.[35]

For the econometric analysis using quarterly data on deposit and lending rates, similar sample selection criteria were applied (substantially complete availability of the relevant data over 1980–97; no microstates, only one country per currency union). This left thirty-seven developing countries for which more or less complete quarterly data on the movements in bank rates can be analyzed. These countries are: Argentina,

---

[34] For example, excluding those who were members of the OECD throughout. In this definition Korea and Mexico are included with the developing countries, as they were not members of the OECD for most of the sample.

[35] We applied a single filter to each country's entire inflation series, rather than using a Kalman filter. A one-sided backward-looking univariate filter on this data would use too little information to provide a credible expectations proxy, especially (but not only) for early periods. This outweighs the obvious drawback of the procedure we have adopted, namely that the expected inflation for time *t* is computed using data that was not available at time *t*. While that would make this approximation questionable for examining issues of informational efficiency, those issues are not a central focus of this chapter (*cf.* Baxter 1994; Edison and Pauls 1993).

Botswana, Brazil, Cameroon, Costa Rica, Côte d'Ivoire, Cyprus, Fiji, the Gambia, Ghana, Guatemala, Guyana, Honduras, Indonesia, Jamaica, Korea, Malawi, Malta, Mauritius, Mexico, Morocco, Nigeria, Papua New Guinea, Philippines, Rwanda, St. Lucia, Sierra Leone, Singapore, South Africa, Sri Lanka, Swaziland, Trinidad and Tobago, Turkey, Uganda, Uruguay, Zambia, and Zimbabwe. For Ghana, Mexico, and Turkey, deposit rate only was used. Argentina and Brazil were excluded from the econometrics because of their outliers. For analysis requiring both whole-sale and bank rates (Table 3.5) the following countries also had to be excluded for want of data: Botswana, Cameroon, Costa Rica, Cyprus, the Gambia, Guatemala, Honduras, Malta, Nigeria, Rwanda, and Uruguay. That left twenty-one countries in the standard sample used. Data for nineteen industrial countries were used as controls: Australia, Belgium, Canada, Denmark, Finland, Germany, Iceland, Ireland, Italy, Japan, Netherlands, New Zealand, Norway, Portugal, Spain, Sweden, Switzerland, the United Kingdom, and the United States.

The shortcomings of the data must be acknowledged. Long series like the ones we are using necessarily involve changing definitions of the underlying assets, as institutions and data-collection methods evolve. Furthermore, there is typically a very wide range of interest rates prevalent in any financial market, depending on size, creditworthiness, maturity, and other asset characteristics. The limited number of series available here will capture this diversity very imperfectly.

REFERENCES

Baxter, M. 1994. "Real Exchange Rates and Real Interest Rates: Have We Missed the Business Cycle Relationship?" *Journal of Monetary Economics* 33:5–37.

Beckaert, G., R.J. Hodrick, and D.A. Marshall. 1997. "On Biases in Tests of the Expectations Hypothesis of the Term Structure of Interest Rates." *Journal of Financial Economics* 44:309–48.

Blanchard, O. and L.H. Summers. 1984. "Perspectives on High World Real Interest Rates." *Brookings Papers on Economic Activity* 1984(2):273–324.

Edison, H. and D. Pauls. 1993. "A Re-assessment of the Relationship between Real Exchange Rates, 1974–1990." *Journal of International Economics* 31:165–88.

Edwards, S. 1985. "Money, the Rate of Devaluation, and Interest Rates in a Semi-Open Economy: Colombia, 1968–82." *Journal of Money, Credit and Banking* 17:59–68.

Edwards, S. and M.S. Khan. 1985. "Interest Rate Determination in Developing Countries: A Conceptual Framework." *IMF Staff Papers* 32:377–403.

Froot, K.A. and J.A. Frankel. 1990. "Forward Discount Bias: Is It an Exchange Risk Premium?" *Quarterly Journal of Economics* 104:139–61.

Galbis, V. 1993. "High Real Interest Rate Under Financial Liberalization: Is There a Problem?" *IMF Working Paper* 93/7.

Haque, N.U. and P.J. Montiel. 1991. "Capital Mobility in Developing Countries: Some Empirical Tests." *World Development* 19:1391–98.

Jenkinson, N. 1996. "Saving, Investment and Real Interest Rates." Bank of England Quarterly Bulletin, February.

Kaminsky, G. 1993. "Is There a Peso Problem?" *American Economic Review* 83:450–72.

King, R.G. and R. Levine. 1993a. "Finance and Growth: Schumpeter Might Be Right." *Quarterly Journal of Economics* 108:717–37.

King, R.G. and R. Levine. 1993b. "Finance, Entrepreneurship and Growth: Theory and Evidence." *Journal of Monetary Economics* 32:513–42.

Levine, R. 1991. "An Empirical Inquiry into the Nature of the Forward Exchange Rate Bias." *Journal of International Economics* 30:359–69.

Levine, R.G., N. Loayza, and T. Beck. 2000. "Finance and the Source of Growth." *Journal of Monetary Economics* 46(1):31–77.

McCallum, B.T. 1994. "A Reconsideration of the Uncovered Interest Parity Relationship." *Journal of Monetary Economics* 33:105–32.

Mishkin, F. 1984. "Are Real Interest Rates Equal Across Countries? An Empirical Investigation of International Parity Conditions." *Journal of Finance* 39: 1345–57.

Mishkin, F. 1992. "Is the Fisher Effect for Real?" *Journal of Monetary Economics* 30:195–215.

Nausser K. and M. Kugler. 1998. "Manufacturing Growth and Financial Development: Evidence from OECD Countries." *Review of Economics and Statistics* 80:638–46.

O'Connell, P.G.J. 1998. "The Overvaluation of Purchasing-Power-Parity." *Journal of International Economics* 44:1–19.

Reisen, H. and H. Yechès. 1993. "Time-varying Estimates of the Openness of the Capital Account in Korea and Taiwan." *Journal of Development Economics* 41:285–305.

Tanner, E. 1998. "Deviations from Uncovered Interest Parity: A Global Guide to Where the Action Is." *IMF Working Paper* 98/117.

Williamson, J. and M. Mahar. 1998. "A Survey of Financial Liberalization." *Princeton Essays in International Finance* No. 211.

Wu, Y. and H. Zhang. 1996. "Mean Reversion in Interest Rates: New Evidence from a Panel of OECD Countries." *Journal of Money, Credit and Baking* 28:604–21.

4

Financial Liberalization and Financial Fragility

Aslı Demirgüç-Kunt and Enrica Detragiache[1]

INTRODUCTION

While the link between financial development and economic growth has been documented through careful empirical studies, the connection between financial liberalization and financial fragility has not been the object of systematic econometric investigation so far. This chapter is an attempt to fill this gap.

Financial liberalization, by giving banks and other financial intermediaries more freedom of action, can increase the opportunities to take on risk, thereby increasing financial fragility. This is not necessarily bad for the economy, as high-risk, high-returns investment projects may dominate low-risk, low-return ventures. However, because of limited liability compounded with other forms of implicit and explicit guarantees, bankers' appetite for risk is likely to be greater than what is socially desirable. If prudential regulation and supervision are not effective at controlling bank behavior and at realigning incentives, liberalization may increase financial fragility well above what is socially desirable. Also, to the extent that the skills to screen and monitor risky borrowers and to manage a risky loan portfolio, as well as the skills to perform efficient supervision, can only be acquired gradually and through "learning-by-doing," banks in newly liberalized systems are likely to be more vulnerable.

All these considerations suggest that, other things being equal, the risk of bank insolvency and, more generally, of systemic banking crises may be greater in liberalized financial systems. This chapter presents econometric tests of various aspects of this linkage.

[1] This chapter is adapted from a paper that was prepared for the 1998 World Bank Annual Conference on Development Economics. We wish to thank Gerry Caprio, George Clarke, Stijn Claessens, Ed Kane, Phil Keefer, Ross Levine, Miguel Savastano, and Peter Wickham for helpful comments, and Anqing Shi and Thorsten Beck for excellent research assistance. The views expressed should not be taken as reflecting those of the International Monetary Fund.

Building upon our previous research on the determinants of banking crises (Demirgüç-Kunt and Detragiache 1998), we construct a financial liberalization dummy variable for a large number of developed and developing countries during 1980–95. To date liberalization we choose an observable policy change, namely the deregulation of bank interest rates, since case studies indicate that this is often the centerpiece of the overall liberalization process. The data set encompasses countries that liberalized financial markets well before the 1980s as well as countries that liberalized at different dates during the sample period. Using a multivariate logit framework, we test whether banking crises are more likely to occur in liberalized financial systems when other factors that may increase the probability of a crisis are controlled. The set of control variables includes macroeconomic variables, characteristics of the banking sector, and institutional variables. We also test whether crises are more likely to occur during the transition to a less-controlled financial system, or if fragility is a permanent feature of liberalization.

Another issue often raised in the debate over financial liberalization is whether the dangers of liberalization are greater in countries where the institutions needed to support the efficient functioning of financial markets are not well developed. Such institutions include effective prudential regulation and supervision of financial intermediaries and of organized security exchanges, and a well-functioning mechanism to enforce contracts and regulations. We investigate this issue by testing whether the relationship between banking crises and liberalization is stronger in countries with weaker institutional environments, as proxied by GDP per capita and various indexes of institutional quality. Finally, we subject our results to a variety of robustness checks.

The general result is that banking crises are indeed more likely to occur in countries with a liberalized financial sector, even when other factors (including the real interest rate) are controlled for; furthermore, increased banking sector fragility is not a characteristic of the immediate aftermath of liberalization; rather, it tends to surface a few years after the liberalization process begins. The data also support the conjecture that a weak institutional environment makes liberalization more likely to lead to a banking crisis; specifically, in countries where the rule of law is weak, corruption is widespread, the bureaucracy is inefficient, and contract enforcement mechanisms are ineffective, financial liberalization tends to have a particularly large impact on the probability of a banking crisis. Thus, there is clear evidence that financial liberalization has costs in terms of increased financial fragility especially in developing countries, where the institutions needed to support a well-functioning financial system are generally not well established.

To explore a possible channel through which liberalization may affect bank fragility, we use bank level data to examine the correlation between variables proxying bank franchise values and the financial liberalization dummy variable. We find evidence that franchise values tend to be lower when financial markets are liberalized, possibly because bank monopolistic power is eroded. This suggests that theories attributing increased moral hazard to low bank franchise value may help explain why financial liberalization tends to make banking crises more likely (Caprio and Summers 1993; Hellman, Murdock, and Stiglitz 2000).

These findings raise the question of whether the many benefits of financial liberalization highlighted in the literature may not be offset by the costs in terms of greater vulnerability to banking crises. A rigorous answer to this complex question is beyond the scope of this chapter. Nonetheless, using our data set we attempt to throw some light on one particular aspect of the issue, namely the effect of financial liberalization and banking crises on financial development and growth. First, we show that financial development is positively correlated with output growth in our sample, confirming the results of King and Levine (1993). Second, we find that, conditional on there being no banking crisis, countries/time periods in which financial markets are liberalized have higher financial development than countries/time periods in which markets are controlled. However, countries/time periods with *both* financial liberalization and a banking crisis have approximately the same level of financial development as countries/time periods with neither, so that the net effect on growth through financial development is not significantly different from zero.

To explore this issue further, we split the sample between countries that were financially repressed at the time of liberalization and countries that were financially restrained, where the state of financial repression (restraint) is identified by the presence of negative (positive) interest rates in the period before liberalization. The same tests described above are then performed for the two subsamples. For the restrained group, the results resemble those for the whole sample. In contrast, for the repressed group financial liberalization is accompanied by higher financial development even if a banking crisis also takes place. These findings suggest that financial liberalization is likely to have a positive effect on growth through financial development in countries characterized by financial repression, even if it increases financial fragility.

The chapter is organized as follows: Section 1 describes the data set and explains the methodology used in the empirical tests. Section 2 contains the main results, while Section 3 summarizes the outcome of various sensitivity tests. Section 4 discusses the relationship between liberalization and bank franchise value. Section 5 discusses the effects of financial liberalization and banking crises on financial development and growth. Section 6 concludes.

1 DATA AND METHODOLOGY

The Sample

To select which countries to include in the panel, we began with all the countries in the *International Financial Statistics* of the International Monetary Fund (IMF) except for centrally planned economies and economies in transition (see Table 4.9 for data definitions and sources). To obtain a sufficiently large number of time series, we decided to limit our study to the 1980–95 period; as will be shown below, this period includes a substantial number of banking crises and of financial liberalization episodes, so that the data set is sufficiently rich for the purposes of our investigation.[2] Some countries had to be eliminated because of missing data, or because we could not find sufficient information on financial liberalization. A few countries were left out because their banking systems were in a state of chronic distress for the entire period under consideration, and it was therefore impossible to pinpoint a specific subperiod as a banking crisis period. Finally, two countries (Argentina and Bolivia) were excluded because they are outliers with respect to two of the regressors that we use (inflation and the real interest rate).[3] This process of elimination left us with fifty-three countries in the baseline specification (see Table 4.1).

A Multivariate Logit Model

To identify the impact of financial liberalization on financial fragility we estimate the probability of a banking crisis using a multivariate logit model, and we test the hypothesis that a dummy variable capturing whether the financial system is liberalized or not significantly increases the probability of a crisis when other factors are controlled for. Accordingly, our dependent variable, the banking crisis dummy, is equal to zero if there is no banking crisis, and it is equal to one if there is a crisis. The probability that a crisis will occur at a particular time in a particular country is hypothesized to be a function of a vector of n variables $X_{i,t}$ including the financial liberalization dummy variable and $n - 1$ control variables. Let $P_{i,t}$ denote a dummy variable that takes the value of one when a banking crisis occurs in country i and time t and a value of zero otherwise. β is a vector

---

[2] Due to lack of data, for some countries the observations included in the panel do not cover the entire 1980–95 period.

[3] If the outliers are introduced in the panel, the results do not change much, except that the estimated coefficient for inflation and the real interest rate become smaller. Peru also had a hyperinflation during the sample period, but the hyperinflation years are excluded from the panel because of missing data.

Table 4.1. Interest Rate Liberalization and Banking Crisis Dates

Country	Liberalization[b]	Crisis	Country	Liberalization[b]	Crisis
Australia	81–95		Malaysia	80–95	85–88
Austria	80–95		Mali		87–89
Belgium	86–95		Mexico	89–95	82, 94–95
Canada	80–95		Netherlands	80–95	
Chile	80–95	81–87	New Zealand	80, 84–95	
Colombia	80–95	82–85	Nigeria	90–93	91–95
Denmark	81–95		Norway	85–95	87–93
Ecuador	86–87, 92–95		Paraguay	90–95	95
Egypt	91–95		Peru	80–84, 90–95	83–90
El Salvador	91–95	89	Philippines	81–95	81–87
Finland	86–95	91–94	PN Guinea	80–95	89–95
France	80–95		Portugal	84–95	86–89
Germany	80–95		Sri Lanka	80–95	89–93
Greece	80–95		Sweden	80–95	90–93
Guatemala	89–95		Switzerland	89–95	
Guyana	91–95	93–95	Syria		
Honduras	90–95		Tanzania	93–95	88–95
India	91–95	91–94	Thailand	89–95	83–87
Indonesia	83–95	92–94	Togo	93–95	
Ireland	85–95		Turkey[a]	80–82, 84–95	91, 94–95
Israel	90–95	83–84	Uganda[a]	91–95	
Italy	80–95	90–94	United States	80–95	80–92
Jamaica	91–95		Uruguay	80–95	81–85
Japan	85–95	92–94	Venezuela	89–95	93–95
Jordan	88–95	89–90	Zaire[a]	80–95	
Kenya	91–95	93	Zambia[a]	92–95	
Korea	84–88, 91–95				

[a] This country had additional banking crises during 1980–95, but these crises are not included in the panel because of missing data.
[b] Periods of interest rate liberalization during 1980–95.

of n unknown coefficients and $F(\beta' X_{i,t})$ is the cumulative probability distribution function evaluated at $\beta' X_{i,t}$. Then, the log-likelihood function of the model is:

$$\log L = \sum_{t=1}^{T} \sum_{1}^{n} \left(P_{i,t} \log[F(\beta' X_{i,t})] + (1 - P_{i,t}) \log[1 - F(\beta' X_{i,t})] \right)$$

To model the probability distribution function F we use the logistic functional form, thus the estimated coefficients do not indicate the increase in the probability of a crisis given a one-unit increase in the corresponding explanatory variables as in standard linear regression models. Instead, the coefficients capture the effect of a change in an explanatory variable on $\log\frac{P_{i,t}}{1-P_{i,t}}$. Therefore, while the sign of the coefficient does indicate the direction of the change, the magnitude depends on the slope of the cumulative distribution function at $\beta'X_{i,t}$.

After the onset of a banking crisis, the behavior of some of the explanatory variables is likely to be affected by the crisis itself; since these feedback effects would muddle the estimation, years in which banking crises are under way are eliminated from the panel.[4] Also, the probability that a crisis occurs in a country that had problems in the past is likely to differ from that of a country where no crisis ever occurred. To take this dependence into account, we include different additional regressors in the estimated equations such as the number of past crises, the duration of the last spell, and the time since the last crisis.

The Banking Crisis Variable

To construct a banking crisis dummy variable, we have identified and dated episodes of banking sector distress during the period 1980–95 using primarily two recent studies, Caprio and Klingebiel (1996), and Lindgren, Garcia, and Saal (1996). For an episode of distress to be classified as a full-fledged crisis, we established – somewhat arbitrarily – that at least one of the following conditions must apply: The ratio of nonperforming assets to total assets in the banking system exceeded 10 percent; the cost of the rescue operation was at least 2 percent of GDP; banking sector problems resulted in a large-scale nationalization of banks; extensive bank runs took place or emergency measures such as deposit freezes, prolonged bank holidays, or generalized deposit guarantees were enacted by the government in response to the crisis. In Section 4 that follows we explore the sensitivity of the results to the definition of a crisis. To establish the length of the crisis, we relied solely on the dates provided by the case studies. A list of the crisis episodes is presented in Table 4.1.

The Financial Liberalization Variable

Empirical studies of financial liberalization have often used the real interest rate as a proxy for financial liberalization (Fry 1997, but see Bandiera et al. 2000). Real interest rates, however, especially when measured ex post, are likely to be affected by a variety of factors that have little to do with changes in the regulatory framework of financial markets. This problem may be limited in a cross-country study, in which interest rates are averaged over long periods of time, but in a panel study like ours with an

---

[4] See Section 4 on sensitivity analysis for alternative approaches.

important time-series dimension proxying financial liberalization with the real interest rate would be potentially misleading. For instance, a positive correlation between real interest rates and the probability of a banking crisis may simply reflect the fact that both variables tend to be high during cyclical economic downturns, while financial liberalization plays no role.

To avoid this problem, in this study we construct a financial liberalization variable based on observed policy changes. This strategy, however, is not without its difficulties: First, no available data base records such policy changes, and we had to resort to case studies, IMF country reports, and other miscellaneous sources of information. Furthermore, the process of financial liberalization has taken many different forms: Some countries eliminated some restrictions before others; some countries, such as Greece or Japan, opted for a very gradual approach, while others like Egypt or Mexico switched regime quite rapidly. Also, in some cases, there were temporary reversals. After reviewing our information sources, it became clear that in most countries the removal of interest rate controls was the centerpiece of the liberalization process; thus, we chose this policy change as the indicator of financial liberalization. This left us with the choice of what to consider as the beginning date in countries where the process was gradual. Lacking a good theoretical ground for preferring one option over another, we chose the first year in which some interest rates were liberalized as the beginning date because it was easier to identify. Table 4.1 shows the dates of interest rate liberalization for the countries in our sample. For some countries, two sets of dates are entered because liberalization was temporarily reversed. While 63 percent of our observations are classified as periods of liberalization, 78 percent of banking crises occurred in periods of financial liberalization.

The Control Variables

The set of control variables is taken from our previous study of banking crises (Demirgüç-Kunt and Detragiache 1998), and it reflects both the theory of the determinants of banking crises and data availability.[5] The first group of control variables captures macroeconomic developments that affect bank performance especially through the level of nonperforming loans; this group includes the rate of growth of real GDP, the external terms of trade, and the rate of inflation. The real short-term interest rate is also introduced as a control variable because, whether financial markets are liberalized or not, banking sector problems are more likely to

---

[5] For more details on the relationship between the theory of banking crises and the choice of control variables, see Demirgüç-Kunt and Detragiache (1998). Table 4.9 identifies data sources.

emerge if real interest rates are high.[6] The second set of control variables includes characteristics of the banking system, such as vulnerability to sudden capital outflows (measured by the ratio of M2 to foreign exchange reserves, as suggested by Calvo 1996), liquidity (measured by the ratio of bank cash and reserves to bank assets), exposure to the private sector (measured by the ratio of loans to the private sector to total loans), and lagged credit growth. This last variable is introduced because high rates of credit expansion may finance an asset price bubble that, when it bursts, causes a banking crisis. Finally, GDP per capita is used to control for the level of development of the country.

Measures of Institutional Quality

Since the quality of institutions may affect the degree to which financial liberalization increases the probability of a banking crisis, in alternative specifications we interact proxies of institutional quality with the liberalization dummy variables, and introduce the interaction term as a separate variable in the regression. We experiment with six alternative measures of institutional quality, GDP per capita and five indexes measuring the degree to which the rule of law is respected ("law and order"), the extent of bureaucratic delays, the quality of contract enforcement, the quality of the bureaucracy, and the degree of corruption. These indexes are increasing in the quality of the institutions.

2 EMPIRICAL RESULTS

Table 4.2 contains the results of the logit regressions estimating the probability of a banking crisis as a function of the financial liberalization dummy variable and of a set of control variables. The table also presents the usual diagnostic tests to assess the goodness of fit of the model.[7] The

---

[6] To minimize potential endogeneity problems, to measure the real interest rate we use the rate on short-term government paper or a central bank rate, such as the discount rate, and not a bank interest rate. In six countries, however, neither measure was available, and we used the bank deposit rate.

[7] The model χ^2 tests the joint significance of the regressors by comparing the likelihood of the model with that of a model with the intercept only. The Akaike Information Criterion (AIC) is computed as minus the log-likelihood of the model plus the number of parameters being estimated, and it is therefore smaller for better models. This criterion is useful in comparing models with different degrees of freedom. The percentage of crises that are correctly classified and the total percentage of observations that are correctly classified are reported to assess the prediction accuracy of the model. A crisis is deemed to be accurately predicted when the estimated probability exceeds the frequency of crisis observations in the sample (around 5 percent). This criterion tends to downplay the performance of the model, because in a number of episodes the estimated probability of a crisis increases significantly a few years before the episode begins and those observations are considered as incorrectly classified by the criterion (see Demirgüç-Kunt and Detragiache 1998, for some examples).

Table 4.2. Financial Liberalization and Banking Crises

	(1)	(2)	(3)	(4)	(5)	(6)	(7)
Control variables:							
Growth	−0.168**	−0.164**	−0.163**	−0.162**	−0.167**	−0.168**	−0.191**
	(0.040)	(0.039)	(0.039)	(0.039)	(0.039)	(0.039)	(0.044)
TOT change	−0.052*	−0.050*	−0.043*	−0.043*	−0.049*	−0.049*	−0.050*
	(0.023)	(0.022)	(0.020)	(0.020)	(0.022)	(0.022)	(0.025)
Real interest	0.047**	0.046**	0.048**	0.050**	0.051**	0.050**	0.044**
	(0.015)	(0.015)	(0.015)	(0.015)	(0.015)	(0.015)	(0.015)
Inflation	0.027**	0.027**	0.027**	0.027**	0.027**	0.028**	0.022*
	(0.009)	(0.008)	(0.009)	(0.009)	(0.009)	(0.009)	(0.011)
M2/Reserves	0.022**	0.021**	0.016**	0.017**	0.017**	0.017*	0.024**
	(0.007)	(0.007)	(0.007)	(0.007)	(0.007)	(0.007)	(0.007)
Private/GDP	0.007	0.007	0.006	0.006	0.006	0.006	0.013
	(0.012)	(0.013)	(0.012)	(0.012)	(0.012)	(0.012)	(0.013)
Cash/Bank	−0.018	−0.019	−0.020	−0.020	−0.021	−0.020	−0.022
	(0.014)	(0.014)	(0.014)	(0.014)	(0.014)	(0.014)	(0.016)
Credit growth$_{t-2}$	0.023	0.022	0.023	0.023	0.023	0.023	0.013
	(0.013)	(0.013)	(0.013)	(0.013)	(0.013)	(0.013)	(0.014)
GDP/Cap	−0.108**	−0.103*	−0.078	−0.077	−0.079	−0.080	−0.101
	(0.051)	(0.051)	(0.051)	(0.051)	(0.051)	(0.051)	(0.057)
Financial liberalization:							
Financial	1.76**	1.42**	0.488	0.639	0.892*	0.811*	1.45*
liberalization[a]	(0.634)	(0.589)	(0.434)	(0.415)	(0.415)	(0.418)	(0.712)
Finlib ×							−0.026
Initial Int.							(0.020)
Past Crisis:							
Duration	0.108*	0.115*	0.139**	0.147**	0.139**	0.140**	0.130*
	(0.051)	(0.051)	(0.051)	(0.050)	(0.050)	(0.051)	(0.062)
No. of crises	32	32	31	32	32	32	26
No. of obs.	639	639	602	639	632	632	525
% correct	77	77	77	76	76	77	78
% crisis correct	63	63	68	59	59	56	62
model χ^2	61.4**	58.8**	52.5**	54.5**	57.3**	56.5**	56.0**
AIC	217	219	218	224	219	221	177

* and ** indicate significance levels of 5 and 1 percent respectively.
[a] The financial liberalization variable in each regression is as follows:
1: Finlib; 2: Finlib (R); 3: Finlib (3); 4: Finlib (4); 5: Finlib (5); 6: Finlib (6); 7: Finlib.

columns correspond to different definitions of the financial liberalization dummy: In the first column, which is the baseline specification, the dummy is zero for periods in which interest rates are subject to controls, and one when liberalization begins. The dummy remains one even if the liberalization is temporarily reversed under the assumption that the effects of liberalization persist even through short reversals. In the second column, the dummy variable is modified by treating periods of reversal as zeroes.

The baseline specifications fits the data well, and it classifies correctly 77 percent of the observations. The macroeconomic control variables are all significant at least at the 5 percent level, and have the expected signs: Banking crises tend to be associated with low GDP growth, adverse terms of trade changes, high real interest rates, and high inflation. Of the characteristics of the banking sector, vulnerability to a speculative attack against the currency is significant at the 1 percent level, while credit growth lagged by two periods is significant at the 10 percent level. The other variables are not significant. Finally, GDP per capita is significantly negatively correlated to the probability of a banking crisis, suggesting that, other things being equal, developing countries are more vulnerable.

More interestingly, the financial liberalization dummy variable is strongly positively correlated with the probability of a banking crisis; as evident from column two, this is true regardless of the treatment of reversals. These results suggest that financial liberalization is a significant factor leading to banking sector fragility; furthermore, this effect is at work even after controlling for variables capturing the state of the macroeconomy (including the level of the risk-free short-term real interest rate). This suggests that, even if it is carried out after macroeconomic stabilization is achieved as recommended by McKinnon (1993), financial liberalization still increases financial fragility.

An important question is whether the effect of liberalization on the probability of a crisis tends to be a transitional effect, that is to manifest itself only during the years immediately following the change in policy. To test this hypothesis, in columns 3 to 6 of Table 4.2 we present estimates of the baseline regression using a liberalization dummy that takes the value of one only in the first three, four, five, and six years after liberalization, as opposed to the entire period following the policy change. The redefined dummies are all less significant than the baseline one, and the overall goodness of fit of the model does not improve. In fact, the dummy corresponding to a transition of only three years is not significant, and that corresponding to a transition of four years is significant only at the 10 percent confidence level. Thus, the effect of financial liberalization on banking fragility does not appear to be characteristic of the immediate aftermath of the change in policy, but rather it manifests itself only over time. This result may also be due to the fact that in a number of countries interest rate deregulation was gradual, and we chose the beginning of deregulation as the date of the policy change.

Another interesting question is whether the effects of financial liberalization on financial fragility differ in countries that were severely repressed at the time of liberalization relative to countries that were only financially restrained. To explore this issue, we interact the financial liberalization dummy variable with the average real interest rate in the three years prior to liberalization, and introduce this interaction term as an additional regressor. A negative and significant coefficient for the new variable would suggest that fragility is less severely affected by liberalization in countries that were more financially repressed at the beginning of liberalization. As shown in column 7 of Table 4.2, the estimated coefficient is negative but it is not significantly different from zero.

Table 4.3 provides an illustration of the magnitude of the effect of financial liberalization on financial fragility according to our empirical model: The third column contains the probability of a crisis as estimated by the baseline model for the twenty-six crisis episodes that took place in a liberalized regime. For those episodes, the probability of a crisis is then recalculated after setting the liberalization dummy equal to zero (column 4, Table 4.3). As it is apparent, for all countries the predicted crisis probability falls substantially, and of the twenty episodes that were correctly classified as crises, eleven would have switched to noncrisis status in the absence of financial liberalization. Thus, the effect of financial liberalization on the probability of a banking crisis not only is statistically significant, but it is also of a nontrivial magnitude.

The Role of the Institutional Environment

The theory reviewed in Section 2 suggests that the adverse effect of financial liberalization on banking sector fragility is stronger where the institutions needed for the correct functioning of financial markets are not well established. To test whether this effect is supported by the data, in Table 4.4 we add to the baseline regression various alternative variables in the form of interaction terms between the liberalization dummy and proxies of the quality of the institutional environment. Negative and significant coefficients for the interaction variables mean that a better institutional environment tends to weaken the effect of financial liberalization on the probability of a banking crisis.

The first proxy for the institutional environment is GDP per capita, which was also used as a control variable in the baseline regression. The other five proxies are indexes of the degree to which the rule of law is respected ("law and order"), of bureaucratic delay, of the quality of contract enforcement, of the quality of the bureaucracy, and of the degree of

Table 4.3. Impact of Interest Liberalization on Crisis Probability

Country[a]	Crisis start date	Predicted crisis probability[b]	Predicted crisis probability absent liberalization[c]
Chile	1981	0.174	0.035
Colombia	1982	0.047	0.008
Finland	1991	0.119	0.023
Guyana	1993	0.028	0.005
India	1991	0.221	0.047
Indonesia	1992	0.306	0.071
Italy	1990	0.028	0.005
Japan	1992	0.071	0.012
Jordan	1989	0.786	0.387
Kenya	1993	0.412	0.108
Malaysia	1985	0.170	0.034
Mexico	1994	0.207	0.043
Nigeria	1991	0.044	0.008
Norway	1987	0.031	0.006
Papua New Guinea	1989	0.259	0.057
Paraguay	1995	0.114	0.022
Peru	1983	0.347	0.084
Philippines	1981	0.052	0.009
Portugal	1986	0.133	0.026
Sri Lanka	1989	0.104	0.019
Sweden	1990	0.033	0.006
Turkey	1991	0.221	0.047
	1994	0.443	0.121
United States	1980	0.459	0.126
Uruguay	1981	0.358	0.087
Venezuela	1993	0.424	0.113

[a] Probabilities for Mali, Mexico 1982, El Salvador, Israel, Tanzania, and Thailand are not reported since these countries had not liberalized prior to the banking crisis.
[b] By baseline estimate at crisis date.
[c] Baseline prediction assuming the country had not liberalized by the crisis date.

corruption.[8] All six interaction variables have the expected negative sign, and all except the index of bureaucratic delay are significant at least at the 10 percent confidence level. The degree of law enforcement, GDP per capita, and corruption have the highest significance levels. Furthermore, the size of the effect is not trivial: For instance, consider the "law and order

---

[8] The indexes measuring "law and order," the quality of the bureaucracy, and corruption range between zero and six, while the index of bureaucratic delay and that of contract enforcement range from zero to four.

Table 4.4. Financial Liberalization and Banking Crises – Institutional Environment

	(1)	(2)	(3)	(4)	(5)	(6)
Control variables:						
Growth	−0.171**	−0.214**	−0.233**	−0.238**	−0.219**	−0.223**
	(0.040)	(0.054)	(0.072)	(0.070)	(0.054)	(0.054)
TOT change	−0.054*	−0.040	−0.056	−0.060	−0.042	−0.040
	(0.023)	(0.027)	(0.034)	(0.033)	(0.026)	(0.026)
Real interest	0.045**	0.052*	0.053*	0.050**	0.049*	0.049*
	(0.015)	(0.024)	(0.021)	(0.021)	(0.024)	(0.023)
Inflation	0.026**	0.024	0.022	0.020	0.021	0.022
	(0.009)	(0.015)	(0.013)	(0.013)	(0.015)	(0.015)
M2/Reserves	0.022**	0.018	0.025*	0.025*	0.022*	0.019*
	(0.007)	(0.010)	(0.012)	(0.012)	(0.010)	(0.010)
Private/GDP	0.002	−0.003	0.005	0.006	−0.003	−0.003
	(0.011)	(0.011)	(0.012)	(0.012)	(0.011)	(0.011)
Cash/Bank	−0.018	−0.030	0.020	0.015	−0.030	−0.027
	(0.014)	(0.023)	(0.026)	(0.026)	(0.022)	(0.021)
Credit Growth$_{t-2}$	0.024	0.013	0.045**	0.043**	0.011	0.009
	(0.013)	(0.018)	(0.017)	(0.016)	(0.018)	(0.018)
Financial liberalization and institutions:						
Finlib	1.96**	1.77	4.05**	4.73**	1.80	1.82
	(0.657)	(0.986)	(1.542)	(1.557)	(1.082)	(1.030)
Liberalization	−0.089	−0.405*	−0.727	−0.938	−0.380	−0.403
interactions[a]	(0.048)	(0.205)	(0.678)	(0.574)	(0.223)	(0.215)
Past crisis:						
Duration	0.112*	0.181*	0.028	0.031	0.171*	0.156*
	(0.051)	(0.081)	(0.067)	(0.067)	(0.079)	(0.078)
No. of crises	32	22	21	21	22	22
No. of obs.	639	425	406	406	418	418
% correct	77	72	78	80	72	73
% crisis correct	63	55	67	71	59	59
Model χ^2	60.1**	35.7**	49.6**	51.3**	34.2**	34.8**
AIC	218	161	140	138	162	162

* and ** indicate significance levels of 5 and 1 percent respectively.
[a] The liberalization interaction term in each regression is as follows: 1: Finlib × GDP/Cap;
2: Finlib × Law & Order; 3: Finlib × Delay; 4: Finlib × Cont. Enforcement; 5: Finlib × Bur.
Quality; 6: Finlib × Corruption.

index." For a country with a score of zero (the lowest score), the net impact of financial liberalization on the crisis probability is 1.770, while for a country with an intermediate score of three the net impact falls to 0.555, and for a country with the maximum score of six the net impact becomes negative, namely financial liberalization tends to make banking crises less likely. Similarly, moving from the worst quality of contract enforcement to the best (a change in the index from zero to four) reduces the impact of liberalization on the crisis probability from 4.732 to 0.980.

These results suggest that improving the quality of the institutional environment, especially reducing the amount of corruption and strengthening the rule of law, can curb the tendency of liberalized financial markets to harbor systemic banking crises.[9]

3 SENSITIVITY ANALYSIS

We performed a number of robustness tests on the baseline regression. The first test concerns the treatment of years during which the crisis is under way. Those years are omitted from the baseline specification, an approach that requires accurate information on the year in which a crisis ended. Since the end of a crisis may be difficult to determine in practice, we also estimated the baseline regression using three alternative panels: one that omits all years following a crisis, one that treats all crisis years as ones, and one that treats all crisis years (except the first) as zeroes. The liberalization dummy remains strongly significant in all of these specifications (details of the sensitivity tests are reported in Demirgüç-Kunt and Detragiache 1999).

A second set of sensitivity tests uses a more stringent definition of a banking crisis relative to the baseline (ratio of nonperforming loans to total loans of at least 15 percent and/or a cost of crisis of at least 3 percent of GDP) as well as a looser definition of crisis (ratio of nonperforming loans to total loans of at least 5 percent, and/or cost of the crisis of at least 1 percent of GDP). Nothing much changes concerning the control variables, and the liberalization dummy remains significant, albeit only at the 10 percent confidence level.

A third methodological issue, which always arises in panel estimation, is whether to include country (time) fixed effects to allow for the possibility that the dependent variable may vary across countries (years) independently of the explanatory variables included in the regression. In logit estimation, including fixed effects requires excluding from the panel countries (years) in which there was no crisis during the period under consideration (Greene 1997, p. 899), and hence it excludes a large amount of information. For this reason, we omit fixed effects from the baseline, and estimate a model with fixed effects as part of the sensitivity analysis. In the case of both country and time fixed effects, the hypothesis that the

---

[9] It is worth noticing that the proxies do not measure the quality of the laws and regulations in a particular country, but rather factors that affect the extent to which laws and regulations are enforced.

coefficients of the country and time dummies are jointly significantly different from zero is rejected, suggesting that there are no fixed effects. In any case, the liberalization dummy is still positively and significantly correlated with the probability of a crisis.

Another sensitivity test involves using lagged values of the explanatory variables to reduce the risk that the regressors may not be exogenous determinants of a crisis. The drawback of using lagged values on the right-hand side, of course, is that if the macroeconomic shocks that trigger the crisis work relatively quickly, then their effect would not be evident a year before the crisis erupts. In this regression, most macroeconomic control variables lose significance (except for the real interest rate), while the other controls remain significant; more interestingly, the liberalization dummy continues to be positively and significantly correlated to the probability of a crisis.

To summarize, the relationship between financial liberalization and banking sector fragility appears to be robust to various changes in the specification of the logit regression.

4 FINANCIAL LIBERALIZATION AND BANK FRANCHISE VALUES

The results of the previous sections suggest that liberalization increases the fragility of the financial system. One reason why financial liberalization may lead to increased banking sector fragility is that the removal of interest rate ceilings and/or the reduction of barriers to entry reduces bank franchise values, thus exacerbating moral hazard problems. As discussed in Caprio and Summers (1993) and Hellmann, Murdock, and Stiglitz (2000), interest rate ceilings and entry restrictions create rents that make a banking license more valuable to the holder. It is the risk of losing this valuable license which induces banks to become more stable institutions, with better incentives to monitor the firms they finance and manage the risk of their loan portfolio. Thus, when a reform – such as financial liberalization – leads to increased bank competition and lower profits, this erodes franchise values, distorting the risk-taking incentives of the institutions. Unless the reform effort incorporates adequate strengthening of the prudential regulations and supervision to realign incentives, lower franchise values are likely to lead to increased fragility.[10]

In this section we use bank-level data from the BankScope data base of IBCA to investigate whether there is any empirical evidence that bank

---

[10] Keeley (1990) presents empirical evidence that supports this view. First, he shows that in the 1970s U.S. thrift institutions began to lose charter value owing to the relaxation of various regulatory entry restrictions and because of technological changes. Second, he shows that banks with larger charter value were less risky, as measured by the risk-premium on uninsured bank CDs.

franchise values fall with financial liberalization. The data set includes bank-level accounting data for eighty countries over the 1988–95 period. In most countries, the banks covered in the IBCA survey account for at least 90 percent of the banking system. For each bank we construct three profitability measures: net interest margin, after-tax return on assets, and after-tax return on equity. Since none of these measures is a perfect indicator of future profitability, we also look at additional balance sheet ratios which may be associated with a fall in franchise value: a measure of capital adequacy (the book value of equity divided by total assets); a measure of liquidity (the ratio of liquid assets to total assets); and the share of deposits to total liabilities. These ratios are country averages of bank-level figures. Both high capitalization and high liquidity should have an adverse effect on bank franchise value, since they decrease the amount of loans that a bank can extend for any given amount of deposits.[11] Also, we examine the behavior of an indicator of market concentration (the ratio of assets of the largest three banks to total banking assets) and an indicator of foreign bank penetration (the proportion of foreign bank assets in total bank assets). More market concentration and less foreign bank penetration should be associated with more monopolistic powers for domestic banks, and, therefore, with higher franchise values.

Table 4.5 reports the correlations of these banking variables with the financial liberalization dummy variable. Of course, simple correlations do not imply causality. However, this exercise can at least tell us whether the hypothesis that financial liberalization leads to lower bank franchise values can be dismissed out-of-hand or needs to be taken seriously. The correlations in the first column of the table are calculated using a dummy variable that is equal to one in all periods in which the financial market is liberalized, and zero otherwise; in the remaining columns, the liberalization dummy is redefined to take a value of one during the transition to a liberalized system (where the transition is taken to last three, four, five, or six years alternatively), and zero otherwise. Thus, by comparing these sets of correlations we can see to what extent the fall in bank franchise value (if there is one) is a temporary or permanent effect of liberalization.

The results in the first column indicate that liberalization leads to permanently lower bank profits measured as return on equity, while neither the net interest margin nor the return on assets are significantly correlated with the liberalization dummy. There is also evidence that financial liberalization leads to higher capitalization (which should reduce bank profitability), and lower liquidity (which should have the opposite effect).

[11] Of course, for given franchise value, large capitalization and large liquidity should create less incentives to take on risk.

**Table 4.5. Correlation Coefficient between Financial Liberalization
and Bank Franchise Value Indicators**

	Finlib	Finlib 3	Finlib 4	Finlib 5	Finlib 6
Net interest margin	0.024	0.175**	0.150**	0.157**	0.158**
	0.653	*0.001*	*0.006*	*0.004*	*0.004*
Return on assets	0.088	0.202**	0.168**	0.167**	0.132*
	0.139	*0.001*	*0.006*	*0.006*	*0.030*
Return on equity	−0.118*	0.120*	0.097	0.077	0.068
	0.028	*0.029*	*0.076*	*0.158*	*0.212*
Capital	0.207**	0.058	0.119*	0.116*	0.121*
	0.000	*0.289*	*0.028*	*0.032*	*0.026*
Liquidity	−0.155**	0.154**	0.184**	0.152**	0.168**
	0.004	*0.005*	*0.001*	*0.005*	*0.002*
Deposit share	−0.033	0.069	0.161**	0.170**	0.121*
	0.541	*0.210*	*0.003*	*0.002*	*0.026*
Market concentration	−0.087	0.092	0.053	0.042	0.035
	0.137	*0.121*	*0.377*	*0.476*	*0.552*
Share of foreign banks	0.109*	−0.012	0.015	0.020	0.031
	0.062	*0.840*	*0.799*	*0.734*	*0.606*

Note: Pearson correlation coefficients are reported. P-values are given in italics. * and **
indicate significance levels of 5 and 1 percent respectively. Net interest margin is given by
interest income minus interest expenses divided by total assets. Return on assets is given by
net profits divided by total assets. Return on equity is given by net profits divided by book
value of equity. Capital is the book value of equity divided by total assets. Liquidity is the
ratio of liquid assets to total assets. Deposit share is the share of deposits (customer and
short-term funding) in total liabilities. Market concentration is measured as the ratio of assets
in the largest three banks to total bank assets. The share of foreign banks is the ratio of
foreign bank assets to total bank assets. All bank level variables are average ratios for all
banks in the BankScope data base in a country in a given year.

The extent of deposit mobilization in the long run does not appear to
change significantly with liberalization. More interestingly, liberalization
appears to be permanently associated with a lower bank concentration
ratio (albeit significant only at the 13 percent confidence level) and a
greater presence of foreign banks. Both of these effects are consistent with
lower bank franchise values due to reduced monopolistic profits resulting
from greater competition.

When we look at the correlations with the transition to a liberalized
system, we see that bank margins, profits, capital, liquidity, and deposit
mobilization are all higher during the transition period. However, a comparison with the correlations in the first column suggests that most of these
effects do not survive in the long run. During the transition, we do not see

a significant coefficient for bank concentration or foreign bank penetration, suggesting that the structure of the banking sector changes only slowly after the liberalization process begins.

Despite the cursory nature of the analysis, these results are broadly consistent with the theories that conjecture that liberalization would lead to increased bank fragility due to its negative impact on bank franchise values. The next logical step would be to test whether low bank franchise values are associated to increased bank fragility; unfortunately, we are unable to examine this issue because the number of banking crises that take place during the period covered by the BankScope data set is too small.

5 FINANCIAL LIBERALIZATION, BANKING CRISES, FINANCIAL DEVELOPMENT, AND GROWTH

So far, we have established that financial liberalization has a cost in terms of increased financial fragility. Do these results imply that policymakers should abandon liberalization in favor of increased direct intervention in financial markets? Of course, the answer depends on whether the welfare costs of financial fragility exceed the welfare benefits of liberalization, and on whether governments can be expected to design and implement regulations that correct market failures rather than reinforce them. An answer to these complex questions is well beyond the scope of this chapter. Nonetheless, it is possible to use our data set to explore one aspect of this issue, namely whether financial liberalization and banking crises affect economic growth through their effect on financial development.

The focus on growth effects through financial development is suggested by the large existing literature documenting how financial development increases long-run growth rates (King and Levine 1993; Levine 1997): Presumably, one of the main benefits of financial liberalization is that it fosters financial development and, through it, increases long-run growth. Conversely, the disruption caused by a systemic banking crisis is likely to have a direct adverse effect on financial development (at least in the short or medium term) and, through that avenue, have a negative impact on growth. The question addressed in this section is whether these effects can be detected in our data set, and, if so, how the magnitude of the adverse effect of banking crises on financial development compares with that of the positive effect of financial liberalization.

To verify whether financial development tends to increase growth in our sample, we estimate growth regression using a panel obtained by splitting the sample period (1980–94) into three subperiods of five years each. The regressors include a set of control variables and four alternative indicators of financial development proposed by King and Levine (1993).[12] These indicators are the ratio of liquid liabilities of the financial system to GDP (liquidity), the share of bank credit that goes to the private sector (private credit), the ratio of domestic bank assets to the sum of central bank assets and domestic bank assets (bank assets), and the ratio of central bank domestic assets to GDP (central bank). The first three indicators are increasing with financial development, while the fourth is decreasing. The results of the growth regressions are reported in the top panel of Table 4.6: Although the R^2 are generally quite low, two out of four indicators have significant coefficients of the expected sign (bank assets and central bank). Thus, there is some evidence that financial development is positively correlated with growth in our panel.

To assess the impact of financial liberalization and banking crises on financial development, we then regress each financial development indicator on a constant, the liberalization dummy, and the banking crisis dummy, using the same panel as in the growth regressions.[13] The estimated coefficients have a simple interpretation: The constant is the mean level of financial development for observations with neither financial liberalization nor a banking crisis. The coefficient of the liberalization dummy, on the other hand, indicates the difference between the level of financial development in a country/time period with financial liberalization but no banking crisis and the level of financial development in countries/time periods with neither liberalization nor a banking crisis. Similarly, the coefficient of the banking crisis dummy, if significantly less than zero, would indicate that, on average, observations corresponding to banking crises are accompanied by lower financial development, conditional on no liberalization having occurred. Finally, if the difference between the coefficients of the two dummies is significantly greater than zero, then a country/period with both financial liberalization and a banking crisis has, on average, a higher level of financial development than one with no crisis and controlled financial markets.

---

[12] The control variables, also similar to those used by King and Levine (1993), are the logarithm of GDP per capita and of the secondary school enrollment ratio at the beginning of the subperiod, the share of government consumption expenditure in GDP, the inflation rate, the ratio of the sum of imports and exports to GDP, the real interest rate, and a period dummy variable.

[13] The financial liberalization dummy variable takes the value of one if interest rate liberalization began in any of the years of the subperiod or if markets were liberalized in the preceding subperiod; the banking crisis dummy variable takes the value of one if a crisis was ongoing in any of the years of the subperiod. The results are robust to redefining the dummy variables by treating a subperiod as a one only if the change in policy (crisis) occurs in the first three years of the subperiod. If the change in policy (crisis) takes place in the last or second-to-last period, then the dummy for the *following period* is set to one.

Table 4.6. Growth, Financial Development, Financial Liberalization, and Banking Crises – Full Sample

	Liquidity	Private credit	Bank assets	Central bank
Growth regressions[a]				
Financial development	−0.407	0.243	3.450*	−2.010
	(0.765)	(1.007)	(1.633)	(1.166)
Adjusted R^2	0.11	0.11	0.14	0.11
No of observations	136	136	137	134
Financial development regression[b]				
Constant	0.466**	0.252**	0.682**	0.187**
	(0.044)	(0.032)	(0.028)	(0.048)
Financial liberalization	0.108*	0.202**	0.152**	−0.103*
dummy	(0.050)	(0.044)	(0.034)	(0.043)
Banking crisis dummy	−0.104	−0.085	−0.066	0.040
	(0.055)	(0.047)	(0.037)	(0.039)
Adjusted R^2	0.03	0.09	0.10	0.03
No. of observations	156	156	159	153
Aggregate impact of	0.004	0.117*	0.086	−0.063
dummies on finance	(F = 0.00)	(F = 4.62)	(F = 3.32)	(F = 0.88)
Impact of finance on growth	0.002	0.028	0.297	0.127

[a] The dependent variable is the real per capita GDP growth rate. Each growth regression includes an alternative financial development indicator, as specified in the column header. Liquidity is ratio of liquid liabilities of the financial system to GDP. Private credit is the ratio of bank credit to private sector to GDP. Bank assets is ratio of deposit money bank domestic assets to deposit money banks domestic assets plus central bank domestic assets. Central bank is the ratio of central bank domestic assets to GDP. Besides the financial development indicators, the regressions include the logarithm of initial real per capita GDP, the logarithm of initial secondary school enrollment, the ratio of government consumption expenditure to GDP, inflation rate, ratio of exports plus imports to GDP, the real interest rate, dummy variables for 5-year periods. White's heteroskedasticity-consistent standard errors are given in parentheses. * and ** indicate significance levels of 5 and 1 percent respectively.
[b] The dependent variable is the financial development indicator listed in the column header. Regressions include a constant.

Table 4.6 contains estimation results. The coefficient of the liberalization dummy is positive and significant in all the specifications, while the banking crisis dummy has a negative coefficient which is significant in all specifications except one. Thus, both financial liberalization and the occurrence of banking crises appear to significantly affect financial development. Turning now to the difference between the two coefficients, it appears that countries/periods with both banking crises and financial liberalization have greater financial development but only if financial development is measured by private credit or by bank assets. For liquidity and central bank, the difference in the coefficients is not significantly different from zero. Private credit, however, does not have a significant impact on growth in our panel, as shown in the first row of Table 4.6. Only in one regression, the one using bank assets as an indicator of financial development, are both the net effect of the dummies on financial development and the effect of financial development on growth significant. Thus, these tests do not show clear evidence that choosing financial liberalization at the cost of experiencing a banking crisis pays off in terms of higher growth through higher financial development, or vice versa, at least in a medium-term time frame.[14]

Additional insights on this issue can be obtained by splitting the sample between countries that were repressed at the time of financial liberalization and countries that were only restrained. Countries are classified as repressed if they had a negative interest rate (on average) during the three years preceding financial liberalization, and they are classified as restrained if they liberalized from a position of positive interest rates.[15] Countries that maintained controlled financial markets during the entire sample period are omitted from this panel, since they cannot be classified in either group.[16] When the sample is split in this fashion, for the restrained countries the results are quite similar to those for the sample as a whole (bank assets and central bank are significant), while for the repressed group, private credit is significant also (Tables 4.7 and 4.8).

More interestingly, when we regress the financial development indicators on the liberalization dummy and on the crisis dummy, banking crises do not seem to lead to significantly lower financial development in repressed countries (where financial development is in any case lower than in the restrained group), while they do so in restrained countries, at least in two out of four regressions (Tables 4.7 and 4.8). In contrast, the positive impact of financial liberalization is present in both groups of countries. Thus, based on these estimated coefficients, a country that liberalized from a position of financial restraint and experienced a banking crisis has a level of financial development similar to a country that did not liberal-

---

[14] When we estimate a growth regression including the banking crisis dummy and the financial liberalization dummy, however, the coefficients are not significant, suggesting that the dummies have a negligible direct impact on growth.

[15] Roubini and Sala-i-Martin (1992) find the negative growth effects of financial repression to be stronger in financially repressed countries than in financially restrained countries.

[16] The panel includes countries that liberalized well before the beginning of the sample period. It may be argued that whether those countries were financially repressed or restrained at the time of liberalization should not affect their economic performance in 1980–94. As a robustness test, we repeated the tests described below dropping those countries from the panel. The basic results remain unchanged.

Table 4.7. Growth, Financial Development, Financial Liberalization,
and Banking Crises – Financially Restrained Countries

	Liquidity	Private credit	Bank assets	Central bank
Growth regressions				
Financial development	−0.735	−0.775	12.418**	−13.417
	(0.841)	(1.007)	(4.757)	(7.362)
Adjusted R^2	0.09	0.09	0.25	0.13
No of observations	64	64	64	62
Financial development regressions				
Constant	0.518**	0.363**	0.788**	0.094**
	(0.075)	(0.059)	(0.030)	(0.012)
Financial liberalization	0.157	0.173*	0.112**	−0.038**
dummy	(0.084)	(0.074)	(0.033)	(0.014)
Banking crisis dummy	−0.019	−0.082	−0.074	0.038*
	(0.111)	(0.082)	(0.040)	(0.019)
Adjusted R^2	0.01	0.04	0.14	0.10
No. of observations	72	72	72	69
Aggregate impact of	0.138	0.091	0.038	0.000
dummies on finance	(F = 0.86)	(F = 0.75)	(F = 0.51)	(F = 0.00)
Impact of finance on growth	−0.101	−0.071	0.472	0.000

Note: See Table 4.6.

ize and escaped banking sector problems. In contrast, for countries that liberalized from a position of financial repression, the level of financial development is higher with liberalization even if the country experiences a banking crisis. Based on the coefficient estimated in the growth regression, the net positive effect on growth for this group of countries is of the order of 0.7–0.9 of a percentage point per year (Table 4.8).

To summarize, this section has shown some empirical evidence supporting the hypothesis that financial liberalization is associated with higher financial development and, through it, with higher output growth, while banking crises have the opposite effects. For countries that liberalize from a position of financial restraint, the gains from liberalization in terms of financial development are comparable to the costs of having a banking crisis, while in the case of financially repressed countries the gains from financial liberalization are larger.

Although these results are suggestive, it is important to stress that they are tentative, and that the methodology used in deriving them leaves a lot to be desired: First, growth regressions are intended to study the determinants of long-run growth rates, which are usually taken to be averages of many years of data. To have enough data points, here we are forced to use

Table 4.8. Growth, Financial Development, Financial Liberalization, and Banking Crises – Financially Repressed Countries

	Liquidity	Private credit	Bank assets	Central bank
Growth regressions				
Financial development	0.421	5.189*	4.466*	−2.865*
	(2.217)	(2.266)	(2.018)	(1.453)
Adjusted R^2	0.04	0.12	0.10	0.08
No of observations	57	57	58	57
Financial development regressions				
Constant	0.411**	0.178**	0.607**	0.267**
	(0.065)	(0.024)	(0.048)	(0.100)
Financial liberalization dummy	0.060	0.163**	0.183**	−0.162
	(0.073)	(0.048)	(0.058)	(0.097)
Banking crisis dummy	−0.085	−0.022	−0.009	0.026
	(0.058)	(0.061)	(0.060)	(0.079)
Adjusted R^2	0.00	0.08	0.11	0.02
No. of observations	64	64	66	64
Aggregate impact of	−0.025	0.141**	0.174*	−0.136
dummies on finance	F = 0.09	F = 6.17	F = 5.68	F = 0.97
Impact of finance on growth	−0.011	0.732	0.777	0.390

Note: See Table 4.6.

five-year averages, which may not really capture the long-run rate of economic growth. In fact, the low R^2 in the growth regressions may indicate that cyclical and other factors not controlled for are important in explaining the dependent variable. If there are omitted variables, and these variables are correlated with the development indicators, the estimates of the coefficient of the financial development indicator would be biased. This criticism, however, concerns only the growth regressions, where the linkage between financial development and growth is established for our panel. Since this linkage has already been documented in other, more rigorous studies, we are not excessively worried by this shortcoming.

The more interesting part of the exercise is the test of the relationship between financial development, financial liberalization, and banking crises. Here our tests, besides being confined to a short- and medium-term horizon, are limited because they are basically differences of means, and ignore that factors other than liberalization and banking crises affect financial development. Also, the effect of financial liberalization on the probability of a banking crisis is not explicitly incorporated in the analysis. We leave more sophisticated explorations of this important issue to future research.

6 CONCLUDING REMARKS

Increased liberalization of financial markets in general and of the banking sector in particular have been major items in the economic policy agenda of many countries during the last thirty years. In this time period, the frequency of systemic banking problems has increased markedly all over the world, raising the issue of whether greater fragility may be a consequence of liberalization. In this paper we have attempted to shed light on the issue by studying a large panel data set, covering fifty-three developed and developing economies during the period 1980–95. The panel includes countries that liberalized their financial markets several years before 1980, and others that liberalized at different dates over the sample period; also, countries that experienced one or more banking crises are represented along with countries that had a stable banking system throughout the period. Thus, the data set covers a large variety of experiences, from which it would be impossible to draw lessons without the help of econometric techniques.

The first result that emerges from the analysis is that financial fragility is affected by a multiplicity of factors, including adverse macroeconomic developments, bad macroeconomic policies, and vulnerability to balance-of-payments crises. When these factors are controlled for, financial liberalization exerts an independent negative effect on the stability of the banking sector, and the magnitude of the effect is not trivial. However, a strong institutional environment, characterized by effective law enforcement, an efficient bureaucracy, and little corruption, can curb the adverse effects of liberalization on the financial system.

These findings suggest that institutional development needs to be emphasized early in the liberalization process: In countries where the institutional environment is weak, achieving macroeconomic stabilization before or during liberalization would certainly bring an important independent source of financial instability under control. However, even in an otherwise well-functioning economy weaknesses in the institutions and in the regulatory framework necessary for financial markets to operate efficiently may fail to check perverse behavior on the part of financial intermediaries, creating the foundations for systemic financial sector problems. Unfortunately, strong institutions cannot be created overnight, not even by the most reform-oriented government; thus, the path to financial liberalization should be a gradual one, in which the benefits of each further step toward liberalization are carefully weighed against the risks. Another implication of our findings is that more research effort should be focused on the design and implementation of prudential regulations and supervision especially in developing countries.

**Table 4.9. Definitions and Data Sources for Variables Included in
the Logit Regressions**

Variable name	Definition	Source
Growth	Rate of growth of real GDP	IFS where available. Otherwise, WEO.
Tot change	Change in the terms of trade	WEO
Real interest rate	Nominal interest rate less the contemporaneous rate of inflation	IFS. Interest: where available, line 60c. Otherwise, rate for CB lending to banks; otherwise, 60l.
Inflation	Rate of change of the GDP deflator	IFS
M2/Reserves	Ratio of M2 to foreign exchange reserves of the central bank	M2 is money plus quasimoney (IFS lines 34 + 35) converted into US$. Reserves: IFS line 1dd.
Private/GDP	Ratio of domestic credit to the private sector to GDP	Domestic credit to the private sector is IFS line 32d.
Cash/Bank	Ratio of bank liquid reserves to bank assets	Bank reserves: IFS line 20. Bank assets: IFS lines 21 + lines 22a to 22f.
Credit growth	Rate of growth of real domestic credit to private sector	IFS line 32d divided by the GDP deflator.
GDP/CAP	Real GDP per capita	GDP data are from the World Bank National Accounts data base. Population is IFS line 99z.
Law and order	Index ranging from 0 to 6	International Country Risk Guide (ICRG), published by Political Risk Service, Syracuse, NY.
Bureaucratic delay	Index ranging from 0 to 4	Business Environmental Risk Intelligence (BERI), Washington DC
Contract enforcement	Index ranging from 0 to 4	BERI
Quality of bureaucracy	Index ranging from 0 to 6	ICRG
Corruption	Index ranging from 0 to 6	ICRG

Support for a gradual approach toward financial liberalization also comes from our findings about the effects of liberalization and fragility on financial development and, through it, on growth: While for countries that were initially in a state of financial repression the positive effect of liberalization on financial development appears to be stronger than the negative effect of a banking crisis, this is not the case for countries that liberalized from a situation of financial restraint, where the two effects roughly offset each other. One way of reading these findings is that, once financial sector reforms are carried out to secure positive interest rates, steps toward further liberalization may not necessary yield gains that offset the negative impact of increased fragility.

REFERENCES

Bandiera, O., G. Caprio, P. Honohan, and F. Schiantarelli. 2000. "Does Financial Reform Raise or Reduce Saving?" *Review of Economics and Statistics* 82(2):239–63.

Calvo, G.A. 1996. "Capital Flows and Macroeconomic Management: Tequila Lessons." *International Journal of Finance and Economics* 1:207–24.

Caprio, G. and D. Klingebiel. 1996. "Dealing with Bank Insolvencies: Cross Country Experience." Washington, D.C.: The World Bank. *Mimeo.*

Caprio, G. and L. Summers. 1993. "Financial Reform: Beyond Laissez-Faire." In D. Papadimitriou (ed.), *Financing Prosperity into the 21st Century*, pp. 400–21. New York: Macmillan.

Demirgüç-Kunt, A. and E. Detragiache. 1998. "The Determinants of Banking Crises: Evidence from Industrial and Developing Countries." *IMF Staff Papers* 45(1):81–109.

Demirgüç-Kunt, A. and E. Detragiache. 1999. "Financial Liberalization and Financial Fragility." In B. Pleskovic and J.E. Stiglitz (eds.), *Annual World Bank Conference on Development Economics 1998*, pp. 303–31. The World Bank.

Fry, M.J. 1997. "In Favor of Financial Liberalization." *Economic Journal* 107:754–70.

Greene, W.H. 1997. *Econometric Analysis.* Upper Saddle River, NJ: Prentice Hall.

Hellmann, T., K. Murdock, and J.E. Stiglitz. 2000. "Liberalization, Moral Hazard in Banking and Prudential Regulation: Are Capital Requirements Enough?" *American Economic Review* 90(1):147–65.

Kaminsky, G. and C.M. Reinhart. 1996. "The Twin Crises: The Causes of Banking and Balance of Payments Problems." Washington, D.C.: Federal Reserve Board.

Keeley, M.C. 1990. "Deposit Insurance, Risk, and Market Power." *American Economic Review* 80:1183–200.

King, R.G. and R. Levine. 1993. "Finance and Growth: Schumpeter May Be Right." *Quarterly Journal of Economics* 108:717–37.

Levine, R. 1997. "Financial Development and Growth: Views and Agenda." *Journal of Economic Literature* 35:688–726.

Lindgren, C.J., G. Garcia, and M. Saal. 1996. *Bank Soundness and Macroeconomic Policy*. Washington D.C.: International Monetary Fund.

Mc Kinnon, R.I. 1973. *Money and Capital in Economic Development*. Washington, D.C.: Brookings Institution.

Roubini, N. and X. Sala-i-Martin. 1992. "Financial Repression and Economic Growth." *Journal of Development Economics* 39:5–30.

LIBERALIZATION EXPERIENCE FROM CONTRASTING STARTING POINTS

5

Financial Restraints and Liberalization in Postwar Europe

Charles Wyplosz[1]

INTRODUCTION

The recent wave of currency and financial crises that have rattled most of the emerging market economies from Asia, Europe, and South America is deeply related to the process of financial liberalization over the preceding decade. The human, economic, and political costs of the crisis are staggering. They must be set against the benefits of financial liberalization. Proponents of liberalization rest their case on the improved allocation of resources which is expected to follow, as well as on the erosion of the effectiveness of restrictions. But just how big are these gains, especially if the controls "do not work"? Ex ante, of course, one cannot offer estimates. Ex post, when the costs of crises are accounted for, the balance is doubtful. Yet, the proponents of financial liberalization feel that they do not have to offer the kind of cost and benefit analysis that is customary in other circumstances. Theory, it is claimed, is unambiguous and since the benefits accrue permanently they must outweigh whatever costs occur in the interim period.

Theory, unfortunately, is not as one-sided as it is often made to be. If financial markets were operating fully efficiently, the case for liberalization would indeed be clear cut. Financial markets, however, are known to suffer from serious defects associated with the phenomenon of asymmetric information.[2] The tendency of financial markets to display extreme instability is well recognized. Indeed virtually all financial markets are subject to public interventions in the form of extensive regulations and careful

[1] I thank the following for their help with the historical material used in this paper: Isabelle Cassiers, Marcel Peter, Riccardo Rovelli, Pierre Sicsic. Useful comments were received from Patrick Honohan and Pierre Sicsic. Xavier Debrun provided effective research assistance.

[2] The macroeconomic role of asymmetric information has been described by Greenwald, Stiglitz, and Weiss (1984). Implications for currency markets are presented in Eichengreen, Rose, and Wyplosz (1995) and for crises in general by Mishkin (1991).

overseeing. That capital opening requires a coordinated international approach is also noncontroversial: The prescriptions of the Basle Committee as well as the emergence of international regulatory bodies (for example, International Organization of Securities Commissions (IOSCO)) represent efforts toward the establishment of international norms. Yet, international organizations such as the Organization for Economic Cooperation and Development (OECD) or the IMF still insist officially that financial liberalization is an end by itself. The OECD has imposed capital liberalization to its new members (Mexico and South Korea) and is currently exerting pressure on transition countries such as Hungary to complete their efforts. The IMF staff has only recently begun expressing a more nuanced view (see IMF 1997) but an official *aggiornamento* is still opposed by the Fund's main shareholders.

In the murky real world of less than perfect markets, balancing the benefits and costs of liberalization is usually impossible ex ante, and ex post it is too late. Fortunately, lessons can be learned from previous experiments. Europe offers a possible test ground. In the postwar era, most European countries have been very slow to liberalize their financial markets. For example, it was not until July 1990 that the European Union fully abolished exchange controls, and even then some late entrants were given grace periods to fully comply with the agreement (see Table 5.1). It has taken the most advanced economies of Europe between thirty and forty-five years after the war to comply with the openness standards that are now sought in emerging markets. Examining that experiment may help shed light on the relative costs and benefits of financial liberalization.

This chapter examines in some detail the process of financial liberalization in three countries: Belgium, France, and Italy. These countries have been chosen because they have long operated with very repressed banking and financial systems and were among the latest to remove capital controls, a step that they unenthusiastically supported. Section 1 describes these three cases, providing background information for the analysis that follows. Section 2 asks four questions: Is there any evidence that financial repression has been hurting? What are the links between internal financial repression and capital controls? What are the effects on money and financial markets of deregulation? And what are the budgetary effects? Section 3 looks at banks, the great casualty of the Latin American and Asian crises. Section 4 offers as conclusion some policy implications.

1 THREE TALES

In the immediate postwar Europe, virtually all goods were in scarce supply. This led to the early adoption of rationing schemes, including in the financial sphere. The acquisition of credit and foreign currency were everywhere

Table 5.1. Financial Restrictions in the Postwar OECD Area: Period of Use

Country	Exchange controls	Credit ceilings and other domestic restrictions
Australia		Early 1960s–82
Austria		1972–75; 1977–81
Belgium	1955–90	Until 1978
Denmark	1950–88	1970–80
Finland		1969–70
France	1950–89	1958–85
Germany	1950–59, 1960–81	None
Ireland	1950–92	1969
Italy	1950–90	1973–83
Japan		1960s
The Netherlands	1950–86	1962–67; 1969–72; 1977–81
New Zealand		Until 1972
Norway		1967–84
Portugal	1950–92	1978–91
Spain	1950–92	1959–66
Sweden		1969–70; 1974–77; 1981–83
Switzerland	1955–66, 1971–80	1962–66; 1969–72; 1973–75
United Kingdom	1950–79	1964–71
United States		1980

Note: The postwar starting date is conventionally set as 1950.
Source: Exchange controls from Bakker 1996, p. 220; credit ceilings mainly from Cottarelli et al. 1986, unpublished appendix.

subject to approval by the relevant authorities. Currencies remained unconvertible for a full fourteen years: Current account convertibility was declared jointly by the founding members of the European Economic Community (EEC) in 1958. Capital convertibility was restored at different speeds and bit by bit. It was made complete in July 1990 following the adoption of the Single European Act (see Table 5.1). The freeing of credit markets has varied considerably from country to country. Germany, for example, opted early on for free banking and universal banks. The U.K. moved quickly toward the reestablishment of London as a financial center. Yet, most of Europe remained far from the idealized model of a market economy for several decades.

The following sections offer a brief description of financial repression in three of the six founding members of the EEC[3]: Belgium, France, and

---

[3] The EEC has been renamed European Union (EU) with adoption of the Maastricht Treaty in 1991. I overlook this distinction, adopting the name EU henceforth.

Italy. These countries have been, perhaps, more persistent in preventing market forces from operating freely, but similar arrangements existed in virtually all others, they were simply lifted faster. The last column in Table 5.1 shows when credit ceilings have been in use in the OECD area.

Most of the changes were the result of domestic travails, yet the process of European integration has played a role too.[4] Exogeneity is, as always, difficult to pinpoint. To a large extent, given the rule of unanimity needed for important changes at the European level, European Union (EU)-wide changes tend to follow domestic changes. Governments support the adoption of new measures by the EU only if they intend to implement them.

Belgium[5]

In postwar Belgium, repression of the banking system was nearly complete. Following the Great Depression, in 1935 Belgian banks were separated into two groups: deposit banks and investment banks. This situation, which resembled the British tradition of clearing banks and merchant banks, lasted until 1993. Deposit banks, the bulk of Belgian financial industry, could only collect deposits and make short-term loans and were prevented from acquiring shares (with few exceptions after 1967). By 1945, deposit banks had become specialized in bankrolling the government: The public debt held by banks represented about 80 percent of all their loans, and most of that debt was short term. As credit demand from the private sector started to rise, the government feared being crowded out from the low interest rate market that it had set up before the war. In 1946 it imposed on deposit banks a number of "structural ratios," including a floor on public debt holdings. The "cover ratio" – the minimum percentage of short-term liabilities that had to be backed by cash or Treasury paper – was set at 65 percent for the larger banks and 50 percent for the smaller ones. This, in effect, forced banks to roll over the public debt. The cover ratio was reduced later on, and finally suppressed in 1962. As a compensation, maybe, banks were allowed to cartelize in 1941. They first adopted ceilings on deposit interest rates and next agreed upon caps on lending rates.[6] Foreign banks, even those established in Belgium, were not allowed to lend directly to the public sector.

---

[4] For a detailed analysis of each country's position in the process of elimination of capital controls, see Bakker (1996).

[5] This section draws on Cassiers (1997) and Cassiers et al. (1996).

[6] Cartels are notoriously fragile and the agreements to refrain from interest competition was continuously challenged, especially after foreign banks started to operate in Belgium in the 1960s. The central bank was often asked to use its influence to bring free riders to heed the cartel's decisions. On this issue, see Vanthemsche (1997), pp. 429–30.

Table 5.2. Growth: Belgium and Europe (Average Annual Growth in Real GDP Per Capita)

	Belgium	France	NW Europe
1950–60	2.40	3.65	3.88
1960–73	4.43	4.31	3.50
1973–90	2.07	1.94	1.92

Note: NW Europe includes Austria, Belgium, Denmark, Finland, France, Germany, Netherlands, Norway, Sweden, Switzerland, and the United Kingdom.
Source: Cassiers et al. 1996.

As a result, banks were working in a relatively riskless environment: no price competition on deposit collection and, since they were lending short term to the private sector and to the public sector, relatively safe loans. With low risk came low returns. Face-to-face contacts between the bank consortium and their main customer, the state, made sure that returns were sufficient to keep the ball rolling. This cozy relationship served well both the public sector and banks, at the expense of under-remunerated depositors and over-charged borrowers.

In the late 1950s, competition came from two sides: saving banks and foreign banks. This prompted deposit banks in 1957 to ask for, and get, the right to extend the maturity of their loans and to lessen the structural ratios which were finally suppressed in 1962. This did not lead to free banking, though. The central bank started to issue "recommendations" that credit to the private sector be "voluntarily" restricted. Autodiscipline followed as commercial banks feared a return to the previous system.

Table 5.2 shows that in the 1960s, the so far sluggish Belgian economy picked up speed. Private demand for credit boomed and the banks responded. With "voluntary" credit ceilings still in place, competition for cheap deposits and status-enhancing market shares took the form of an expanding network of branches. As Figure 5. 1 shows, this expansion set Belgian banks far apart from others. The Belgian banking scene became far more international and credit to the private sector grew considerably. Yet, the public sector remained a key customer and the cozy relationship survived, including guaranteed margins on public paper and the exclusion of foreign banks from this lucrative market. The first oil shock further increased the golden goose effect: High interest rates resulted in a fast buildup of public debt service met by ever larger public borrowing from banks.

Restrictive measures on banks were accompanied by limits to financial exchanges with the rest of the world. Starting in 1955, Belgium (along with Luxembourg, its partner in the monetary union established in 1922)

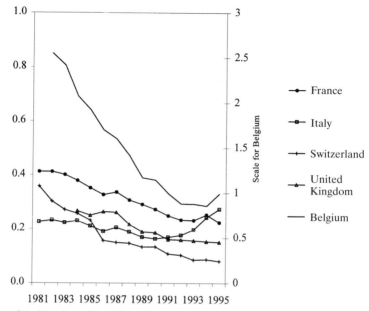

Figure 5.1. Number of bank branches relative to gross income (in DM) (*Source*: OECD Bank Profitability).

operated a dual exchange rate system. The commercial franc was fixed, first to the U.S. dollar and, after the collapse of the Bretton Woods system, to the deutsche Mark (DM). This rate was guaranteed only for current account transactions. Capital transactions had to be carried out on the financial franc market at a floating rate. The authorities could intervene on the financial franc market but had no obligation to do so. A dual exchange market is a market-based form of capital control which insulates the monetary authorities from international flows. This is quite an efficient arrangement for dealing with capital inflows or outflows since the financial exchange rate is free to fully respond to fluctuations without affecting, at least in principle, the commercial exchange rate. In practice, leaks occur and this forces an ever-widening range of control and enforcement measures. Figure 5.2 reports the percentage difference between the two rates, a positive value representing the case where the commercial franc is appreciated vis-a-vis the financial franc. It shows that during tranquil periods the difference is small and grows in the presence of (speculative) outflows. The difference is a measure of the efficiency of the device and its ability to shield domestic markets and the central bank from disturbances.

The oil shocks set in motion a process that led to the big bang of 1989–91, the end of banking system cartelization. With a public debt well

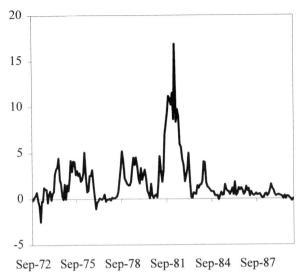

Figure 5.2. Dual exchange rate in Belgium – financial versus commercial franc, percent difference (*Source*: Bakker 1996).

above 100 percent of GDP, the public sector had to trim down its expenses, including the cost of debt service. Inflation had to be brought down from double-digit levels. The chosen strategy was to tie the Belgian franc to the DM. This in turn led to lower risk premia and the integration of the Belgian financial system into the European and global network, a move reinforced by the end of the dual exchange rate system. The big bang took the form of a series of deep reforms. First, the public debt was no longer financed by direct deals with the consortium of banks; after 1989 the Treasury started to issue paper on a market open to all domestic as well as foreign institutions. This seriously affected the banks' profit margins so, in return, the separation between deposit and portfolio investment banks was suppressed in 1993. The oligopolistic setting of deposit rates was abandoned at the same time. In fact, the Single European Act (the so-called "1992 Act") implied that the Belgian banking system had to be fully liberalized.

France[7]

The tale starts in the immediate postwar when the government, led by General de Gaulle and which included communists, nationalized the major banks. The reason was a mixture of punishment for institutions that had

---

[7] This section draws on Icard (1994). See also Melitz (1991) and Wyplosz (1988).

collaborated with the German authorities during the war, and a strongly held view that collusion between financiers and industrialists had led to an excessive concentration of wealth and economic power during the interwar period.

Following banking legislation adopted between 1944 and 1948, monetary policy relied on a combination of discount quota ceilings and selective credits. Each bank was given a quota for its rediscounting, the only source of financing from the central bank. Quotas were not allowed to grow rapidly; in fact their ratio to banks assets continuously declined over the next two decades. The interest rate charged at the discount windows was systematically kept well below the market rate. Emergency funding from the central bank was possible, but at a high penalty rate, aptly called "the rate from hell (*taux d'enfer*)."

Undermining this quantitative control of money supply was the policy of selective credits. Commercial banks could obtain ex ante approval by the Banque de France for credits to selected borrowers. Over time, the criteria for selecting borrowers changed as the authorities adjusted their definition of priority, in line with the Planning Commission's choices. In the early postwar period, rebuilding the capital goods industry was the main priority. Over time priority shifted to encouraging exports and housing. Once a particular loan to a selected borrower had been approved, a commercial bank could discount it with a specialized institution that could in turn borrow directly from the central bank. The special discount rate was even lower than the ordinary discount rate. Unsurprisingly, selected credit grew faster than overall credit, gradually representing the lion's share of overall credit.[8] More importantly, control of the money supply was lax as it unavoidably required restraining credit to priority borrowers, a politically difficult exercise.

In addition, by law, the interest rate on bank sight deposits was set to zero while most other lending and deposit rates were set by the Banque de France. Eventually, bank lending rates were liberalized in 1967. The prohibition on the payment of interest on sight deposits is still in place but may be abandoned soon. A wide range of popular savings accounts remained subject to interest rate restrictions.

In 1957, France underwent an exchange crisis fueled by a widening inflation differential vis-à-vis the United States. The method of monetary control was changed to credit ceilings (*encadrement du crédit*). This method was adapted and refined over the years but basically worked as

---

[8] This explains the puzzling observation that net claims by the Banque de France on the banking system represented an unusually large proportion of total bank credit throughout the 1950s and 1960s. Commercial banks knew that credit to favored causes was automatically refinanced by the central bank, thus guaranteeing an attractive profit margin.

follows. Each bank was given a yearly growth rate for its credit outstanding (less long-term liabilities). Excessive credit was subject to a special reserve requirement which increased quadratically. The authorities would decide each year on the growth rate, allowing smaller banks to expand faster than larger ones.[9] Selective credit was not abandoned, however. A number of exemptions were given to priority borrowers, still benefiting mainly the capital good and housing industries as well as exports. Such credits were not within the ceiling quotas and, naturally, they grew much faster than the credits within the ceiling. Much of this selective credit was also still subsidized. Eventually, to keep money growth under control, selected credit was brought under the ceiling system, but it was still allowed to grow faster than regular credit.

Icard (1994) well articulates the reasoning behind credit ceiling as a classic example of the *n*-th best. Because subsidized credit represented a large share of overall credit, an interest rate policy would be ineffective. Inasmuch as it applied only to a subset of overall credit, the market interest rate would have to be raised to very high levels, if money growth was to be reduced significantly. At the same time (since holding back the "priorities" with a restrictive policy was inconceivable), money supply grew rapidly resulting in nominal interest rates that were already high, and as such thought unsuitable for further increases.[10] Banks had no reason to be seriously concerned with competition or bad loans as the market for credit was in structural excess demand and priority loans had a state guarantee. This led to poor management and weak institutions, and to concerns that high interest rates could destabilize the banking system. The combination of high inflation and a fixed exchange rate, together with fairly abundant credit, meant that the current account was more or less continuously in deficit. The response was to encourage capital inflows through domestic credit rationing.

As in Belgium, the public debt was explicitly first in line for credit. Credit ceilings were also used to that end. Bank loans to the public sector did not enter the ceiling, thus avoiding any competition for funds with the private sector. And as credit rationing implied interest rates below market-clearing level, the budget was the recipient of net transfers from depositors.

It was not until the mid-1980s (forty years after the war) that this approach to monetary policy was abandoned. The immediate cause for

---

[9] It is not clear why smaller banks were favored. Presumably there remained a view that big banks are dangerous, and it was felt that they could find other sources abroad. Another argument was that small banks lend more to small enterprises, a traditional favorite daughter of any French government.

[10] Presumably, this argument involves Modigliani's nonneutrality.

change was the macroeconomic situation following, again, severe exchange crises in 1982 and 1983. Inflation became the priority and the economy started to slow down. Credit demand followed the downtrend so, for the first time, excess demand gave way to unused lending rights: Credit ceilings ceased to bind. As a result, monetary control based on quantitative limits was inoperative. Individual credit ceilings were dropped but quadratically increasing reserve requirements remained. Some degree of credit selectivity was maintained as favored loans were only weighted by two thirds toward reserve requirements.

The second incentive for change came from the authorities' concern with the role of Paris as a financial center. The authorities encouraged the adoption of new instruments such as options and the creation of the MATIF, Paris' futures market. The government found other ways of financing its borrowing requirements. Banks could also tap the growing amount of resources collected by the financial markets.

In 1986, more than four decades after the end of the war, came the last change. The Banque de France adopted the "Anglo-Saxon" approach, relying on the interbank and open markets and on market-set interest rates to influence the volume of credit demand. Credit selectivity was abandoned and replaced by explicit credit subsidies.

The history of capital controls is equally long. Dating back to the restoration of capital account convertibility in 1958, France operated a system of restrictions that varied over time depending upon circumstances, but was not removed until 1989, a few months ahead of the EU-wide deadline of July 1990. At all times capital outflows have been regulated, while restrictions on inflows have been imposed on a few occasions: after the breakdown of the Bretton-Woods system in 1971–73, and when the DM was temporarily weak at the end of the 1970s.

Capital controls have always been of the administrative variety, i.e., based on prohibitions. Banks, which were the required channel for cross-border transfers, were in charge of implementing the controls, and typically complied.[11] By and large, unless specifically authorized, outflows were either forbidden or subject to ceilings. These restrictions applied to firms, banking and financial institutions, and ordinary citizens. The ceilings were frequently modified, being raised when exchange market pressure was seen as less threatening by the monetary authorities. They were lowest at times of acute crisis, in 1973 after the oil shock or after the exchange rate crisis of 1983, at which point French citizens travelling abroad had to purchase a document on which outflows were recorded and could not exceed FF2000 ($270) per person and per year. Simultaneously, the use of credit

---

[11] According to Bakker (1996), this stands in contrast with German banks which displayed opposition to implement controls when they were in force in Germany.

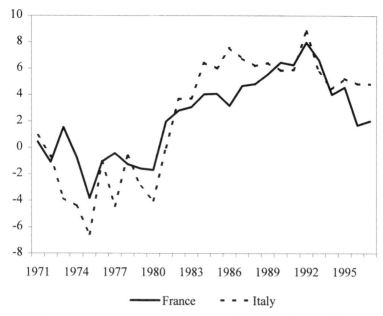

Figure 5.3. Real interest rates – ex post, short term (*Source*: IFS).

cards abroad was forbidden. Leads and lags in international current payments were also the object of specific legislation which set limits (adjusted depending upon circumstances) on the time allowed for repatriation of export earnings as well as on the advance purchase of foreign currency by importers.

When pressure was extreme, these measures were supplemented by others. Between 1971 and 1974, France also operated a dual exchange market similar to the Belgian one: There was a fixed commercial franc and a floating financial franc. In the early 1970s and until the oil shock of 1973, a Chilean-type 100 percent margin requirement was also imposed on bank deposits made by nonresidents.

The motivation for capital controls was varied. Fundamentally, the French authorities wished to "disconnect" the domestic interest rate from foreign ones. The measures proved to be successful during periods of speculative attacks, especially in the early 1980s. This was in line with the policy of credit ceilings which implied nonmarket-clearing interest rates. Figure 5.3 indicates that, together, these measures allowed France (and Italy) to maintain for about a decade (1973–82) negative real interest rates. The stated aim was to prevent runaway increases in public debt and to "support investment." Another objective of controls on outflows was to limit tax

**Table 5.3. France: Money Growth Targets and Outturns
(% Per Annum)**

	Target	Outturn	German outturn
1977	12.5	13.8	9
1978	12	12.2	11
1979	11	14.4	6
1980	11	9.8	5
1981	10	11.4	4
1982	9	11.5	6
1983	12.5–13.5	11.0	7

Source: Bakker 1996, p. 127.

evasion. Finally mercantilist sentiment also played a role in providing support for keeping French savings in France.

As previously noted, the credit ceilings were not preventing money growth from exceeding the central bank's announced targets (see Table 5.3). With inflation far in excess of Germany's, the fixed exchange rate regime was in constant jeopardy. Depreciations were endemic and widely foreseen, giving rise to recurrent exchange market crises. Only controls allowed for the survival of the exchange rate regime.[12] Naturally, these measures had highly visible drawbacks, in addition to efficiency costs. Avoidance was a national sport, and a source of income redistribution. For example, large firms with important operations abroad easily escaped controls, while smaller enterprises were constrained.[13] In addition, banks faced increasingly large administrative costs in enforcing the controls, not to mention the need to manage a dicey relationship with their customers.

The tide turned against capital controls when, after the crises of 1982–83, the government decided that membership of the European Monetary System (EMS) – and of the European Union more generally – implied that inflation must be brought down to the German level in order to eliminate the need for recurrent devaluations. Along with the adoption of a new monetary policy in 1986, this soon made controls unnecessary. The Single European Act which further prevented discrimination among European countries sealed the fate of exchange controls.

---

[12] On the need for capital controls to maintain a fixed exchange rate regime in an inflationary situation, see Wyplosz (1986).

[13] This aspect was made embarrassingly obvious when the two largest carmakers (Renault and Peugeot) set up their financial subsidiaries in Geneva in the early 1980s.

Italy

After the war, most commercial banks were state owned but relatively free to operate. Monetary policy was conducted through standard liquidity creation. On the other side, capital controls were firmly in place, the object of detailed – but often evaded – regulation which was not lessened after the establishment of current account convertibility in 1958. Like their French counterparts, the Italian authorities were convinced that speculation is mostly destabilizing, and regarded controls as a prudential device. In the late 1960s, after two decades of very fast growth and low inflation, Italy started to establish its trademark: endemic budget deficits that ended up being largely monetized and a source of creeping inflation.

By 1970, the Lira was an embattled currency. Capital controls, already extensive, were reinforced. The breakdown of the Bretton System brought another blow. As the dollar weakened, the DM strengthened and the Lira got caught in the middle of this seesaw movement. This led to a deep change in the conduct of monetary policy as well as in a further strengthening of capital controls. A dual exchange market was adopted, but it was quickly evaded, in particular through large exports of cash. The authorities responded with a triple exchange market, setting up a separate floating exchange rate for cash transfers. When none of that worked, a unified exchange rate was reestablished, and temporarily replaced by a 50 percent margin deposit on some type of flows.

A longer-lasting move was the adoption in 1973 of credit ceilings. As they were moving to tighten up monetary policy, the authorities wanted to avoid putting too much pressure on investment by small and medium enterprises. The measure was clearly seen as temporary but it remained in place until 1983.[14] Over time, credit ceilings were used to encourage the financing of current account deficit through capital inflows. The idea of replacing autonomous domestic money creation by private foreign borrowing was an explicit component of the IMF program agreed upon in 1974.

The measure aimed primarily at large, short-term bank loans. The ceilings were frequently (several times a year) revised, at least early on. Special credit institutions – often publicly owned institutions specializing in mortgages – were largely exempt from ceilings. Over time, the range of exemptions expanded: The list grew to include foreign currency loans, loans to local authorities or to particular geographic areas, etc. Noncompliance was also widespread and led to tighter penalties, like the imposition of

---

[14] A general study of this experiment is Cottarelli et al. (1986). See also Caranza and Fazio (1983).

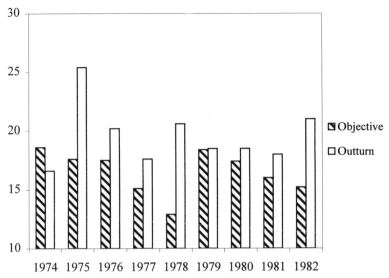

Figure 5.4. Credit ceilings in Italy (*Source*: Caranza and Fazio 1983).

nonremunerated compulsory deposits on delinquent banks. In the end, and in contrast with stated intentions, the credit ceilings mainly hurt small firms. To protect small firms, ceilings were imposed per credit, but large firms and their banks circumvented the size limit by splitting large loans into acceptable small ones.

Figure 5.4 shows that credit ceilings were not very successful, at least in achieving the targets on total domestic credit growth. Part of the reason was noncompliance, but another important part of the story was the budget deficit. As in France and Belgium, credit ceilings were explicitly seen as a way of not crowding out public borrowing without raising interest rates. In the event, interest rates were kept low (see Figure 5.3) and budget deficits continue unabated.[15] Crowding out affected those with less political clout or weak connections to banks.

Summing Up the Cases

For more than forty years Belgium, France, and Italy have adopted a variety of tools aimed at lowering the interest-cost of government borrowing, while orienting credit toward favored industries, regions, or firms. Quantitative credit ceilings were used to unhinge quantity and prices (the

---

[15] "The task of controlling the domestic component of the base is made more difficult by the Treasury's direct access to central bank's financing," Caranza and Fazio (1983), p. 39.

interest rate) but this required preventing international arbitrage also. Capital controls, while primarily motivated by the wish to rein in speculation, were thus a logical companion to domestic financial repression.[16]

In fact, ceilings were seldom "biting," i.e., effectively constraining bank credit. In Italy, Cottarelli et al. (1986) estimate that the constraint was operative from mid-1974 to early 1975, during the first three quarters of 1977, and in 1980–82. The Banque de France had developed its own index which shows a similar sporadic pattern. After a careful analysis Cassiers (1997) reaches the same conclusion for Belgium.

In all three countries, capital controls were mainly used to restrain outflows. Borrowing from abroad was a natural way around credit ceilings, one that was even welcomed by the authorities when the current account deficit was deepening. The banking and financial systems used any crack in the system to develop their lending business. Unsurprisingly, in countries where the Treasury had direct access to central bank financing and the central banks were not independent, monetary control was weak and the three countries exhibited large inflation rates.

Most other European countries followed similar practices well into the 1980s, with similar results. Even in those countries where monetary control was firm, and inflation low, various controls were used either to direct credit to favorite sons and daughters, or to limit speculation. Even Switzerland, the land of private banking, practiced various nonmarket schemes when the Swiss franc came under pressure toward appreciation, as Table 5.4 recalls. For several decades after the war, free financial markets were not a defining characteristic of Europe.

2 MACROECONOMIC EFFECTS

What are the effects of domestic financial repression and capital controls? This section examines both the period of heavy interference and the liberalization process in an attempt to answer this question. It starts by clearing some undergrowth, the relation between domestic and foreign regulation. It then examines the effect of financial repression, and its lifting, on interest rate levels and volatility.

The Link between Domestic Financial Markets and Currency Markets

Among the cases surveyed, all those that repressed their domestic financial markets used capital controls, but the reverse is not true. This is inevitable: Financial repression cannot be achieved if borrowers and

---

[16] For a comparative study on France and Italy that reaches similar conclusions but from a different angle (the focus is on the stability of money demand and control of monetary aggregates), see Dooley and Spinelli (1989).

Table 5.4. Restrictions in Switzerland

Year	Measures
1955–64	"Gentlemen's agreement" among banks to restrict inflows
1964–66	Deposit requirements on foreign deposits
1964–66	Negative interest imposed on foreign deposits
1971–74	Restrictions on foreign deposits (zero, then negative, interest, margin requirements)
1974–80	Restoration of restrictions on foreign deposits (some retroactively); quota on foreign bond issues
1976–77	Prohibition to import foreign banknotes
1977–79	Prohibition of forward sales with short maturities (<1 year); Ceilings on longer term maturities

Source: *Rapport de gestion de la Banque Nationale Suisse*, various issues.

lenders can circumvent it by freely transferring funds to and from abroad. On the other hand there is nothing to prevent free-functioning of domestic financial markets behind a wall of capital exchange controls.[17]

It follows that capital controls cannot be safely removed before financial repression is ended. To do so suddenly disables domestic regulations also, entailing substantial adjustment in the financial sector as rents disappear, implicit guarantees are removed, and competition forces a streamlining of financial firms and the development of new competences. A possible intermediate or transitory step is to allow foreign institutions to operate on the still-sheltered but liberalized domestic scene. This allows for the buildup of human capital, for the strengthening of domestic firms through heightened competition and the weeding out of laggard establishments,[18] and the adoption of adequate regulation.

Though linked in practice, external and internal controls are differently motivated. Financial repression has been motivated, at least in Europe, by a general distrust of financial markets. In addition, it represents an implicit tax that serves to lower the servicing cost of government borrowing,[19] but has the side effect of limited transparency and considerable deadweight losses. Capital controls, on the other hand, are designed to prevent domestic savings from being invested abroad. This is both a form of protection-

---

[17] As occurred during the interwar period (personal communication from Pierre Sicsic).

[18] This presumes that, as liberalization proceeds, state-owned financial institutions are privatized. This has not been the case in France and Italy where, ten years after liberalization, some banks are still state owned.

[19] The ability to keep real interest rates low enough to be below the growth rate can be very important: It prevents an autonomous debt buildup while relying on monetary financing.

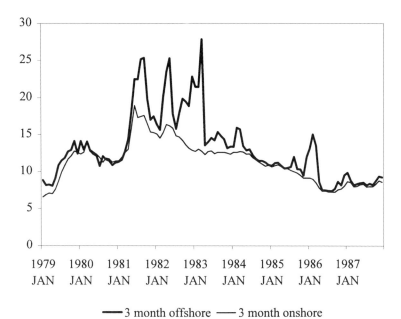

3 month offshore ——— 3 month onshore

Figure 5.5. Capital controls in France, 1979–87 (*Source*: Burda and Wyplosz 1997).

ism (benefiting borrowers and hurting lenders, with the usual efficiency costs) and a way of dealing with destabilizing speculation.[20]

While both capital controls and domestic financial repression are prone to being circumvented, the former can arguably be more effective in the limited role of providing insulation against speculative pressures at times of crisis. As Figures 5.2 and 5.3 show, most of the time credit controls do not have much effect. Capital controls, on the other side, manage to keep down domestic interest rates when needed, at times of crises. This is readily confirmed with Figure 5.5 which shows the three-month French franc interest rates measured in Paris and London. Arbitrage should eliminate any difference between the two centers unless prevented by controls and the costs of circumvention. The figure shows that at times of exchange pressure large differences emerged and could be sustained for months running. In this way, capital controls may permit the maintenance of a fixed exchange rate regime where this is deemed useful.[21] If they are put

---

[20] For a full discussion of modern theory here with references, see Eichengreen, Tobin, and Wyplosz (1995).
[21] Wyplosz (1986) shows how capital controls maintain an exchange rate regime while repeatedly devaluing the peg.

in place primarily to deal with destabilizing speculation, capital controls lose much of their justification when the exchange rate is allowed to float.

There is a link between budget financing and financial repression. By imposing below market-clearing interest rate levels through credit ceilings and locking in domestic saving through capital controls, the public sector implicitly imposes a tax on saving.

Drawing these elements together, a few conclusions emerge.

- Domestic financial repression requires capital controls, thereby adding two sources of distortions.
- The logic of financial repression is to direct saving toward public sector objectives, while capital controls may be limited to the correction of currency market failures.
- Repression prevents the emergence of a competitive financial sector with the implication that capital controls cannot safely be lifted until this sector is strengthened, which may take a substantial amount of time following domestic financial liberalization.

These different aspects are now studied in more detail.

Interest Rates: Level versus Volatility

Limiting the ability of financial markets to operate freely is sometimes justified by the view that these markets tend to display excessive volatility. Clearly, the authorities also sought to keep (real) interest rates low, ostensibly to encourage investment, more selfishly to achieve cheap finance for budget deficits. It is therefore important to ask whether these aims were achieved. On the other side, it is often feared that the removal of competition-stifling regulation will be followed by a period of instability. Several of the European financial crises of the late 1980s and early 1990s (the United Kingdom, Sweden, Finland, and Spain) have been traced to a once-off adjustment that went awry.

Case studies are suggestive, but formal evidence is needed to help assess these various propositions. This section offers some econometric evidence. Table 5.1 presents in a compact form the main regulatory changes affecting both domestic financial markets and capital controls. Were these changes associated with measurable effects on interest rates? Exchange rates are left out of the picture because European countries have experimented with various regimes. In addition, even if the EMS implied a fixed exchange rate regime as far as the conduct of monetary policy was concerned, European currencies have been floating since 1973 vis-á-vis the U.S. dollar and the yen, which may be as important for the behavior of interest rates.

The postwar period provides few regulatory regime changes per country, making country-based analyses problematic. The approach adopted here is to pool countries together. As usual, pooled cross-section analysis is open to the criticism that it assumes identical effects of the relevant explanatory variables in different countries. This is the price for avoiding the small sample hurdle. Sensitivity checks are performed to assess how high that price is.

I proceed as follows. The information provided in Table 5.1 is used to build two dummy variables, setting the value unity to years when capital controls or credit restraints were in place, and zero otherwise. Two other dummy variables are meant to capture the effect of liberalization: They take the value unity in the year that follows liberalization of the capital account or of the credit market, zero in all other years. This is done for the eleven countries for which complete information is available.

Table 5.5 first asks whether the volatility of the nominal interest rate is related to financial market restrictions. It focuses on the short-term interest rate representative of monetary condition (code 60b in the IMF's *International Financial Statistics*). Volatility is measured as the annual standard deviation of monthly rates.[22] To allow for a worldwide effect, each country's volatility is regressed on volatility in the U.S. interest rate: This variable is found to affect volatility in Europe. The other explanatory variables are the four dummy variables previously described. Both postliberalization dummy variables turn out never to be significant and are not reported, although they are used as regressors (suppressing them has a negligible effect on the results). In both panels of Table 5.5, the two first columns show the ordinary least squares (OLS) panel estimates using heteroskedasticity-consistent estimators. In the first column, country-specific constants are allowed (fixed effects) while in the second column random effects are estimated. Credit ceilings do not affect interest rate volatility but capital controls increase volatility, the opposite of the sought-after effect. The last two columns provide results from alternative procedures designed to take into account heteroskedasticity and/or covariances among countries' error terms: generalized least squares (GLS) in Column 3 and seemingly unrelated regressions (SUR) in Column 4. That capital controls raise volatility may be related to the finding by Eichengreen, Tobin, and Wyplosz (1995) that capital controls tend to weaken monetary policy discipline.[23]

---

[22] Similar results are obtained when defining volatility by the coefficient of variation. I choose to present estimates using the standard deviation because financial repression typically imposes low interest rates, which tend to increase the coefficient variation. Following liberalization, the coefficient of variation could decline because of higher average nominal rates even though the standard deviation increases. I am grateful to Patrick Honohan for pointing this out.

[23] I have also carried out the same tests using the (ex post) real interest rate (r) and the capitalization factor (1/r). For the real interest rate, the results are very similar, which is not surprising since interest volatility far exceeds inflation volatility. For the capitalization factor there is weak evidence that credit restraints *increase* volatility.

Table 5.5. Effects of Financial Regulation on the Volatility of Nominal Interest Rates (Pooled Time Series/Cross Section Estimates)

	OLS Fixed effects (1)	OLS Random effects (2)	GLS Fixed effects (3)	SUR Fixed effects (4)	OLS Fixed effects (5)	OLS Random effects (6)	GLS Fixed effects (7)	SUR Fixed effects (8)
Variance of U.S. interest rate	0.39** (0.07)	0.40** (0.09)	0.41** (0.03)	0.39** (0.05)	0.40** (0.06)	0.39** (0.08)	0.40** (0.02)	0.37** (0.05)
Capital controls	0.36** (0.13)	0.38* (0.16)	0.14** (0.05)	0.18* (0.09)	0.19 (0.11)	0.22 (0.15)	0.08 (0.04)	0.10 (0.08)
Credit restraints	0.22 (0.14)	0.18 (0.17)	0.08 (0.07)	-0.13 (0.09)	-0.01 (0.12)	-0.01 (0.16)	-0.10 (0.05)	-0.21** (0.08)
Fixed exchange rate regime					-1.03** (0.14)	-1.01** (0.15)	-0.87** (0.08)	-0.91** (0.10)
Adj. R^2	0.28	0.29	0.28	0.26	0.38	0.39	0.44	0.37
S.E.R.	0.98	0.98	0.96	1.00	0.91	0.90	0.89	0.92
No. observations	280	280	280	280	280	280	280	280

Notes: Standard errors in brackets; ** (*) significant at the 1 percent (5 percent) confidence level. White heteroskedasticity-consistent standard errors. Estimation period: 1957–97, unbalanced panel. Annual data are averages of monthly data over the year.
Countries: Belgium, Denmark, France, Germany, Italy, Netherlands, Switzerland, Ireland, Spain.
Not reported: constant, postcapital controls and postcredit restraints dummies.
Sources: Interest rates: *IFS*, CD-ROM; Capital controls and credit restraint dummy variables constructed from Table 5.1. The fixed exchange rate dummy is equal to 1 for the Bretton-Woods and EMS periods and countries, 0 elsewhere.

Interestingly, the results change somehow when the exchange rate regime is taken into account. The rightmost panel of Table 5.5 shows the effect of adding a fixed exchange rate dummy variable, set to unity for the Bretton-Woods period (1957–71) and for EMS membership. This dummy consistently predicts less interest rate volatility under a fixed-but-adjustable exchange rate regime. The capital control variable retains its positive sign, but it becomes either insignificant or significant only at the 7 percent confidence level (columns 5 and 7). Credit restraints now appear to reduce volatility, although the evidence does not seem robust.[24]

These results suggest some collinearity among the three dummy variables. And indeed, during both the Bretton-Woods years and most of the EMS period capital controls and credit restraints were frequently used. Is this just historical coincidence or is there a deeper link? There are good reasons to restrict capital movements to strengthen a fixed exchange rate regime (see Wyplosz 1986). The EMS collapsed in 1992 soon after the removal of capital controls in 1990 (see Eichengreen and Wyplosz 1993). Similarly Mexico and Korea had to abandon their exchange rate pegs following the quasi elimination of capital controls.

A plausible conclusion is that countries which adopt a fixed exchange rate regime typically engage in some form of financial repression, either to defend the regime or because they generally wish to harness financial markets, or both. Pegs unambiguously reduce interest rate volatility, as do, maybe, credit restraints. Capital controls may have the opposite effect unless it is speculative pressure which both raises volatility and leads the authorities to adopt capital controls.

The other hoped-for effect is to reduce interest rates. Tables 5.6 and 5.7 have the same structure as Table 5.5 but the dependent variable is now the nominal, respectively real, interest rate (annual averages of end-of-month observations). The influence of U.S. nominal and real interest rates on European rates is confirmed.

Financial restraints significantly reduce the real interest rate. The effect is highly significant, estimated at 150–200 basis points. The result is quite robust to the estimation procedure, as a comparison across columns in Table 5.7 shows. Capital controls tend to lower, and credit ceiling to raise, the nominal rate, but these effects are not statistically significant. They suggest that the stronger real interest effect of capital controls is accompanied by less inflation, while the weaker effect of credit restraints on the real interest rate is accompanied by more

---

[24] I thank Patrick Honohan for suggesting the use of a Bretton-Woods and EMS dummy.

**Table 5.6. Effects of Financial Regulation on Nominal Interest Rate Levels
(Pooled Time Series/Cross Section Estimates)**

	OLS Fixed effects	OLS Random effects	GLS Fixed effects	SUR Fixed effects
U.S. interest rate	0.59**	0.59**	0.59**	0.78**
	(0.04)	(0.05)	(0.03)	(0.06)
Capital controls	−0.68	−0.62	−0.71*	−0.57
	(0.42)	(0.41)	(0.34)	(0.34)
Credit restraints	0.36	0.36	0.01	0.09
	(0.39)	(0.45)	(0.27)	(0.37)
Adj. R^2	0.64	0.63	0.83	0.61
S.E.R.	2.55	2.58	2.54	2.63
No. of obs.	281	281	281	281

Notes: Standard errors in brackets; ** (*) significant at the 1 percent (5 percent) confidence level. White heteroskedasticity-consistent standard errors.
Estimation period: 1957–97, unbalanced panel. Annual data are averages of monthly data over the year.
Countries: Belgium, Denmark, France, Germany, Italy, Netherlands, Switzerland, Ireland, Spain.
Not reported: constant, postcapital controls and postcredit restraints dummies.
Sources: Interest rates: *IFS*, CD-ROM; Capital controls and credit restraint dummy variables constructed from Table 5.1.

inflation.[25] Being part of the Bretton-Woods system or of the EMS leaves the nominal interest rate unaffected (results not reported) but raises the real interest rate by 150–200 basis points, which presumably represents the cost of defending the regime. Countries which adopt both a fixed exchange rate regime and capital control leave their interest rates unaffected. Adopting in addition credit restraints results with lower real interest rates.

All in all, the statistical analysis shows that financial restraint succeeds in keeping real interest rates lower than they would have been otherwise. There is no clear sign of any effect on the nominal interest rate, presumably because authorities who avail themselves a shelter against financial markets do not dislike or do not fear inflation. Surprisingly perhaps,

---

[25] Some capital controls (e.g., in Germany) and some credit restraints (e.g., in Switzerland) were designed to make the domestic currency less attractive. Changing the sign of entries in the corresponding dummy variables does not affect the results much. This procedure is not adopted because the assessment of the intent with financial restraints would require a detailed analysis and would still be arbitrary.

Table 5.7. Effects of Financial Regulation on Real Interest Rate Levels (Pooled Time Series/Cross Section Estimates)

	OLS Fixed effects	OLS Random effects	GLS Fixed effects	SUR Fixed effects
U.S. interest rate	0.56**	0.55**	0.30**	0.48**
	(0.12)	(0.09)	(0.08)	(0.09)
Capital controls	−2.52**	−2.01**	−1.52**	−1.82**
	(0.50)	(0.48)	(0.30)	(0.32)
Credit restraints	−1.91**	−1.49**	−2.65**	−1.84**
	(0.49)	(0.50)	(0.33)	(0.27)
Fixed exchange	1.35*	2.26**	1.93**	1.02**
Rate regime	(0.53)	(0.43)	(0.38)	(0.39)
Adj. R^2	0.41	0.38	0.64	0.39
S.E.R.	3.17	3.24	3.07	3.21
No. of obs.	288	288	288	288

Notes: Standard errors in brackets; ** (*) significant at the 1 percent (5 percent) confidence level. White heteroskedasticity-consistent standard errors.
Estimation period: 1957–97, unbalanced panel. Annual data are averages of monthly data over the year. Ex post real interest rates.
Countries: Belgium, Denmark, France, Germany, Italy, Netherlands, Switzerland, Ireland, Spain.
Not reported: constant, postcapital controls and postcredit restraints dummies.
Sources: Interest rates: *IFS*, CD-ROM; Capital controls and credit restraint dummy variables constructed from Table 5.1.

capital controls, which in principle alleviate external pressure, actually result in more short-term interest rate volatility. Finally, the abolition of financial restraints are not followed, within a year, by more interest rate volatility.

On the other hand, the experience with the EMS shows that a fixed exchange rate regime rarely survives the removal of capital controls. As shown by Eichengreen and Wyplosz (1993) and Jeanne (1996), the EMS crisis of 1992–93 can be directly related to the lifting of restrictions to capital movements. This has created the conditions for multiple equilibria which are at the root of the self-fulfilling attacks on the French franc and other otherwise healthy currencies. The adoption of 30 percent wide bands of fluctuations in August 1993 in effect meant the end of the fixed exchange regime to which European countries had displayed great attachment. A year earlier, Italy and the United Kingdom had found no other solution than to withdraw from the EMS and let their currencies float freely.

Table 5.8. The Budget Surplus and Financial Regulation (Pooled Time Series/Cross Section Estimates; Dependent Variable: Budget Surplus (Percent of GDP))

	OLS Fixed effects	OLS Random effects	GLS Fixed effects	SUR Fixed effects
Output gap	0.28**	0.28**	0.35**	0.24**
(% of potential)	(0.09)	(0.08)	(0.07)	(0.04)
Capital controls	−0.85*	−0.86*	0.31	1.17**
	(0.42)	(0.39)	(0.31)	(0.25)
Credit restraints	2.03**	2.02**	1.56**	0.92**
	(0.45)	(0.48)	(0.37)	(0.22)
Adj. R^2	0.53	0.54	0.48	0.48
S.E.R.	2.54	2.52	2.59	2.67
No. of obs.	254	254	254	254

Notes: Standard errors in brackets; ** (*) significant at the 1 percent (5 percent) confidence level. White heteroskedasticity-consistent standard errors.
Estimation period: 1960–97, unbalanced panel. Countries: Belgium, Denmark, France, Germany, Italy, Netherlands, Ireland, Spain.
Not reported: constant.
Sources: Budget and output gap: OECD *Economic Outlook* 64, December 1998; Capital controls and credit restraint dummy variables constructed from Table 5.1.

Budgetary Effects

Keeping real interest rates low may have two opposite effects on the budget deficit.[26] By reducing the interest charge, it contributes to lower the overall deficit. On the other side, a lower debt service may encourage governments to run a higher primary surplus resulting in limited effect on the overall budget. The end effect of financial restraints on, respectively, the overall and primary budget surpluses is studied in Tables 5.8 and 5.9.

In addition to the dummy variables constructed from Table 5.1, these regressions include the output gap to account for cyclical effects. Domestic credit restraints clearly improve the overall budget surplus, by about two percentage points on average in the sample (Table 5.8). The lack of discipline effect is detected but it is not statistically significant (Table 5.9).

Capital controls, on the other hand, are accompanied by deeper deficits, by about one percentage point, but the effect is weakly measured.[27] One possible interpretation is that protection from capital movements relaxes

---

[26] For work along similar lines, see Alesina et al. (1994).

[27] The result is weak. Depending on the regression technique, the effect of capital controls on the overall budget changes sign. Based on goodness-of-fit criteria, it seems reasonable to conclude that the effect is mildly negative.

Table 5.9. The Primary Budget Surplus and Financial Regulation (Pooled Time Series/Cross Section Estimates Dependent Variable: Primary Budget Surplus (Percent of GDP))

	OLS Fixed effects	OLS Random effects	GLS Fixed effects	SUR Fixed effects
Output gap	0.25**	0.25**	0.33**	0.22**
(% of potential)	(0.09)	(0.08)	(0.04)	(0.04)
Capital controls	−2.08**	−2.09**	−1.25**	−0.59**
	(0.35)	(0.39)	(0.16)	(0.19)
Credit restraints	−0.56	−0.53	−0.17	0.29
	(0.54)	(0.48)	(0.27)	(0.19)
Adj. R^2	0.28	0.29	0.27	0.20
S.E.R.	2.50	2.46	2.55	2.63
No. of obs.	248	248	248	248

Notes: Standard errors in brackets; ** (*) significant at the 1 percent (5 percent) confidence level. White heteroskedasticity-consistent standard errors.
Estimation period: 1960–97, unbalanced panel. Countries: Belgium, Denmark, France, Germany, Italy, Netherlands, Ireland, Spain.
Not reported: constant.
Sources: Budget and output gap: OECD *Economic Outlook* 64, December 1998; Capital controls and credit restraint dummy variables constructed from Table 5.1.

fiscal discipline: The primary budget declines by about two percentage points. This conclusion should be handled carefully as causality may well run in the opposite direction: Governments which run large deficits may be tempted to "bottle in" domestic savings. Controls can be seen as an implicit tax that may be optimal to include in the overall battery of taxation. This applies to the inflation tax as well, which may help explain the association between financial repression and inflation previously documented.[28]

---

[28] There is no discernible growth effect of financial restraints in the European sample studied here (regressions not reported). It may be that the effect exists but is too small to be detected. This suggests that, for a host of reasons, the much trumpeted distortions of such measures are less serious than (simple) theory predicts. After all France and Italy were considered as stunning postwar successes, as were Korea and Japan, while they were actively stifling financial freewheeling. Reviewing the postwar performance of France, Sicsic and Wyplosz (1996) find, however, that the high growth rates of the 1960s and early 1970s might have been even higher absent widespread public intervention. Their conclusion is based on evidence of a severe misallocation of resources toward favorite and ultimately declining industries. The state control of financial markets evidently played a role, but a host of other institutions as well, including price controls and pervasive subsidies, education, the structure of the labor market, and a slow ending of trade protection.

3 BANKING EFFECTS

Financial repression, affecting both domestic markets and capital movements, is widely understood to stifle competition in the banking sector. Credit ceilings, in particular, when applied bank by bank, in principle freeze market shares. In their detailed analysis of the Italian experiment, Cottarelli et al. (1986) conclude that indeed, credit ceilings reduce competition but they note a number of mitigating factors:

- the possibility that quotas are traded, officially or not,
- the Darwinian adaptability of the banking system to credit ceilings,
- the existence of other regulations (e.g., limits on deposit and/or lending rates, on branch openings, etc.) which already stamp out competition,
- separate collusive agreements (clear in Belgium, France, and Italy) which also reduce competition,
- circumvention of ceilings through the creative use of exemptions and/or loopholes.

This section asks whether the removal of financial restraints has had a visible effect on the banking industry. It is often argued that enhanced competition reduces profitability, hence the franchise value of banks, possibly leading to crises.[29] Figure 5.6 presents the celebrated British case. Deep deregulation of the British banking system in the early 1980s led to a shake-up of the industry. Fueled by cut-throat competition on the mortgage market, rent prices (the figure displays the ratio of rent prices to the CPI) more than doubled in real terms in a few years, resulting in what is customarily considered a bubble. The bubble burst in the mid-1980s as bad loans came due, prompting a severe bank crisis. Interestingly, as if developers and investors recognized the phenomenon as temporary, the volume of new construction did not follow, even slowing down when the bubble started to grow even faster. Did the removal of credit constraints and capital controls produce similar effects in the three countries reviewed in Section 2?

Market Structure

Figure 5.7 displays the real rent price index for the three countries surveyed in Section 2, along with the United Kingdom for comparison. It confirms the conclusion by Cottarelli et al. (1986): In the case of Italy housing prices declined vis-á-vis the CPI when credit ceilings were imposed in 1973, and recovered some of the lost ground in 1983 when the ceilings

---

[29] See Caprio and Summers (1996) and Hellmann et al. (1998).

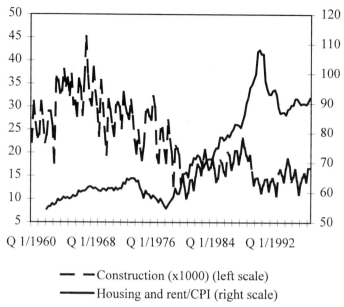

Q 1/1960   Q 1/1968   Q 1/1976   Q 1/1984   Q 1/1992

— —Construction (x1000) (left scale)
———Housing and rent/CPI (right scale)

Figure 5.6. The housing market in the United Kingdom, 1960–97 (*Source*: OECD).

were removed. The pattern for Belgium and France is less clear. In all three cases, the end of domestic financial repression is not marked by the spectacular rise observable in the United Kingdom. In France, Jaillet and Sicsic (1998) show that only in Paris did housing prices exhibit a behavior resembling the British one. This suggests that other factors may have continued to restrain competition.

One possibility is collusion. In France the largest banks remained state owned for several years afterward and regulation regarding interest rates remains in place; in fact a large part of mortgage credit is subsidized and the corresponding interest rates are set by the authorities. Similarly in Belgium, the banking industry remained officially cartelized until 1992. Another possibility is that competition in the banking sector may be muted because of restrained market behavior in the labor market. The next section evaluates this hypothesis.

Rent-shifting

The top graph in Figure 5.8 presents a customary measure of bank profitability, net income as percent of total assets, for the three same countries and for two comparator countries with a very developed banking sector, the United Kingdom and Switzerland. The graph suggests two observa-

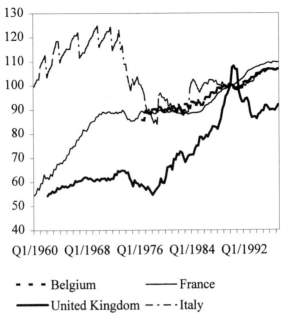

Figure 5.7. The real price of housing, 1960–97 (*Source*: OECD).

tions. First, the sheltered banks of Belgium and France are less profitable than the others. This could be due to a Belgian-type quid pro quo, whereby, in exchange for protection, banks agree to limit their profit margins: Low risks are accompanied by low returns. Alternatively, this could reflect low returns from lending to the authorities' favorite firms.[30]

In both cases, one would then expect profits to be related to changes in the regulatory and competitive environment. The removal of protection should lead, possibly after a shake up of the industry, to improved margins thanks to more lucrative, possibly riskier loans. The second observation, however, is that there is no visible link between profitability and the changing competitive environment of banks. Looking at a large sample of developed and developing countries, Demirgüç-Kunt and Detriagache (Chapter 4) also fail to detect a clear link between financial repression (or liberalization) and bank profitability.

Does deregulation affect the way banks operate at all? One possibility is that, as other financial institutions enter the loan market when it is deregulated, bank intermediation declines. The lower graph of Figure 5.8

---

[30] Profitability is measured after tax, which may explain some of the differences observed in Figure 5.7.

Net income
percent of balance sheet total

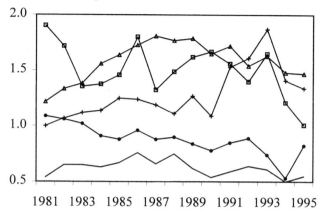

Net interest income
percent of balance sheet total

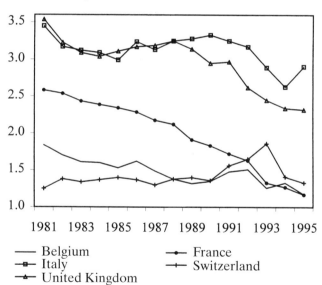

Figure 5.8. Bank profitability (*Source*: OECD).

displays a measure of intermediation, net profits as a share of total bank assets. There is a clear downward trend in France – but it dates back to the early 1980s, prior to deregulation – and in the United Kingdom after the wave of crises.

Clearly, if deregulation produced important changes in the banking industry, it did not operate through profitability of the banks' portfolio of activity. Figure 5.9 suggests another explanation. The top chart shows that staff reduction has been a general phenomenon of the last twenty years in Europe. However, the lower chart indicates that this has not been accompanied by savings in labor costs. A number of plausible interpretations arise.

A first possibility is technological change. From labor intensive, the banking industry has become capital intensive. A large staff of cheap low-skill, low-wage personnel has been replaced with less but better-paid high-skill personnel. A second possibility is that the pressure of increased competition has led banks to seek to economize on labor costs but that strong unions have managed to preserve labor's share of income. The contrast between Switzerland and the United Kingdom on one hand, with the three EU countries on the other hand, would tend to support the second assumption: In the United Kingdom and Switzerland, two countries where union power has been either low (Switzerland) or sharply declining (the United Kingdom), labor costs have followed a declining trend while there is no discernible trend in Belgium, France, and Italy, where union power in banking has been and remains strong.

Putting together these observations, a plausible hypothesis runs as follows. The end of financial repression increases competition in the banking industry but without affecting profitability. Rents simply shift. In the repressed regime, banks are sheltered and collusion is officially sanctioned; the resulting rent is captured by the government through cheap debt financing. Once repression ends, banks adjust from simple trouble-free low value-added activities to producing more sophisticated and higher value-added products. However, banking services are known for strong brand loyalty, largely because of heavy switching costs, so rents do not fully dissipate. Instead they are captured by the more professional staff on which banks now crucially depend.

4 CONCLUDING REMARKS

This overview of financial repression and liberalization in Europe, as well as other work surveyed, suggests the following conclusions.

The imposition of quantitative controls on banks does not improve the effectiveness of control over monetary aggregates. In fact, inflation tends to be higher where such controls exist. The reason is clear. Such controls

Number of employees
relative to gross income (in DM)

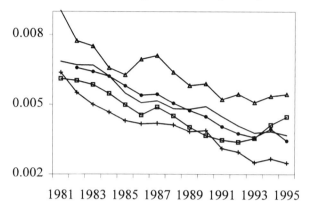

Staff costs relative to gross income

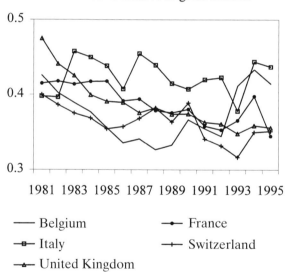

Figure 5.9. Bank staffing and bank profitability (*Source*: OECD).

are usually motivated by two objectives: to provide readily available and cheap financing for public sector deficits and to support an industrial policy targeted at specific firms and industries or other objectives (e.g., regional development). As a consequence credit remains abundant, and monetary policy becomes far too political to be tightened easily when the need arises.

Domestic financial repression brings about capital controls. There is no point in preventing some activities or imposing quantitative ceilings if domestic agents can legally and easily circumvent these restrictions by operating on foreign financial markets and transferring funds across borders as they see fit. On the other hand, capital controls can be applied to fully liberalized domestic financial markets. This clearly implies a certain sequencing of liberalization.

By reducing nominal interest rates domestic credit restraints reduce the debt burden and result in lower budget deficits *ceteris paribus*. The finding that the primary budget deficit worsens in the presence of credit restraints and capital controls may indicate that financial repression is often imposed with a view to loosening market-induced fiscal discipline in the public sector.

Restriction of domestic financial activity reduces competition in banking. Administrative rules lessen the need to compete and, through the associated capital controls, shelter banks from foreign competition. The rent is usually captured by the public sector in an implicit quid pro quo. In Belgium, France, and Italy liberalization does not seem to have greatly enhanced competition. Rents appear to have shifted toward personnel.

The effects of financial restraints on interest rates are mostly disappointing. Credit ceilings do not reduce volatility or the level of nominal interest rates but they may succeed in lowering the average real interest rate level, presumably through rationing. Capital controls keep interest rates down but increase their volatility. On the other hand, there is no indication that the suppression of financial restraints raised nominal interest rate volatility in Europe.

It may well be that one additional main reason for internal and external financial repression lies in the authorities' wish to maintain the exchange rate regime. A fixed but adjustable exchange rate system tends to lower interest rate volatility but to raise real interest rates. The combined effect of a fixed exchange rate regime, capital controls, and credit ceilings is to reduce interest rate volatility and to deliver lower real short-term interest rates, leaving the level of nominal interest rates unaffected.

Capital liberalization should not be seen as a precondition for growth. The view that developing countries should aim at liberalization as soon as possible is certainly not vindicated by the case of Europe.

Credit restrictions seem generally more harmful than capital controls. Since domestic restraints require the presence of capital controls, a reasonable approach is to proceed through liberalization in two steps: First lift domestic restraints, next remove capital controls. The last step should follow the establishment of a competitive domestic banking system with an accompanying regulatory capacity.

The lifting of capital controls requires the end of any fixed exchange rate regime that might have been in place. To reverse that order, by liberalizing first and hoping to leave the float until later, is virtually to guarantee an exchange crisis which may develop into full-blown financial crisis. Floating often comes too late.

REFERENCES

Alesina, A., V. Grilli, and G.M. Milesi-Ferretti. 1994. "The Political Economy of Capital Controls." In L. Leiderman and A. Razin (eds.), *Capital Mobility: The Impact on Consumption, Investment and Growth*, pp. 289–321. Cambridge University Press.

Bakker, A.F.P. 1996. *The Liberalization of Capital Movements in Europe*. Dordrecht: Kluwer Academic Publishers.

Caprio, G. and L. Summers. 1996. "Finance and its Reform: Beyond Laissez-Faire." In D.B. Papadimitriou (ed.), *Stability in the Financial System*, pp. 400–21. Jerome Levy Economics Institute Series. New York: St. Martin's Press; London: Macmillan Press.

Caranza, C. and A. Fazio. 1983. "L'evoluzione dei metodi di controllo monetario in Italia: 1974–1983." *Bancaria* 39(9):819–33.

Cassiers, I. 1997. "La Générale de Banque de 1935 à nos jours: une mise en perspective macroéconomique." In E. Buyst et al. (eds.), *La Générale de Banque, 1822–1997*. Bruxelles: Editions Racine.

Cassiers, I., P. de Villé, and P.M. Solar. 1996. "Economic Growth in Postwar Belgium." In N. Crafts and G. Toniolo (eds.), *Economic Growth in Europe Since 1945*, pp. 173–209. Cambridge University Press.

Cottarelli, C., G.P. Galli, P. Marullo Reedtz, and G. Pittaluga. 1986. "Monetary Policy Through Ceilings on Bank Lending." *Economic Policy* 3:673–94.

Dooley, M.P. and F. Spinelli. 1989. "The Early Stages of Financial Innovation and Money Demand in France and Italy." *The Manchester School* 57(2):107–24.

Eichengreen, B. and C. Wyplosz. 1993. "Unstable EMS." *Brookings Papers on Economic Activity* 1:51–124.

Eichengreen, B., J. Tobin, and C. Wyplosz. 1995. "Two Cases for Sand in the Wheels of International Finance." *Economic Journal* 105:162–72.

Eichengreen, B., A. Rose, and C. Wyplosz. 1995. "Exchange Market Mayhem: The Antecedents and Aftermath of Speculative Attacks." *Economic Policy* 21:249–312.

Greenwald, B., J. Stiglitz, and A. Weiss. 1984. "Information Imperfections in the Capital Markets and Macroeconomic Fluctuations." *American Economic Review, Papers and Proceedings* 74:194–99.

Hellman, T., K. Murdock, and J. Stiglitz. 2000. "Liberalization, Moral Hazard in Banking and Prudential Regulation: Are Capital Requirements Enough?" *American Economic Review* 90(1):147–65.

Icard, A. 1994. "Monetary Policy and Exchange Rates: The French Experience." In J.O. de Beaufort Wijnholds, S.C.W. Eijffinger, and L.H. Hoogduin (eds.), *A Framework for Monetary Stability*. Financial and Monetary Policy Studies, Vol. 27. Dordrecht and Boston: Kluwer Academic.

International Monetary Fund. 1997. *International Capital Markets*. Washington D.C.

Jaillet, P. and P. Sicsic. 1998. "Asset Prices: Relationships with Demand Factors and Credit, and Implications for Monetary Policy." In *The Role of Asset Prices in the Formulation of Monetary Policy.* Basle: Bank for International Settlements.

Jeanne, O. 1996. "Would a Tobin Tax Have Saved the EMS?" *Scandinavian Journal of Economics* 98(4):503–20.

Melitz, J. 1991. "Monetary Policy in France." Centre for Economic Policy Research Discussion Paper 509.

Mishkin, F. 1991. "Anatomy of a Financial Crisis." *NBER Working Paper* No. 3934.

Wyplosz, C. 1986. "Capital Controls and Balance of Payments Crises." *Journal of International Money and Finance* 5:167–79.

Wyplosz, C. 1988. "Monetary Policy in France: Monetarism or Darwinism?" *Financial Markets and Portfolio Management*, May.

6

The Role of Poorly Phased Liberalization in Korea's Financial Crisis

Yoon Je Cho

INTRODUCTION

Although not the immediate trigger of Korea's financial and currency crisis in November 1997, poorly implemented financial liberalization contributed to the scale and pace of the crisis by weakening the financial structure of both the financial and nonfinancial corporate sectors during the preceding years. There were errors in sequencing of market and price liberalization as well as inadequate prudential regulation and supervision. The downturn was characterized, not by the bursting of an asset-price bubble, as was the case in many other countries, but instead by widespread insolvency among manufacturing firms, in particular the large chaebols.

The immediate cause of the crisis was the run of foreign creditors. This in turn was critical because of the level of short-term foreign debt which had risen to a multiple of usable foreign exchange reserves. The Thai crisis from mid-1997 contributed to the doubts of foreign creditors, but what really triggered their refusal to rollover loans to Korean banks was the rapid increase in the banks' nonperforming assets, with six of the thirty largest Korean conglomerates (chaebols) failing after January 1997. The fundamental reasons for this string of chaebol bankruptcies lay in the distorted incentive structure of the economy, which encouraged overexpansion of corporate investment and was reflected in excessive real wages, an overvalued exchange rate and other misaligned relative prices (Cho 1998a).

But there was also a contribution from the uneven, poorly phased approach to financial liberalization. Korea had launched its policy of financial liberalization in the early 1990s by implementing a four-stage interest rate liberalization plan and encouraging competition among the financial institutions. However, the actual implementation of financial liberalization deviated from what had been formally announced. It maintained a proper balance neither between banks and nonbank financial institutions (NBFIs), nor between short- and long-term domestic and foreign borrowing. Above all, a shortening of the maturity of the financial liabilities of Korean corporate borrowers and in the foreign liabilities of Korean banks and nonbank financial intermediaries (NBFIs) made the economy very vulnerable to external shocks. The authorities retained de facto control of many bank interest rates and corporate bond yields, while completely deregulating interest rates for short-term securities such as commercial paper (CP).

Against a background of poor credit risk assessment and supervision of the institutions active in the short-term securities market, short-term financing was quickly made available on a large scale to firms engaged in high-risk expansion of long-term investment in steel, automobiles, petrochemicals, and so on. Total corporate investment and debt increased quickly despite the declining profitability of firms during this period.

The accelerated opening up to international capital flows from 1994 without adequate supervision also contributed to the currency crisis. Here again, short-term bank borrowing was liberalized while long-term borrowing was regulated. For nonfinancial borrowers too it was the short-term trade and other credits that were liberalized, while long-term suppliers' credit and foreign access to bond markets remained restricted. Furthermore, the government allowed the entry of many new merchant banking companies (MBCs) during 1994 96. These new MBCs borrowed heavily in the short term but invested in long-term assets. This increasing mismatch in maturity between foreign liabilities and assets in MBCs, along with the fact that financial institutions were not properly monitored or supervised by the authorities, made the Korean system very vulnerable to a foreign exchange crisis.

When the domestic recession and a disruption in the terms of trade aggravated the cash flows of highly indebted firms, corporate insolvency became widespread. The authorities' efforts to prevent massive bankruptcy among the big chaebols by organizing a Creditors' Coordination Committee and providing rescue financing were unable to prevent a snowballing of nonperforming assets in the banks which in turn prompted an increase in the spread of their borrowing costs on the international capital markets, as their credit ratings were lowered.

Section 1 discusses the process of financial liberalization and its impact on the development of financial market structure. Using the balance sheet data of individual firms, Section 2 explains how changes in the financial market affected the corporate sector's financing pattern and its debt structure. Based on the previous two sections, Section 3 discusses the ways in which the process of financial liberalization contributed to the financial crisis. Section 4 draws some generally applicable lessons.

1 FINANCIAL LIBERALIZATION AND CHANGES IN THE FINANCIAL MARKET STRUCTURE

Uneven Liberalization and the Composition of Financial Assets

The Plan and Its Implementation

The Korean government started to liberalize the financial system in the early 1980s, but implementation was haphazard and lacked a comprehensive strategy at that time.[1] The government announced a comprehensive four-stage interest rate deregulation plan in 1991. However, the incoming Kim Young-Sam administration accelerated the process with *Blueprint for Financial Liberalization and Market Opening* (July 1993) and *Foreign Exchange Reform Plan* (December 1994). Many restrictions on the financial markets and foreign exchange transactions were relaxed or abolished in order to expedite the "globalization" of the Korean economy. Korea's financial deregulation was implemented ahead of schedule in order to meet the goal of becoming a member of the OECD by the end of 1996. The financial reforms undertaken in Korea since the early 1990s were wide ranging in their scope. By July 1997, most interest rates had been liberalized, while entry barriers to the banking and nonbanking sector had been significantly relaxed. Restrictions on foreign capital flows were substantially removed.

The four-stage interest rate plan seems to have been based on the principle of progressing gradually from long-term to short-term rates, from the securities market to bank interest rates, and from large- to small-denomination instruments. However, in the end, the sequence lacked a clear logic (see Appendix).

Furthermore, actual implementation of liberalization deviated substantially from the officially announced plan. Interest rates for short-term bills such as commercial paper (CP) were formally liberalized in 1991, but it was 1993–94 before they were fully liberalized in practice. Bank interest rates continued to be controlled through moral suasion or administrative guidance until 1996, despite formal liberalization in 1993. For instance, according to the official announcement, bank loan rates (except for policy-based loans supported by the rediscount window of the central bank) were completely liberalized by November 1993. But the fluctuation of bank loan rates (prime rate) clearly shows that they were not fully deregulated at that stage (Figure 6.1). Corporate bond rates were indirectly controlled

[1] See Cho (1998c) for a discussion of the major experiences of financial reform in Korea during the last three and a half decades.

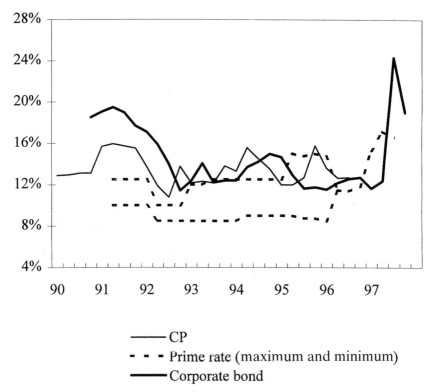

Figure 6.1. Bank loan rates and yield on CPs and corporate bonds (*Source*: Bank of Korea, *Monthly Bulletin*, various issues, Merchant Banks Association of Korea).

until mid-1997, through the control of the amount of issuance following formal liberalization in 1991.[2]

As a consequence, for most of the period 1994–97, three-month CP yields were above three-year corporate bond yields, which in turn were higher than bank prime lending rates (Figure 6.1). Interest rates on time deposits of less than one year's maturity were liberalized in July 1995, but they were indirectly controlled until the middle of 1996, and remained below the rates of close substitutes (Figure 6.2).

---

[2] The government allowed the Securities Association to determine who would be able to issue the bonds, the overall amount of which was guided by the government. Usually, the Securities Association allocated the amount between applicants. The reason why the government was so conscious of the level of corporate bond yield was because it was the most observable market rate.

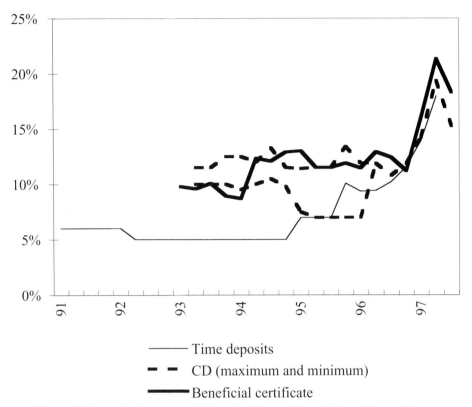

Figure 6.2. Interest rates on bank deposits, CDs, and beneficial certificates (*Source*: Bank of Korea).

Shift of Funds to the Short-term Market

The unbalanced liberalization of interest rates caused a rapid shift of funds toward the short-term CP market[3] between 1993 and 1996 (Table 6.1). The corporate sector became increasingly reliant on CPs for its financing (Table 6.2). Accounting for only 2.5 percent during 1990–92, the share of CPs in total corporate financing increased to 13.1 percent during 1993–96, peaking at 17.5 percent in 1996.

---

[3] In Korea, CPs are accepted by finance and investment companies (FICs) and merchant banking companies (MBCs), and are then discounted by individuals or institutional investors.

Table 6.1. Growth of Financial Markets (Outstanding Basis)

Won trn	Commercial paper	Corporate bonds	Bank loans	M3
1991	21.6	43.5	113.0	244.8
1992	25.5	50.1	132.9	298.3
1993	36.1	59.5	152.0	354.9
1994	44.4	72.2	187.1	442.7
1995	61.0	87.5	218.8	527.0
1996	80.8	111.4	254.6	615.0
Growth rates (%)				
(91–96)	26.4	18.8	16.2	20.8

Source: Bank of Korea, *Monthly Bulletin*, various issues.

Table 6.2. Sources of Finance for Corporate Sector, 1990–97

(%)	1990	1991	1992	1993	1994	1995	1996	1997
Direct financing	42.4	37.9	41.4	52.9	38.1	48.1	47.2	37.1
CPs	3.7	−3.8	7.6	13.9	4.9	16.1	17.5	4.1
Bonds	21.5	24.2	12.1	14.5	14.2	15.3	17.9	22.9
Stocks	11.8	11.5	13.1	14.7	14.8	14.4	10.9	7.7
Indirect financing	38.4	41.8	36.3	31.4	44.5	31.8	29.1	37.9
Banks	15.8	19.8	15.1	13.1	20.7	14.9	15.2	12.9
Nonbanks	22.6	22.0	21.1	18.3	23.8	17.0	13.9	24.3
Overseas	6.4	4.1	7.1	1.5	6.6	8.4	10.4	6.1
Others	12.8	16.1	15.3	14.2	10.8	11.7	13.2	18.9
Total	100	100	100	100	100	100	100	100
(Won trn)	(50.7)	(58.2)	(54.9)	(65.0)	(89.0)	(100.0)	(118.8)	(117.0)

Source: Bank of Korea, *Monthly Bulletin*, various issues.

Constraints on Bank Liberalization: Policy Loans and Instruments of Monetary Control

One of the reasons the Korean authorities were slow to liberalize bank interest rates was that they could not abolish policy-based lending completely. Most of the directed loans earmarked to support specific industries had been abolished, leaving only a general guideline to allocate a minimum share of bank loans (40 percent) to the manufacturing sector. However, the authorities continued providing policy loans to small and medium-sized firms, through the central bank's rediscount window. When the commercial banks discounted bills for small- to medium-sized firms, the central bank (Bank of Korea) rediscounted a certain portion of the banks' discounts. As a result, the BOK's outstanding loans to commercial

**Table 6.3. BOK's Lending to Banks and Monetary
Stabilization Bonds Issued (in Trillions of Won)**

Year	Loans & discounts to deposit money banks	Monetary stabilization bonds issued
1990	11.0	15.6
1991	12.9	13.9
1992	16.4	20.6
1993	15.9	24.4
1994	13.4	25.3
1995	11.1	25.8
1996	6.7	25.0
1997	10.9	23.5

Source: Bank of Korea, *Monthly Bulletin*, various issues; *Economic Statistics Yearbook*, various issues.

Table 6.4. Reserve Requirements of Deposit Money Banks (%)

Effective date	Time & savings deposits	Demand deposits
1985 (July 23)	4.5	4.5
1987 (February 20)	4.5	4.5
(November 23)	7.0	7.0
1988 (December 23)	10.0	10.0
1989 (May 8)	10.0 (30.0)	10.0 (30.0)
1990 (February 8)	11.5	11.5
1990 (March 8)	11.5	11.5
1996 (April 23)	9.0	9.0
(November 8)	7.0	7.0
1997 (February 23)	2.0	5.0

Note: Figures in parentheses show the marginal reserve ratio applied to the increment of each half-monthly average deposit compared with the first half-monthly average deposits of April 1989.
Source: Bank of Korea, *Monthly Bulletin*, various issues.

banks were substantial. To offset this, the central bank had to issue large amounts of Monetary Stabilization Bonds below market rates; these were allocated to banks and NBFIs (Table 6.3).

Furthermore, in order to offset the monetary impact of the policy-based loans, the BOK imposed a high reserve requirement on banks. Because of this high reserve requirement ratio (and the implicit control on lending rates), banks could not afford to offer competitive deposit rates even though they were formally liberalized (Table 6.4).

Expansion of Trust Business

In Korea, banks have been allowed to do trust business, mobilizing funds by issuing beneficiary certificates. While returns on beneficiary certificates should, in principle, be determined ex post by the actual rate of return on the investment portfolio of the trust fund in question, it was common practice in Korea for banks to post a fixed interest rate for beneficiary certificates. The authorities had indirectly controlled this rate by requiring the trust account portfolio to purchase a certain minimum proportion of public securities, including the Monetary Stabilization Bonds, which were issued at below market yields. But from 1993, portfolio restrictions were gradually relaxed, and furthermore the gap between yields on public securities and market rates diminished. These changes effectively further liberalized the rate of return on bank beneficiary certificates, which were in competition with the beneficiary certificates of the Investment and Trust Companies (ITCs). With funding costs increasing in 1993, the authorities allowed the trust account of the banks to purchase CPs, for which the interest rates were completely free. This further facilitated the expansion of the CP market.

One of the reasons for the authorities' asymmetric treatment of liberalization between bank trust accounts and general accounts was the fact that they had chosen M2 as the target for monetary control, and that aggregate includes only deposits made in banks. When it became difficult to meet the M2 growth target in 1993 (with deposit growth resulting from the partial liberalization of long-term deposit rates), the authorities reacted by further liberalizing trust account instruments and CPs, which were not included in M2. As a result, funds shifted back from deposit to trust accounts in the banks and to the CP market (Table 6.5), and the growth of M2 (and M3) accelerated in 1994 (Figures 6.3 and 6.4).[4]

Increasing Risk with Inadequate Supervision

The Shift to High-risk Assets

Banks increased their holdings of marketable securities both in their general accounts and in trust accounts. From 1993, trust funds were allowed to be invested in CPs, relaxing the previous requirement that they be either invested in long-term securities or loaned to firms. At the same time, the maximum share of securities investments allowed in the total asset portfolio increased from 40 percent to 60 percent in trust accounts. Thereafter, the share of corporate bonds, CPs, and other securities in trust

---

[4] Within the bank's deposit business, the share of CDs and long-term deposits expanded at the expense of short-term deposits, whose interest rates remained under control.

Table 6.5. Bank Liabilities

Won trn (%)	Deposits		CDs	Trust funds	Foreign liabilities
	Short-term	Long-term			
1990	56.77	27.29	6.80	29.18	7.30
	(29.3)	(14.1)	(3.5)	(15.1)	(3.8)
1991	65.29	33.22	9.94	36.62	10.52
	(28.3)	(14.4)	(4.3)	(15.9)	(4.6)
1992	69.55	37.69	11.94	53.02	11.57
	(25.2)	(13.6)	(4.3)	(19.2)	(4.2)
1993	71.21	44.52	16.50	71.32	11.97
	(21.7)	(13.6)	(5.0)	(21.7)	(3.6)
1994	80.79	54.40	21.41	93.42	16.76
	(20.4)	(13.7)	(5.4)	(23.5)	(4.2)
1995	91.50	62.63	31.17	124.89	24.51
	(18.3)	(12.5)	(6.2)	(24.9)	(4.9)
1996	102.85	78.88	25.50	151.09	36.67
	(17.5)	(13.4)	(4.3)	(25.7)	(6.2)
Growth rate 1990–96 (%)	9.9	17.7	22.0	27.4	26.9

Note: Figures in parentheses express the percentage share.
Source: Bank of Korea, *Monthly Bulletin*, various issues.

Table 6.6. Share of Securities Holdings in Bank Assets

Won trn (%)	1991	1992	1993	1994	1995	1996	1997
Bank account	16.75	18.69	23.12	30.53	41.38	51.07	71.93
	(12.2)	(12.3)	(13.9)	(15.2)	(15.9)	(16.4)	(17.1)
Trust account	14.98	21.69	40.55	58.67	87.92	105.98	124.52
	(46.9)	(46.8)	(59.8)	(61.2)	(64.0)	(65.2)	(66.2)

Source: *Statistics on Bank Management*, Office of Banking Supervision, various issues.

funds increased rapidly (Table 6.6), growing from 47 percent in 1991 to 65 percent in 1997, mainly reflecting the rapid increase in their holdings of CPs. Most depositors did not distinguish between a time deposit account and a trust account offered by the same bank, and easily shifted between the two in response to yield differentials. (No Korean bank had ever failed, and depositors assumed that both instruments carried essentially zero risk.) The result was that that depositors' money was being used to finance the long-term risky investments of corporate firms through the purchase of their short-term CPs.

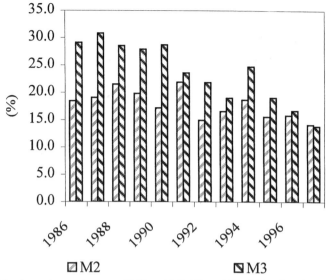

Figure 6.3. Annual growth rates of M2 and M3 (*Note*: M2 = M1 + Quasi-Money (time & savings deposits and residents' foreign currency deposits at monetary institutions). M3 = M2 + other financial institutions' deposits + debentures issued + Commercial Paper sold + CD + RP + Cover bills. Include debentures, commercial paper sold, CDs sold, deposits with credit unions, mutual credits of National Federation of Fisheries Cooperatives, community credit cooperatives, mutual savings & finance cooperatives situated in locality and reserve of life insurance companies since Jan. 1980, RP sold since Jan. 1986, and cover bills since Nov. 1989. *Source*: Bank of Korea).

Supervision of Trust Investments

While responsibility for supervising bank accounts rested with the Office of Banking Supervision (OBS), under the aegis of the central bank (BOK), responsibility for supervising trust accounts in banks and in most NBFIs rested with the Ministry of Finance and Economy (MOFE). The Auditor's Office of the MOFE lacked the personnel and expertise to carry out an adequate monitoring and supervisory role in relation to trust accounts in the banks and NBFIs. The OBS and MOFE also failed to share information closely or to coordinate supervision with each other. Banks also took advantage of a serious gap in the prudential regulations limiting a bank's lending to individual borrowers in that these ceilings applied only to loans from banks' general accounts, and not to loans from trust accounts, and not to CPs or corporate bonds held by the banks' trust accounts, even where the money was lent by the same bank to the same firm.

The banks were thus happy to expand lending or purchasing of CPs through trust accounts, because they could get a higher interest return by

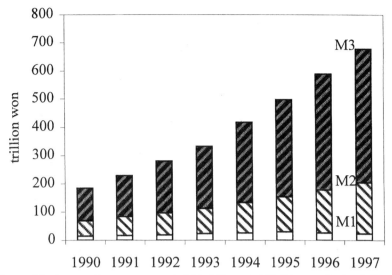

Figure 6.4. Outstanding money stock M1, M2, and M3 (*Source*: Bank of Korea, *Monthly bulletin*, various issues).

doing so than they would get by lending through bank accounts (since interest rates on the latter were still controlled). The depositors were happy to shift their deposits from bank accounts to trust accounts since these generated a higher rate of return. The monetary authorities were also happy because they could meet the monetary aggregate (M2) target without discouraging corporate investment or compromising the achievement of rapid economic growth.[5] Now corporate firms could easily finance their investment expansion by issuing CPs, because there was ample demand for them and they were not subject to cumbersome supervisory requirements. It was easy for firms to satisfy the credit rating criteria required for issuance of CPs, and their monitoring of the associated investment projects was lax.

Quality of Credit Rating

In fact, an analysis of the record of credit rating carried out by the two credit rating agencies in Korea reveals that their credit assessments of

---

[5] In Korea, ultimate authority over, and responsibility for, monetary policy resided with the Ministry of Finance and Economy rather than with the Bank of Korea (BOK) until February 1998. The Minister of Finance and Economy automatically became the chairman of the Board of Monetary Policy and the Governor of the BOK became the deputy chairman. MOFE was also responsible for overall macroeconomic performance, including achievement of a high growth rate.

Table 6.7. Credit Rating: Korean Agencies and S&P

	Korean agencies' average			Standard & Poors (U.S.)	
	1997	1996	1995		1995
A1	8.4%	8.2%	6.4%	AAA	1.2%
A2	17.9%	22.0%	21.1%	AA	5.4%
A3	31.1%	33.8%	32.5%	A	16.2%
B	40.6%	35.9%	40.0%	BBB	19.5%
C	0.4%	0.2%	0	BB	26.1%
D	1.3%	0	0	B	28.6%
No Action	0.3%	0	0	CCC	1.1%

Source: Korean Information Service.

corporate firms lacked reliability and expertise. Investigating the credit rating records of the forty bankrupt companies in 1997, I found that Korean rating agencies were extremely lax and unreliable compared to their counterparts in more advanced economies. Table 6.7 compares the distribution of the ratings awarded by Korean agencies with that of the U.S. company, Standard & Poors.

While the ratings from *A1* to *A3* make up about 65 percent in Korea, equivalent ratings from *AAA* to *A* make up only 22 percent in the United States. The minimum rating required to issue CPs in Korea is *B*. Ninety-eight percent of Korean companies received a *B* or above in 1997, while only 42 percent of U.S. companies received *BBB* (the equivalent rating) or above. *AAA*, the highest rating for securities, was conferred on only 1.2 percent of the total listed companies in the United States, while *A1* companies made up about 8 percent in Korea in 1997. I also traced the ratings between 1991 and 1997 for forty companies that went bankrupt during 1997–98. During that period, there were almost no changes in the ratings and no difference between the two agencies. Even in 1997, the year of greatest financial distress, there were only two adjustments in the ratings for these firms.

Increased On-balance Sheet Portfolio Risk

In addition to the growing risk in the trust accounts, a further twist can be seen in a bank's own assets. As long-term deposit rates were gradually deregulated, the cost of deposits for banks increased. But, as mentioned previously, the lending rate for corporate firms continued to be controlled. In response, banks sharply increased the rate for consumer loans, where interest rates were not controlled. The relaxation of the restrictions on consumer loans as part of the financial liberalization plan also facilitated this development. Loans to households increased from 7 percent of the

Table 6.8. Bank Loans by Type of Borrower

End-year	Large firms	Medium-small firms	Household	Public and others
1990	37.1	49.8	8.3	4.8
1991	36.5	52.0	7.7	3.8
1992	37.1	52.4	7.0	3.6
1993	33.3	54.8	8.7	3.2
1994	27.5	54.9	14.7	2.9
1995	21.1	55.9	17.5	5.5
1996	20.7	54.3	19.5	5.4
1997	19.9	43.9	20.0	16.3

Source: Banking Supervisory Authority, *Bank Management Statistics*, various issues.

total in 1992 to 19.5 percent in 1996. Although further study is required, it seems likely that the rapid increase in consumer loans between 1994 and 1996 may also have contributed to the reduction in the national savings rate and to the increased current account deficits during this period (Table 6.8).

Capital Account Liberalization

Korea took a cautious approach to the liberalization of foreign capital flows. Fearing massive capital inflows that could destabilize the domestic macroeconomic environment, Korea liberalized capital accounts on a gradual basis. The gap between domestic and foreign interest rates was large (Figure 6.5) and there was strong corporate demand for cheap foreign capital.

With a view to obtaining membership of the OECD, Korea began to accelerate the opening of the capital market in 1994. This caused firms to expect an appreciation of the Korean currency; and as a result domestic interest rates gradually declined to converge on foreign interest rates, encouraging increased borrowing and investment.

Three measures were central in opening the capital market. First, the ceiling on foreign investments in the domestic stock market was gradually increased. Second, restrictions on short-term trade-related borrowing were further relaxed. Third, control over the issuance of Korean firms' securities in the foreign capital market and offshore borrowing was relaxed. However, foreign investments in government securities and corporate bonds issued in the domestic market remained under strict control. It was only after the crisis that the Korean capital market was completely opened up. But from earlier on there had been no significant restrictions

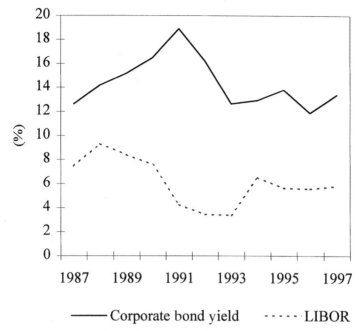

Figure 6.5. Gap between domestic and foreign interest rates (*Source*: Bank of Korea, *Monthly Bulletin*, various issues).

on foreign borrowing by Korean banks and merchant banking companies, especially on short-term borrowing.[6]

In retrospect, however, the opening of the capital market could have been done in a more prudent manner. First, there was no symmetry in the treatment of lending and borrowing by financial institutions in foreign currencies. From 1993 the positive list of uses for which financial institutions might provide foreign currency-denominated loans was expanded. Furthermore, short-term foreign borrowing by banks had been freely allowed. But, in order to help manage overall capital flows, the authorities continued to maintain quantitative restrictions on long-term foreign borrowing. The result was a dramatic increase in the short-term foreign debts of financial institutions, incurred to finance the strong investment demands of the corporate sector as the economy entered a boom in 1994.

Second, as mentioned previously, the number of financial institutions dealing in foreign currency-denominated activities jumped. Some twenty-

[6] A broad limitation on long-term borrowing was guided by the balance-of-payment projection (or target) for the year.

Table 6.9. Number of Financial Institutions

	1989	1990	1991	1992	1993	1994	1995	1996	1997
Banks		23	25	26	26	26	26	26	26
Merchant banking companies	6	6	6	6	6	15	15	30	30
Insurance companies	43	45	49	49	49	49	49	49	50
Securities companies	25	25	31	32	32	32	33	34	36
(Foreign branches)[a]	(–)	(–)	(2)	(7)	(8)	(11)	(14)	(19)	(22)

[a] i.e., branches of foreign-owned companies.

four finance companies were transformed into merchant banking corporations between 1994 and 1996, while banks opened twenty-eight new foreign branches in the same three-year period. The large-scale transformation of finance companies into MBCs led to a corresponding increase in the number of participants in the international financial markets, since finance companies were not allowed to deal in foreign exchange transactions (Table 6.9).

These two changes in the institutional framework contributed to the strong growth in foreign currency-denominated assets in the financial sector since 1994 and to the maturity mismatch problem. Of course, the adverse effects could have been obviated if appropriate strengthening of the supervisory structures was synchronized with these changes. But reforms within the supervisory sector were gradual, or simply absent. Though banks and MBCs were rapidly accumulating long-term assets in foreign currencies financed by short-term liabilities, it was not until June 1997 that the Office of Bank Supervision belatedly introduced a liquidity ratio; while the Ministry of Finance and Economy, which was the supervisory authority for MBCs, had not, until the crisis erupted, established any measures to deal with the problem (Shin and Hahm 1998).[7] The only restriction imposed on the banks' foreign borrowing was a floor of 60 percent for the share of long-term liabilities and a ceiling on the net open foreign exchange position.

As the inexperienced MBCs borrowed heavily from abroad at short term, competition in the foreign currency lending business on the domestic market became severe. In order to remain competitive in the foreign

[7] Weakness of prudential regulation of the MBCs' operations was not confined to supervision of foreign currency–liquidity conditions. Even basic regulations such as minimum capital adequacy ratios were not in place. Moreover, supervision by the MOFE was extremely poor, as witness the MBC frauds which came to light after the crisis (Shin and Hahm 1998).

Table 6.10. External Debts by Sector

US$ bn	1992	1993	1994	1995	1996	1997
Public sector	5.6	3.8	3.6	3.0	2.4	18.0
Long-term	5.6	3.8	3.6	3.0	2.4	18.0
Short-term	0	0	0	0	0	0
Corporate sector	13.7	15.6	20.0	26.1	35.6	42.3
Long-term	6.5	7.8	9.0	10.5	13.6	17.6
Short-term	7.2	7.8	11.0	15.6	22.0	24.7
Financial sector	23.5	24.4	33.3	49.3	66.7	60.5
Long-term	12.2	13.0	13.9	19.6	27.7	33.9
Short-term	11.3	11.4	19.4	29.7	39.0	26.6
Total	42.8	43.9	56.8	78.4	104.7	120.8
Long-term	24.3	24.7	26.5	33.1	43.7	69.6
Short-term	18.5	19.2	30.4	45.3	61.0	51.2
Total (% GNP)	14.0	13.3	15.1	17.3	21.8	27.5

Source: Bank of Korea.

Table 6.11. Mismatch Gap Ratios of the Seven Largest Banks (%, March 1997)

Bank A	Bank B	Bank C	Bank D	Bank E	Bank F	Bank G	Average
21.9	27.5	22.4	23.3	20.2	16.8	11.3	20.3

Source: Shin and Hahm 1998.

currency lending business, the commercial banks lobbied hard for the authorities to lower the floor on long-term liabilities. In 1994 this ratio was reduced from 60 percent to 40 percent. As a result, not only did foreign debt increase rapidly, but its structure became more oriented toward the short term from 1994 on.

The volume of foreign-currency denominated assets of banks grew from 20.2 percent of GNP in 1992 to 28.9 percent in 1996, while the ratio for MBCs more than doubled to 3.8 percent over the same period. The ratio of external debt to GNP rose to 21.8 percent in 1996 from 14.0 percent in 1992, where the major debt holders were financial institutions as shown in Table 6.10.

Foreign exchange liquidity risk grew substantially in the system, essentially because of maturity mismatches. The one-month mismatch gap and the three-month liquidity ratio (Shin and Hahm 1998) both deteriorated as shown in Tables 6.11 and 6.12.[8] Each of the seven largest banks vio-

---

[8] The former is the difference between assets and liabilities due within one month, expressed as a ratio of total assets; the latter is a ratio of liquid (maturity less than three months) assets to liquid liabilities.

**Table 6.12. Liquidity Ratios of the Ten Largest Banks:
Distribution**

No. of banks within:	1995	1996	1997.3	1997.9
80%–90%	1	3	2	2
70%–80%	2	2	1	1
60%–70%	4	2	4	5
Below 60%	3	3	3	2
Average Ratio (%)	59.9	61.7	62.0	63.2

Source: Shin and Hahm 1998.

lated the standard which had recently been proposed by the Korean supervisory authority for the mismatch gap, namely 10 percent; indeed, all but two had ratios in excess of 20 percent. Likewise, during 1997, most banks had liquidity ratios of less than 80 percent, well below the goal of 100 percent announced by the authority in 1998.

Thus in its foreign debt position as in the domestic liability structure, the Korean financial system moved to the short term in a way that made the economy increasingly vulnerable to a financial and currency crisis.

2 LIBERALIZATION AND CORPORATE FINANCIAL STRUCTURE

Differential Impact by Group and Firm Size

Financial liberalization and the consequent changes in the structure of the financial market had a substantial impact on the financial structure of the nonfinancial corporate sector. As the capital market was opened up, domestic firms could borrow more easily from abroad. However, it was mainly the five largest chaebols,[9] that had already established their reputation in the international market, and that could take advantage of the deregulation applied to the issuing of bonds and equities in the foreign capital market. Smaller chaebols (the sixth to the thirtieth largest) and other corporate firms could also borrow more easily from abroad, but they did so mainly through the intermediation of banks or merchant banks, since they did not have firmly established reputations in the international market. As a result, from 1993–94 the five largest chaebols increased their borrowing from abroad by issuing long-term convertible bonds and were thereby able to improve the maturity structure of their debts. Since foreign loans were cheaper than domestic credit, the average cost of their debt also declined with the deregulation of capital accounts.

---

[9] They are Hyundai, Samsung, Daewoo, Lucky-Goldstar (LG), and Sunkyung (SK).

Table 6.13. Six Bankrupt Conglomerates in 1997

	Hanbo	Sammi	Jinro	KIA	Haitai	New-core
Date of default	Jan 23	Mar 19	Apr 21	July 15	Nov 1	Nov 4
Size ranking	14th	25th	19th	8th	24th	28th

While the five largest chaebols increased their reliance on the international capital market for their funding needs, domestic financial institutions tried to fill the vacuum by seeking second-tier customers, mainly from among the smaller chaebols. With the increased availability of funds in the domestic financial markets these smaller chaebols expanded their investments heavily. But this was largely financed in the short term leading to a deterioration in the financial structures of these smaller chaebols. When their product and sales could not generate sufficient cash flow to service their debt, they quickly became insolvent.

This section shows how financial liberalization affected the corporate financial structure with firms[10] classified in three groups: Group I: firms belonging to the five largest chaebols; Group II: firms belonging to the sixth through thirtieth largest chaebols; and Group III: nonchaebol firms. It was bankruptcy among chaebols in Group II that triggered the crisis of 1997 (Table 6.13).

Debt Ratio

Aggregate leverage of the corporate sector slightly increased during the 1990s (Figure 6.6): The average debt/asset ratio increased from 68 percent in 1990 to 72 percent in 1996. Looking at the data for each group, we find that the debt ratio for Group I was stable at around 75 percent, but for the remaining groups the debt ratio increased after 1993, with Group II increasing from 74.8 percent in 1990 to 77.8 percent in 1996, whereas Group I had a debt ratio of less than 70 percent. From 1994, Group I switched their reliance from domestic to foreign debt, whereas the increase in the debt of the other two groups was mainly from domestic sources (Figures 6.7, 6.8, and 6.9).

Maturity Structure of Debt

Taking advantage of the newly introduced opportunity to raise long-term capital in the foreign market, Group I improved the maturity of their debt structure. But the opposite was true for other firms, which had to rely on

---

[10] The data set contains more than 500 listed companies for each year between 1990 and 1996 and was obtained from the Korean Information Services.

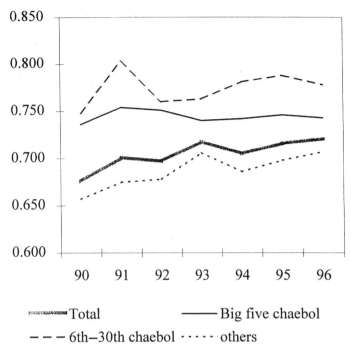

Figure 6.6. Debt ratio of Korean firms (*Source*: Korean Information Services).

the domestic financial market as it became more short-term oriented (Figure 6.9). This was a predictable consequence of the sequencing of liberalization as discussed previously.

Cost of Borrowing

Interest rates on the domestic market had risen during 1994–95 (Figure 6.1). But there appears to have been an increase in the average cost of borrowing only for Group II (Figure 6.10). Group I actually reduced their average cost of borrowing significantly during 1993–96, because they could rely on foreign funds on which the interest rates were substantially lower. Average borrowing costs for Group III remained stable or declined slightly, perhaps because they had privileged access to bank loans due to the government policy of increasing bank lending to small- and medium-sized firms.

Debt Service Capacity

The debt service capacity of firms is closely linked with the domestic business cycle, and this is reflected in Figure 6.11 which shows the ratio of

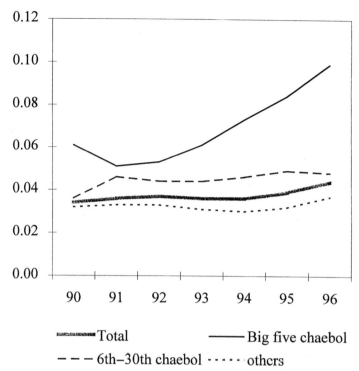

Figure 6.7. Foreign debt/assets ratio (*Source*: Quoted partly from Jong Hwa Lee, Young Su Lee 1998).

interest rate payments to total earnings before interest and tax (EBIT): We see evidence of the recession of 1991–93, and the boom of 1993–95. With the start of the recession in late 1995, debt service capacity deteriorated rapidly, and was lowest in Group II, whose capacity had hardly improved even during the 1993–95 boom, because of their heavy borrowing in the high-cost domestic market. This burden rapidly brought many of the firms in this group to insolvency in the downturn.

Debt service capacity of Group I also deteriorated from 1996; here one of the main causes was the collapse of the international price of semi-conductors, which is the main export item of the five largest chaebols. The key unit price of semiconductors fell from about $60 in 1995 to $8 in 1996. Furthermore, with the fall in the international price of steel and petro-chemical products the terms of trade deteriorated sharply in 1996, which, together with the domestic recession, aggravated the cash flow of domestic firms (Figure 6.12).

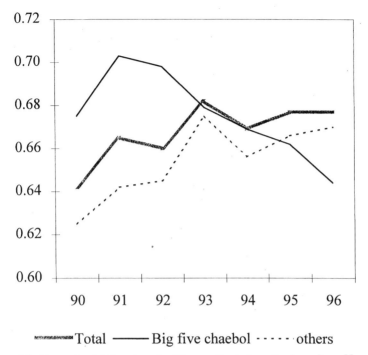

Figure 6.8. Domestic debt/assets ratio (*Source*: Quoted partly from Jong Hwa Lee, Young Su Lee 1998).

3 THE CONTRIBUTION OF MISMANAGED FINANCIAL LIBERALIZATION TO THE CRISIS

By early 1997 it was apparent that the Korean economy faced financial crisis. Nonperforming assets of the financial sector were estimated at up to half of Korean GNP at the end of 1997.

Did financial liberalization cause the financial crisis in Korea, and if so, how? The discussions in the previous two sections provide only a limited answer. There are many factors that have not been discussed in this chapter that could have caused the financial and currency crisis in Korea.[11] However, the analysis here suggests that unbalanced financial liberalization, which completely liberalized the short-term securities market without having established an appropriate supervisory function and capital market infrastructure (including a reliable credit assessment capacity,

---

[11] See Cho (1998a; 1998b) for a comprehensive discussion of the structural problems that caused corporate insolvency.

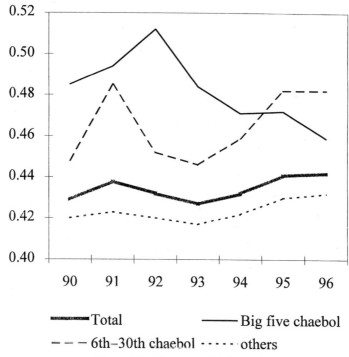

Figure 6.9. Short-term debt/assets.

transparency in accounting and audit, and disclosure requirements), was a significant factor.

A rigid approach to monetary policy, involving adherence to a target for the money stock M2, continued to restrict growth in bank deposits and loans, while controls were being relaxed on financing opportunities for firms through the expansion of the unregulated short-term bills market.

Continuation of some policy-based lending also limited the competitiveness and growth of the banks in the liberalized financial market. Furthermore, even after liberalization of corporate bond yields, the authorities continued to maintain downward pressure on yields by intervening to control the issue of corporate bonds by the firms.

Depositors shifted their funds to the trust departments of banks who invested in CPs which had been recklessly underwritten and brokered by NBFIs such as MBCs and finance and investment companies. Only the on-balance sheet arm of the banks' activities were supervised by the OBS while the other arm, the trust account, was (lightly) supervised by the MOFE.

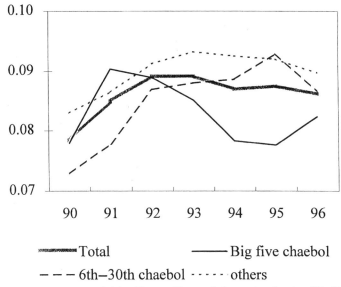

Figure 6.10. Average cost of debt (*Source*: Korean Information Service; Kis-Fas Database *Note*: cost of debt = interest expenses/interest bearing debt).

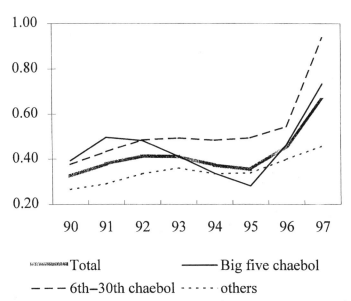

Figure 6.11. Debt service capacity (*Note*: Shows interest payments as a share of earnings before interest rate and tax payments).

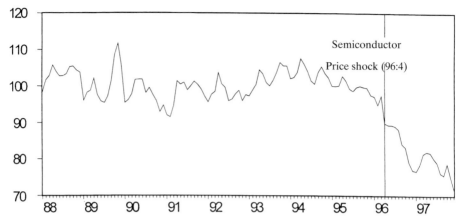

Figure 6.12. *Terms of trade* (*Source*: Quoted from Jong Hwa Lee, Young Su Lee 1998).

As a result, the credit appraisal, monitoring, and corporate governance function of the financial market shifted from the more experienced banking sector to the less experienced NBFIs and short-term securities markets. Short-term financing expanded without adequate supervision and governance, and corporate financial structures deteriorated. This was an unintended consequence of financial liberalization. It was not caused by financial liberalization itself, but rather by a poorly sequenced, unbalanced, and confused implementation of liberalization in the different financial sectors.

The liberalization differentially affected the cost of and access to borrowing by different classes of firms. In practice, deregulation of foreign borrowing gave only the largest chaebols access to foreign funds. Their departure created a vacuum in the domestic capital market which was filled by the second-tier chaebols (Group II above). Thus, deregulation of the capital account led to adverse selection with domestic financial institutions ending up with riskier customers. As shown in Figure 6.13, Group II had the lowest profitability of the three groups.

There was some asset-price inflation, but both real-estate and stock markets were stable or somewhat bearish from 1992 to 1996 (Figure 6.14). What caused the financial crisis in Korea was not the bursting of the real-estate bubble, as was the case in many other countries, but overexpansion of investment and the consequent insolvency of corporate firms, especially the second-tier chaebols. To the extent that financial liberalization and the resulting financial market development encouraged these chaebols to expand their investment recklessly, it certainly contributed to the financial crisis.

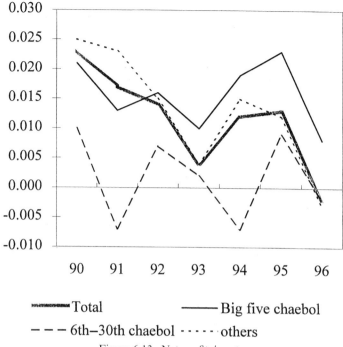

Figure 6.13. Net profits/assets.

Other factors also contributed to the financing of reckless investment by the chaebols. One of these factors was crosssubsidization among affiliated firms, a matter which has not been adequately regulated in Korea. Firms in chaebols crossguaranteed loans from affiliated firms, and subsidized each other through internal transactions. Disclosure of their balance sheets by listed firms was required only once a year, and anyway, accounting and audit practices lacked credibility and transparency. Chaebols were not required to prepare and disclose consolidated balance sheets. The belief that financial institutions would never fail, and that the government would not allow large chaebols to go bankrupt, also meant that domestic depositors and creditors paid little attention to credit appraisal and monitoring of the investment behavior of chaebols.

The domestic financial crisis soon led to a currency crisis in Korea. Korea's currency crisis was not caused by speculative short-term portfolio flows, but rather by the refusal of many foreign creditors to roll over their short-term credit to Korean banks and merchant banking companies. This too can be traced back to a critical supervisory oversight. New entry on a massive scale into the merchant banking industry (which was allowed

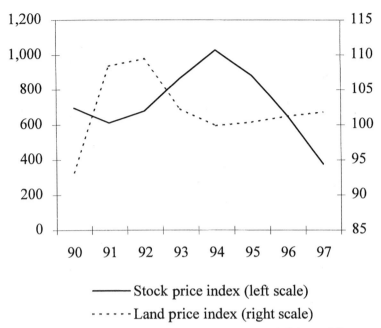

Figure 6.14. Stock price index and land price index (*Source*: Ministry of Construction and Transportation, Korean Stock Exchange).

to deal in foreign capital) resulted in severe competition for foreign currency business within the banking system. Total short-term debt within the banking system increased sharply. It was the bankruptcies of certain chaebols and a rapid, visible increase in nonperforming assets within the banking system in 1997 that triggered a run of foreign creditors, occurring in conjunction with the outbreak of the East Asian crisis in late 1997.

The twin maturity foreshortening – the move to shorter-term maturities in corporate debt structure as well as in the foreign liabilities of banks and MBCs – coupled with poor supervision, eventually led to crisis in the Korean economy.

4   LESSONS AND CONCLUDING REMARKS

We suggest five general policy lessons from the Korean experience of financial liberalization and crisis. The first two relate to sequencing, reflecting our view that the phasing of a gradual liberalization can have important implications.

First, long-term financial instruments should be liberalized before short-term ones to avoid a rapid expansion of short-term financing and a deterioration in the financial structure of corporations.

Second, the banks should be treated equally with the nonbanking financial sector. To this end, government policy-driven lending programs affecting banks should be phased out, and indirect monetary control or other more coherent methods of monetary policy should be adequately developed in order to allow a consistent and balanced liberalization of the banking system to be implemented. Otherwise, liberalization may cause a rapid expansion of the short-term financing market, dominated by NBFIs. Because NBFIs in developing countries usually have less experience and pay less attention to corporate risk and monitoring, a rapid swing to NBFIs can have adverse consequences for the risk assessment and corporate governance functions of the financial market.

Third, without proper development of a credit assessment capacity in the market and adequate supervision on the part of the authorities, liberalization of the short-term securities market can lead to an overall increase in the riskiness and vulnerability of financial markets in general.

Fourth, effective development of the infrastructure necessary to support an efficiently functioning liberalized financial market requires a parallel development of the regulatory framework on a wider front, including rules on fair trade, disclosure, crossguarantee, accounting and auditing practice, and so on. After all, for example, when cross-subsidization among affiliated firms is allowed, and no transparent consolidated balance sheet is available, how can anyone adequately assess the risk status of individual firms?

Finally, one may question the viability of complete deregulation of the domestic financial system where corporate leverage has gotten too high. High debt ratios in the corporate sector will make an economy extremely vulnerable to external shocks, and limit the capacity of the authorities to socialize the risks (by cutting interest rates, providing relief loans to troubled firms, etc., *cf.* Cho and Kim 1997). Likewise, where (as was the case in Korea) average corporate leverage is above 300 percent, with many major firms at more than 600 percent, it may be too much to expect that prudential regulations will always be strictly enforced. Fearing that a curtailment of loans to such firms might trigger a string of bankruptcies, regulators will hesitate to take drastic action even when they see banks lending to heavily overleveraged firms. Only when average leverage in the economy is down to 200 percent or lower can normal conditions for supervision and credit risk assessment be said to prevail. To help facilitate a reduction in the corporate debt ratio steps should be taken to develop equity markets rapidly.

APPENDIX: THE FOUR-STAGE LIBERALIZATION
OF INTEREST RATES

The various financial instruments were to be liberalized as follows.

Phase I: November 1991

Deposits: *Banks*, CD, large denomination RPs, commercial bills and trade bills, time deposits with maturity of three years (new). *NBFIs*, large denomination CPs, time deposits with maturity of at least three years, time deposits of mutual savings and finance companies with maturity of at least two years, etc.

Loans: *Banks*, overdrafts, discounts on commercial paper apart from loans assisted by BOK rediscounts, overdue loans. *NBFIs*, discounts on commercial bills of trust, mutual savings and finance companies, insurance, discounts on CPs and trade bills of investment finance corporations, etc. Corporate bonds with maturity of at least two years.

Phase II: November 1993

Deposits: (a) Bank: time deposits with maturity of at least two years, installment-type deposits with maturity of at least three years such as installment savings, mutual installments, etc. (b) NBFI: time deposits with maturity of at least two years, installment-type deposits with maturity of at least three years such as installment savings, mutual installments, etc. *Cf.* mutual savings and finance companies: time deposits with maturity of at least one year and installment savings with maturity of at least two years, etc.

All loans from banks and nonbanking financial institutions except policy loans. Corporate bonds with maturity of less than two years, financial debentures, government and public bonds. Minimum maturity of CPs reduced to two months.

Phase III: From July 1994

(i) Partially implemented in July 1994:
     Minimum maturity of CP shortened from ninety-one days to sixty days; issue of cover bills by banks allowed.
(ii) Partially implemented in December 1994:
     Time deposits with maturity of less than two years and installment savings with maturity of two to three years.
     Prime rate on loans within aggregate credit ceiling system of BOK.

(iii)   Partially implemented in July 1995:
        Time deposits with maturity of six months to one year and install-
        ment savings with maturity of one to two years. Expanded liber-
        alization of short-term marketable products (minimum maturity
        shortened and minimum issue denomination lowered).
        All loans within aggregate credit ceiling system of BOK.
(iv)   Fully implemented in November 1995:
        Time deposits with maturity of less than six months and install-
        ment savings with maturity of less than one year, etc. Preferential
        savings and company savings with maturity of at least three months.
        Expanded liberalization of short-term marketable products.

Phase IV: July 1997

Banks: savings deposit accounts, preferential savings with maturity of less
than three months and MMDA, company savings with maturity of less
than three months and MMDA. *Merchant Banks*: bills issued with maturity of less than one month. Trust-type securities savings. *Investment Trust*:
passbooks.
Mutual Savings: preferential time and savings deposits with maturity of
less than three months. *Mutual Credits and Credit Unions: Community
Credit Cooperatives*: deregulation of the maturity of short-term marketable products (CD, RP, CP, etc.), minimum denomination, repurchasing
fee of trust companies, interest rate of time deposits with maturity, etc.

REFERENCES

Cho, Y.J. 1998a. "The Structural Reform Issues of the Korean Economy."
    Institute of International and Area Studies Working Paper 98-01.
Cho, Y.J. 1998b. "Financial Crisis of Korea: The Causes and Challenges."
    Institute of International and Area Studies Working Paper 98-05.
Cho, Y.J. 1998c. "Financial Reform Experience of Korea." *Institute of Interna-
    tional and Area Studies Working Paper* 98-04.
Cho, Y.J. and J.K. Kim. 1997. "Credit Policies and the Industrialization of Korea."
    KDI Research Monograph 9701.
Shin, I.S. and J.H. Hahm. 1998. "The Korean Crisis – Causes and Resolution."
    KDI Working Paper 9805 Korea Development Institute. *Mimeo.*

7

Interest Rate Spreads in Mexico during Liberalization

Fernando Montes-Negret and Luis Landa[1]

INTRODUCTION

In periods of increased volatility and crisis the concept of economic liberalization comes under rigorous scrutiny, and even attack. In Mexico as elsewhere, stressful conditions often lead to liberalization being blamed for all the ills of the domestic and international economies. A closer examination of Mexican financial liberalization reveals a much more complex story.

The particular objective of this chapter is to examine the interest rates and bank spreads in Mexico during a financial liberalization which took place against a background of relatively high and volatile rates of interest and inflation, and under diverse exchange-rate regimes.

The chapter begins with an overview of Mexico's process of financial liberalization in a rapidly changing macroeconomic and external environment. We then examine the consequences of liberalization for monetary aggregates and for the evolution of interest rates and interest spreads, showing in particular that while spreads may not be necessarily lower under financial repression, they are certainly much less transparent. Finally, we compare elements of the Mexican experience with other high inflation cases, before offering some concluding remarks.

1 THE FINANCIAL LIBERALIZATION PROCESS AND MACROECONOMIC TURNING POINTS

Turning Points

Mexico's recent financial and macroeconomic history is punctuated by several major turning points. The first one occurred in 1982, with an

---

[1] Our thanks to the Banco de México for their valuable comments and to Andrea Semaan for her assistance.

exchange-rate crisis, high inflation, and the nationalization of the banking system. The second (1988–89) involved interest rate liberalization and an end to high inflation. The third (1991–92) consisted of bank reprivatization, which took place under manageable yet unstable macroeconomic conditions. The fourth and final turning point (1994) was precipitated by the shock of the Tequila Crisis.

In the 1960s and 1970s interest rates in Mexico were kept low and stable.[2] By the 1970s this often meant negative real rates, and little financial deepening. As a result of directed allocation of bank credit to preferential sectors of the economy, commercial bank credit to the private sector in Mexico declined dramatically from 19.5 percent of GDP in 1972 to only 10.4 percent in 1988.

The Lopez Portillo presidency ended with the 1982 balance of payments crisis and the nationalization of the Mexican banking system. Banks were accused of making excessive profits, behaving monopolistically, and facilitating capital flight. To make the nationalization process more difficult to reverse, Articles 28 and 123 of the Constitution were changed to prohibit private bank ownership. All but two[3] of the sixty banks were nationalized, the owners being compensated by indemnification bonds. The new De la Madrid administration started a process of consolidation and restructuring in 1983, closing nine banks and merging the remaining forty-nine into twenty-nine banks.[4]

Until the end of the 1980s, and as in much of Latin America, Mexican financial markets continued to be repressed through *dirigiste* policies including high reserve requirements, credit rationing, and controlled interest rates for deposits and loans.

The Liberalization of 1988–89

In the late 1980s, policies on credit and interest rates began to change. Success in implementing a fiscal adjustment program allowed a reduction in crowding out of the private sector. The budget strengthened from a deficit of 13 percent of GDP in 1988 to a surplus in 1992, and inflation declined from 99 percent in 1988 to a still high 16 percent in 1992. It was in October 1988 that the authorities took the first legal steps[5] toward

---

[2] Interest rate variation never exceeded 200 basis points in a given year. The rate on savings accounts was fixed at 4.5 percent for years on end.

[3] Citibank and the trade union-controlled Banco Obrero.

[4] Two more rounds of bank consolidation in 1985 and 1986 meant that there were just eighteen state-owned banks on the eve of privatization in 1991–92 (Unal and Navarro 1999).

[5] Though the most significant liberalization was in 1988, financial repression began to be eased as early as 1982, when interest rate ceilings on initial public offerings of government-issued Treasury Bills were removed, allowing institutional investors to place competitive bids at the central bank auctions.

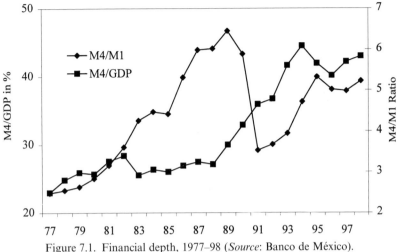

Figure 7.1. Financial depth, 1977–98 (*Source*: Banco de México).

elimination of credit rationing by allowing banks free allocation of funds raised by the issuance of acceptances and debentures (instead of these being compulsorily channeled to selected priority sectors).

Liberalization of banking[6] continued in 1989 with deregulation of interest rates, and other measures including (i) the elimination of maximum tenors for traditional deposit-based instruments; (ii) substitution of obligatory reserve requirements for a "liquidity coefficient" (which had required 30 percent of bank assets to be invested in government securities); (iii) elimination of credit rationing; and (iv) elimination of financing to the government at below market rates.

The impact of financial liberalization on monetary holdings is shown in Figure 7.1. Having stagnated around an average of less than 27 percent during 1980–88, financial depth (M4/GDP)[7] jumped to 30 percent in 1989,

---

[6] Measures to foster access to capital by firms listed in the Mexican Stock Exchange were also introduced in 1989. Firms were allowed to issue nonpreferential shares aimed at attracting foreign investors. Before this reform, foreign investment in most stocks was limited to 49 percent of the total. In December of that year, Congress approved laws promoting the placement of a greater number of Mexican securities in international financial markets. A "special section" within the National Stock Registry was created for stocks in Mexican firms issued on foreign markets. Specialized firms were also authorized to offer rating services for securities, and rating requirements for issues of new commercial papers were established (Babatz 1997).

[7] M4 = M1 + time deposits + bankers' acceptances + government securities + commercial papers + government pension fund (SAR) + all debentures in both local and foreign currencies. The definition excludes equity holdings.

to 33 percent in 1990, and by 1994 had reached 45 percent, before falling back to 43 percent by 1998.

The ratio of M4 to M1 (also shown in Figure 7.1) reached its peak in 1989, coinciding with the historic peak in the stock of government securities (over 20 percent of GDP). But, despite the decline in the budget deficit which began in 1990, the trend in the composition of M4 continued to be away from narrow money, with the ratio of M4 to M1 growing from less than three in the later part of the 1970s to over five by the end of the 1990s.

Bank Privatization

The financial liberalization process culminated in 1991–92 when ownership of the state-owned banks was transferred to the private sector and most of the industry's barriers to local entry were eliminated.[8]

The preconditions for privatization and liberalization of the banking system were poor, and failure to take corrective action planted the seeds of the subsequent crisis. To begin with, sufficient account was not taken of the fact that banking and supervisory skills in general had deteriorated in the previous two decades, as the banking system degenerated into a collector of funds for the government. Despite a number of enactments especially during the early years of the Salinas administration 1989–91 (Ortiz 1994), regulatory and supervisory structures remained generally weak, and important needed reforms in banking and commercial legislation (for example in relation to secured lending and bankruptcy) had not been accomplished, and this left the system vulnerable to moral hazard. In the privatization, many of the banks were purchased by individuals or consortia with little prior banking experience and dubious ethical standards. Prior due diligence reviews were inadequate, the new owners paid unrealistically high prices,[9] and the quantity and quality of capital was less than desirable.

Overoptimism following liberalization led to a rapid "explosion" in credit during the years when macroeconomic conditions were favorable. Bank credit to the private sector grew eight times faster than GDP in the years prior to the 1994 crisis. Commercial bank credit to the private sector grew from less than 15 percent of GDP during 1980–89 and from 29 percent in 1992 to over 40 percent by 1994, as shown in Figure 7.2.

In short, having paid premium prices for the banks, the new bankers were under considerable pressure to make loans in order to recover their

[8] *Cf.* Arellano and Rojas 1995; Aspe 1992. Note that restrictions on foreign investors in the larger Mexican banks remained until late 1998.

[9] Admittedly, the economic reforms had increased the prospective profitability of banks, but it was clear even before the crisis of 1994–95 that the prices paid – a multiple of book value – reflected excessive optimism.

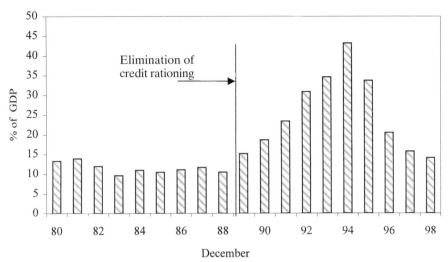

Figure 7.2. Commercial bank financing of the private sector (*Source*: Banco de México).

investment. Insider and related lending was also a common problem. This combination of factors, in an environment of lax banking supervision, led to excessive risk taking that rendered the banking system highly vulnerable to a crisis, especially as it occurred against the background of ominous macro-economic developments: a strongly appreciating real exchange rate and a deteriorating current account in the balance of payments. As an increasing share of the banks' portfolios started to perform badly, banks raised their lending spreads to cover these losses, which depressed investment demand.

2 INTEREST RATE MOVEMENTS DURING THE LIBERALIZATION

Intermediation Spreads

An important, though less dramatic, aspect of financial liberalization is the degree to which it affects interest rates, and in particular, bank inter-mediation spreads. On the liability side, increased competition between banks would eventually be reflected in higher deposit rates, encouraging savings. On the asset side, increased competition would be reflected in lower lending rates, encouraging investment. Increased efficiency in bank intermediation – an important goal of liberalization – should result in a narrowing of the gap between the two rates. The discussion below con-siders the behavior of the intermediation spread in Mexico before and after the financial reforms.

Methodology

Two alternative sets of data were used to construct the intermediation spread. The first comes directly from the balance sheets and income statements of the banking industry. The second comes from a survey of the financial cost of bank loans to local Mexican corporations reporting to the central bank, less the average cost of funds within the banking system (Banco de México 1998).

Using the banks' quarterly and annual balance sheets and income statements, a time series was constructed to approximate the intermediation spread for the period 1985–98. Data from 1985 through 1990 are year-end annual and data from 1991 through mid-1998 are annualized from quarterly accounts. The average lending and deposit rates are ex post rates from the banks' financial statements. They are calculated respectively as the ratio of interest and commissions received to interest-generating assets, and interest and commissions paid to interest-generating liabilities.

Monthly survey data of the financial cost of loans to large Mexican corporates can be broken down into the explicit (contractual) interest charges and the effective cost of loans which include other additional costs such as fees and commissions, compensating balances, and so on. In order to determine the effective intermediation spread, the effective rate on loans was compared to the weighted average cost of bank liabilities as reflected by the monthly average cost of funds published by the central bank, *Costo Porcentual Promedio* (CPP), for June 1978 to August 1998. It should be noted that the CPP overestimates the banks' cost of funds by excluding the cost of demand deposits (and consequently underestimates the true size of the spread).

Both sources are less than perfect. In particular, the shortcomings of Mexico's accounting system prior to January 1997,[10] combine with the well-known limitations of spreads constructed from bank accounting information. Survey data may be a more reliable source of information, with the caveat that they only represent a partial view of economywide bank spreads, to the extent that they cover only working capital loans and other loans contracted by large Mexican companies. Such companies are traditionally charged lower rates than their retail and medium-sized loan counterparts. Moreover, the survey data lead to an estimate of the banks'

---

[10] Until 1997, Mexican bank accounting standards differed markedly from U.S. Generally Accepted Accounting Practice (USGAAP) standards. Note that, given the importance of FOBAPROA (Deposit Insurance Fund) bonds received by the banks in exchange for bad assets, and the characteristics of those bonds (zero coupon maturing in a ten-year period), interest income does not reflect actual cash flows, since interest on these bonds accrues and (for most banks) does not generate cash revenues.

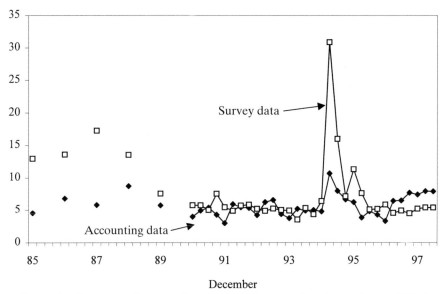

Figure 7.3. Intermediation spreads: survey and accounting data (*Source*: CNBV Statistical Bulletins and Banco de México).

marginal lending rates, while the accounting information calculates the average return on assets influenced by the inertia of banks' past lending. In this sense, the two data sets are not strictly comparable.

Figure 7.3 shows a comparison between the intermediation spread resulting from each set of data.

The spreads from survey data averaged 7.63 percent over the twenty-year monthly sample period, with a standard deviation of 4.57 percent. In contrast, spreads arising from accounting information averaged 5.8 percent over the sample period 1985–mid-1998, with a standard deviation of 1.7 percent.

The data indicate that both series roughly coincide in times of financial stability (1989–94), when both fluctuated around 4–7 percent, and diverge at times of financial difficulty. Two of these latter periods are identified in the figure: The first is during 1987–88 when Mexico experienced inflation in three figures; the second is during the 1995 financial crisis. In 1997–98 the figures also diverge, partly because of the adoption of the new accounting standards. Given the comparative advantage of survey data over accounting information for the construction of spreads, the former, despite being more volatile than the latter, will be used for further discussion.

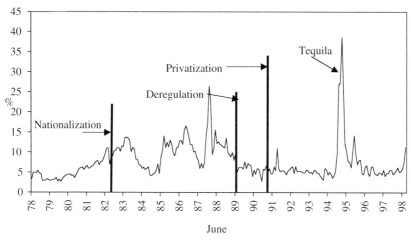

Figure 7.4. Intermediation spreads: effective corporate loan and CPP rates (*Source*: Banco de México).

Interpreting Movements in the Intermediation Spread

Figure 7.4 shows the intermediation spread, and Figure 7.5 shows commissions (as implied by the survey data) in more detail. Commissions are shown as the difference between effective and contractual lending rates.

The fluctuations in intermediation spreads and bank commissions (shown as the difference between effective and contractual rates) follow the same pattern. They rise before and during the period of bank nationalization, with a drop following interest rate liberalization. The decline was reinforced by increased price competition in the wake of bank privatization.

This is an important finding, showing that during periods of financial restriction, when interest rates are subject to controls, banks bypass these restrictions with other charges which must be covered by nonpreferential borrowers. Liberalization leads to a rapid decline in these implicit charges (commissions), making interest rates reflect more accurately and transparently the actual cost of borrowing.

Preliberalization Trends

From 1978 until April–August 1989, when interest rates were deregulated and credit rationing was finally abandoned, intermediation spreads were affected by two important factors besides the financially restrictive

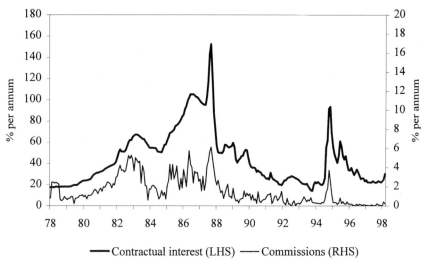

— Contractual interest (LHS) —— Commissions (RHS)

Figure 7.5. Nominal lending rates: effective and contractual (*Source*: Banco de México).

Table 7.1. **Intermediation Spreads and Commissions**

% per annum	Preliberalization period		Postliberalization period		
	1978–1982[a]	1982–1989[b]	1989–1994	1995	1996–1998
	Interest rate spreads				
Mean	5.2	10.5	5.5	16.3	5.6
Volatility[c]	2.1	3.8	1.4	10.5	1.5
	Commissions and other charges				
Mean	1.7	3.0	0.7	1.1	0.2
Volatility[c]	0.9	1.4	0.4	1.1	0.2
Memo item: Inflation[d]	27	90	17	35	25

Notes: [a] Through September 1982 when banks were nationalized. [b] Through April 1989 when interest rates were deregulated and credit-rationing abolished. [c] Measured by the standard deviation. [d] Mean monthly year-on-year inflation rates.
Source: Authors' estimates based on data provided by the Banco de México.

environment: 1) the nationalization of the banking industry; and 2) a decade of high inflation with significant episodes of financial and economic turmoil. The combination of these two factors was immediately translated into high intermediation spreads as seen in Table 7.1.

Prior to the nationalization of the banks, both the intermediation spread and bank commissions were on the rise. This was partly due to accelerating inflation, which climbed from 16 percent in 1978 to 74 percent by September 1982 when the banks were nationalized. At that point the banking community was accused by President Jose Lopez Portillo of facilitating capital flight, and of predatory market practices at the expense of Mexican workers' welfare. In response, banks were nationalized by the Constitutional reforms of September 1982, which initiated the "lost decade" of the eighties. This decade was characterized by practically no economic growth and periods of high inflation, particularly during 1987–88, when average inflation rates were consistently over 100 percent.

The effect of bank nationalization on interest rate spreads is difficult to isolate because it occurred at the height of the 1982 financial crisis, which initiated the inflationary process that lasted until the end of the decade. Spreads increased from an average of 520 basis points prior to nationalization, at a time when monthly (year-on-year) inflation rates averaged 27 percent, to 1050 basis points during the height of the nationalization period (1982–89), when inflation rates rose to an average of 90 percent. However, some evidence suggests that factors other than increased inflation accounted for the rising intermediation spread during this period.

During the years of state ownership, banking losses arising from government financing at below market rates were transferred to the private sector by means of higher rates and a higher bank spread (cross-subsidization). Bank financial statements show this practice, since the industry's net profits increased consistently in real terms between 1982 and 1989–90. Return on assets (ROA) also increased consistently during this period, from 0.44 in 1982 to 1.17 in 1990, with a peak in 1988 of 1.86. Noninterest revenue, comprised almost entirely of commissions charged for banking services, increased by 100 percent in real terms between 1982 and 1990. This transfer of wealth from the private sector to the government-owned banking industry worked as an additional intermediation tax on private borrowers.

Postliberalization Trends

After April–August 1989, the resources released from reduced reliance of the government's budget on the commercial banks,[11] combined with interest rate liberalization, allowed banks to engage in more profitable activities than before. Larger volumes of domestic and external resources were now available to be channeled to the private sector at more attractive rates. Since the beginning of the liberalization process, one of the goals of commercial banks was to encourage individuals and small businesses who had

---

[11] Beginning to be replaced by alternative means of government financing, namely the sale of government-issued Treasury Bills through central bank auctions.

never used banking services to do so for the first time. Greater market penetration was accompanied by lower lending rates and smaller intermediation spreads, which were also explained by the abolition of cross-subsidization, lower inflation, and increased competition. As a result, average intermediation spreads during 1989–94 declined to 550 basis points. This lasted until the eve of the next financial crisis, which erupted in December 1994.

During the period June 1991 to July 1992, the eighteen state-owned commercial banks were privatized. The first market-based response to privatization was fierce competition among them to increase their customer base on both the asset and liability fronts. Competition reduced the intermediation spread and the commission charged on banking services. However, the spread was prevented from declining further for several reasons:

1. The very high prices paid for the privatized banks – an average of three-and-one-half times book value. Much of the purchase price paid by new owners was covered by incurring internal and external debt, which required servicing and amortization. This put pressure on the banks to obtain high and quick returns on their investments.
2. The investment required to modernize the technologically outdated banking system after a decade in the hands of the state.
3. The higher risks being taken by banks as new unproven borrowers were accepted.
4. The drag resulting from the less-than-desirable quality of the loan portfolios acquired (which had been hidden by the inadequacy of existing accounting practices).
5. The oligopolistic banking industry created after bank privatization. Three banks (Banamex, Bancomer, and Serfin) alone controlled over 60 percent of the banking industry's assets and liabilities. Their cartel allowed the pricing of banking services above marginal cost, forcing other smaller banks to become price followers.

In 1994, some of the solvency problems in the banking system were already evident, which forced the authorities to intervene in the case of two of the original eighteen privatized banks, and to invite foreign investors to purchase them. Interest spreads widened very sharply prior to and during the December 1994 banking crisis and liquidity crunch.

Risk Profile of Lending

As shown in Table 7.2, real lending exploded following the banks' privatization, while the (highly understated) volume of overdue loans climbed continuously. Owners received a speculative return on their investment in

Table 7.2. Understated Risk Profile of Mexican Banks Before the 1994 Crisis

Concept	1992	1993	1994
Real growth of loans outstanding[a] (%)	30.0	18.3	32.5
Overdue loans[c] (as % of total loans)[a]	5.5	7.3	9.0
Loan loss reserves[d] (% of overdue loans)[a]	48.3	42.2	43.3
Return on equity[b] (%)	43.7	40.7	13.2
Capitalization ratio[b] (%)	9.2	10.3	9.8

[a] Includes banks which suffered intervention.
[b] Excludes banks which suffered intervention.
[c] Under the old accounting standards (prior to January 1997) banks classified as overdue only the unpaid portion of the loan, rather than the whole loan. This grossly underestimated nonperforming loans. Moreover, banks continued to accrue interest on delinquent loans (no interest-suspension clause).
[d] Due to very poor supervision and deficient internal systems, banks had a severely deficient system for classifying loans according to risk, and provisions were accordingly grossly inadequate.
Source: CNBV. *Boletin Estadistico Dic-95*, pp. 23, 27.

undercapitalized and underprovisioned banks, which were going to collapse after the severe external shock. The riskier lending profile of the newly privatized banks, together with (as already mentioned) excessively rapid credit expansion in a very poorly regulated environment and a deficient legal–judicial infrastructure, accelerated a systemic solvency crisis which was detonated by the sharp devaluation of the Mexican peso in December 1994.

By March 1995, the financial condition of the newly privatized banks had deteriorated considerably. The negative effects of the rise in interest rates[12] and the currency devaluation worked themselves into the banks' income statements through the open positions held in the money and foreign exchange markets. The reported condition of the banks was exacerbated by the problem of overdue loans, which until then had been concealed by poor accounting practices.

After the initial shock of the crisis had been absorbed, the interest spread gradually declined. From the peak of 39 percent in March 1995, it dropped to a monthly average of 5.9 percent in 1996, 4.8 percent in 1997, and 6.4 percent in the third quarter of 1998. This was despite local banks focusing on loan loss reserves and capital buildup in order to confront the growing problem of nonperforming loans (on top of the massive sales of nonperforming loans to the Deposit Insurance Fund – FOBAPROA).

---

[12] Interest rates increased to over 65 percent on twenty-eight-day government papers, from approximately 20 percent in the weeks prior to devaluation. See also Ramirez (1997).

After the Crisis

After the shock of the 1994–95 crisis had been absorbed, and more than five years into the liberalization period, other important forces affecting interest spreads were also at work. The following factors exerted upward pressure:

1. The macroeconomic fundamentals improved, initiating an export-led recovery. Once the peso was devalued, Mexican exports were extremely competitive in a booming U.S. market. This boom led to renewed growth as real GDP increased by 5.2 percent in 1996 and 7 percent in 1997, compared to the drastic drop of over 6 percent in 1995. Rapid economic activity increased the demand for credit. However, banks were too weak and too risk averse to lend, and in fact lending to the private sector continued to decline sharply. By the end of 1998, credit to the private sector had fallen by 60 percent in real terms relative to its peak of 1994 (Fernandez 1999).

2. The debate following the government's presentation of a financial package to Congress in March 1998 increased the political uncertainty and reopened the debate over how to allocate the enormous losses resulting from the banking crisis (estimated by the government at $65 billion (U.S. billion), close to 15 percent of GDP). By 1997, thirteen banks had undergone formal intervention, seven of which were newcomers to the industry.

3. The possibility that the banking industry might have to absorb a larger share of the costs resulting from the mountain of nonperforming loans sold to FOBAPROA, either totally or partially, might have led to renewed bank insolvency. The anticipation of further losses and the increased uncertainty resulted in higher intermediation spreads.

4. The financial fragility of the banking system and the worsening situation of many of the debtors, many of them in default, called for additional government financial relief programs.

5. The negative carryover resulting from having to fund FOBAPROA zero-coupon bonds at the interbank rate (TIIE), while these bonds accrued at an interest rate 200 basis points above the domestic currency government bill rate CETES during the first three years and (CETES minus 135 basis points) during the remaining life of the bonds (seven more years).

On the other hand, and exerting downward pressure on the spreads, was the increased competition from newcomers to the industry, particularly the eighteen foreign banks. Given the weak financial state of the Mexican banks, the newcomers could easily compete for corporate clients, who shifted their businesses from already established banks to foreign banks backed by powerful offshore parents.[13] Commercial banks competed to widen their customer base and reduced their spreads to gain market share. Even more important than the enhanced domestic competition in reducing the spreads was the easy access that Mexican exporters had to international sources of funding. In this respect, there was an increasing segmentation of the market and increased disintermediation, as the best corporate clients were able to borrow abroad, while domestically oriented companies and small- and medium-scale enterprises (SMEs) were unable to borrow.

Commissions

The 1995 financial crisis brought credit activity to a standstill, except among the large Mexican corporates and multinational organizations, which were perceived by the banking community as the only creditworthy borrowers in the country. These institutions are very few in number, but they received heavily preferential treatment from the banks. One way the forty Mexican banks competed for the group's potential business was by eliminating or reducing the commission charged for banking services. Prior to the liberalization process, since banks were obliged to grant credit at preferential interest rates, one of the compensating factors was a substantial charge on banking services for nonpreferential borrowers. During 1982–89, commissions represented a surcharge of 300 basis points over contractual interest rates, while during 1989–94 these charges declined to 70 basis points. Following the crisis, commissions represented less than 20 basis points of the total effective lending rates.

The survey data indicate that commissions were practically at zero after the crisis. Strong competition between banks, along with more personalized customer attention, gave large corporate firms a significant degree of negotiating power. This drove down commission charges practically to zero, and interest rates began to reveal more closely the actual cost of credit. Retail banking commissions and fees, however, remained an important and growing source of revenue for the banking industry.

The survey data also indicate that both the spread and the rate of commission have declined over time, as has their potential volatility. Despite the weight of overdue loans, borrowers and savers alike have benefited from declining spreads since the liberalization process began in 1989. However, society as a whole will be confronted with the future cost of eventually bailing out the Mexican banking system.

---

[13] The expansion of foreign banks dates to 1994. By December 1998 their market share of deposits had reached 16.3 percent.

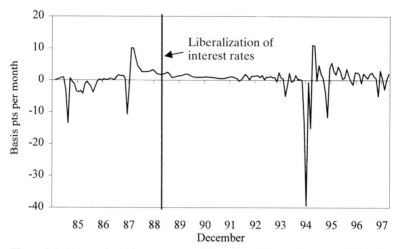

Figure 7.6. International interest rates differentials (*Source*: Banco de México).

International Interest Differentials

In previous sections we examined the *lending rate spread*, defined as the difference between the nominal lending rate and a representative deposit rate. The other key interest differential, sometimes known as the *deposit rate spread* (Vieira da Cunha and Brock 1997) is the gap between domestic wholesale deposit rates and an international equivalent of comparable default risk, adjusted for exchange rate change. It is normally assumed that the first type of spread is driven more by microeconomic factors in the financial sector, while the second type depends more on macroeconomic conditions and expectations.

Uncovered interest rate parity (UIP – which would prevail in a world free of controls and dominated by risk-neutral investors) would imply a zero expected deposit rate spread. After all, why (apart from default risk and the effects of risk aversion) should the domestic peso return of a Mexican government bond be expected to yield more than a comparable U.S. government bond, adjusted for the depreciation or appreciation of the Mexican peso against the U.S. dollar. Ex post deviations from UIP could additionally result from actual deviations and from expected nominal exchange rate changes (*cf.* Tanner 1998).

Figure 7.6 compares the yield $(1 + \hat{r})$ on twenty-eight-day CETES auctioned by the Banco de México on behalf of the government, with the realized yield in Mexican pesos that would have been gained by holding a U.S. Treasury Bill with similar maturity, where the dollar yield on the Treasury Bill is $(1 + i^{us})$ and the rate of exchange rate change is $(1 + x)$. Specifically, it shows, for 1985–98, the ex post excess return on holding domestic currency assets:

$$D = (1 + i^{c}) - (1 + i^{us})(1 + x)$$

For most of the period $D > 0$, implying that it was usually better for investors to place their funds in Mexican pesos than to invest in equivalent dollar-denominated financial assets, even after taking account of the exchange rate change. The much higher domestic rates that prevail in Mexico compared to the United States more than compensated for the potential currency fluctuations. But there were exceptional periods: During episodes of external crisis in which the Mexican peso depreciated abruptly against the U.S. dollar in discrete large amounts, it would have been better for depositors to have dollar-denominated investments. This was particularly true during three particular crises: (i) from the second half of 1985 through most of 1986, which culminated with a sharp depreciation (over 200) of the Mexican peso; (ii) the fourth quarter of 1987, when the peso depreciated by twenty four in just three months; and (iii) the last quarter of 1994 and all of 1995, following the major balance of payments and banking crisis.

The standard explanation for this kind of pattern in Latin American countries subject to large currency instability is as follows:

Expectations of exchange rate depreciation typically are the largest component of a high deposit rate spread. In many countries that undertake exchange rate-based inflation stabilization programs, for example, inflation falls but the public continues to believe that stabilization will only be temporary. Because people lack confidence that exchange rate policies will be maintained, they demand a rate of return on domestic currency-denominated deposits that compensates them for the expected devaluation (the so-called peso problem). As a result ex post real interest rates rise, placing greater strain on firms and banks, slowing growth, and reinforcing expectations of a depreciation (Tanner 1998).

This comment indicates a particular chain of causality, in the sense that it is the perceived high foreign exchange risk that puts pressure on domestic real interest rates. That is, in an effort to defend the parity of the domestic currency, many countries have no choice but to allow very high domestic real interest rates.

Large and persistent deviations from the UIP during the whole period examined (January 1985 to January 1998) are, except for crisis episodes, arguably interpretable as significant real interest rate differentials between Mexico and the United States, likely reflecting the greater country risk expressed by the higher level and variability of Mexican inflation, in addition to other restrictions which make capital flow less than frictionless.[14]

Note that the behavior of foreign financial investors in the Mexican money market appears to be correlated with the excess return differential D. Before the 1994 crisis, these investors, as a group, reduced their exposure to peso-denominated money market instruments prior to the crisis. That is, they switched back to dollars, though perhaps with some hesitation, as suggested by the oscillations during 1993, evident from Figure 7.6. A large peak in the value of D coincided with a slowing of the drain in early 1994, but this was followed by the dramatic decline in D at the time of the December 1994 devaluation. It seems that some months may have elapsed between the decline in D and the abrupt fall in CETES held by foreigners. The absence of foreign investors lasted throughout 1995. However, even small positive values of D were a sufficient inducement to attract them back to peso-denominated papers once confidence was restored in 1996 and 1997.

3 CONCLUDING REMARKS

Weaknesses in macroeconomic management were the first source of Mexico's financial fragility. In Mexico, the "boom-bust" cycle over the last twenty-five years has created widespread uncertainty and perverse reversals in the development of the financial sector. High exchange rate and interest rate volatility, combined with large private capital inflows and terms of trade shocks, followed by recession, have been associated with large potential losses for the banking sector. In addition, high inflation has eroded the information base for business planning and sound credit appraisal, contributing to higher portfolio risks. The demand for bank loans has also been discouraged by high nominal interest rates, hampering the development of financial markets, and particularly of debt instruments with longer maturities.

Policy making during the Salinas administration (1988–94) did not escape the boom-bust cycle. Excessive reliance on volatile short-term external financing, and the defense of an exchange rate that was out of line with market fundamentals, led to a sudden correction of asset prices and the subsequent crisis. The macroeconomic costs are large in terms of growth foregone. The federal government's contingent liabilities arising from the restructuring of the banking system since 1994 now exceed 15 percent of GDP.

---

[14] Note that this finding is not inconsistent with Tanner's results – in which the rational expectations hypothesis cannot be rejected for Mexico – since he is testing for an expected value of $(D_t - D_{t-1})$ equal to zero. In our case, the mean of such differences is also zero.

The second source of financial fragility can be traced to weaknesses in the incentive structure provided by the financial and institutional frameworks, market discipline, and regulatory and supervisory structures. As noted previously, most of what are normally regarded as the essential foundations for sound financial intermediation were absent in Mexico. What is now needed is a more balanced approach, looking at the whole "production chain" for delivering the "complete product" (i.e., abundant, risk-priced, enforceable loan contracts). Without addressing some of the fundamental problems in Mexico's financial infrastructure, which predate the latest banking crisis, financial intermediation will not deliver the expected results in supporting sustainable economic development.

The lack of modern and effective legal, accounting, and regulatory frameworks for banking was a major drawback for the successful achievement of a sound and healthy financial system operating in a liberalized environment. The authorities were far too slow in bringing these frameworks into conformity with international standards.[15]

A third factor contributing to Mexico's financial fragility was the lack of transparency about banks' operations and financial conditions, making it difficult for stakeholders to exercise proper market discipline – rewarding good performers and shunning poor ones. Creditors failed to discipline poor performers because of distorted incentives and a lack of timely and accurate information.[16] Government intervention also blunted incentives to discipline poor performers, by creating strong expectations that owners and creditors would be bailed out. Weak exit policy and universal deposit protection exacerbated moral hazard. Explicit government guarantees also played a role in fueling unsustainable credit booms. Once credit quality had been compromised, regulatory shortcomings and supervisory indulgence aggravated matters by failing to identify problems early and address them in a timely fashion.

The combination of macroeconomic instability and incomplete microeconomic reforms, including inadequate disclosure of timely and accurate information and severe problems of moral hazard, together with the risks of the financial liberalization process per se – such as increased exposure to market and credit risks – finally resulted in technical bank failures.

Despite these problems, the financial liberalization process sowed the seeds essential for more competitive and contestable financial markets.

---

[15] Inadequate laws relating governing corporations, bankruptcy, contracts and private property, as well as ineffectual judicial enforcement, all contributed to a breakdown in credit discipline – leading to a higher incidence of nonperforming loans and a lower collection rate – and inhibited the development of a credit culture.

[16] The move toward USGAAP accounting standards initiated in 1997 is an important measure to increase transparency in commercial bank financial information.

Bank privatization, the elimination of barriers to entry, and unrestricted interest rates have fostered an environment of increased competition among Mexican banks. A competitive environment does not necessarily require a large number of institutions, nor does it exclude the presence of institutions with substantial market share. However, the market must be contestable, in that market shares and prices are market driven, leading to competitive outcomes. The behavior of interest rates in Mexico has provided evidence that liberalization leads to a rapid decline in implicit loan charges (commissions), making interest rates reflect more accurately and transparently the actual cost of borrowing. This has filtered through to other interest rates, especially those of securities traded in the secondary markets, whose contestability has been greatly enhanced by means of widespread information about the behavior of market participants.[17]

As shown above, there has been substantial financial deepening in Mexico since the important reforms of 1988–89, but there is still some way to go, if comparison is made with countries such as Chile. However, the road toward deeper financial markets has been paved. Deeper financial markets will make the system more robust and consequently better prepared to face internal and external shocks.

The behavior of the intermediation spread has shown gains in efficiency since the liberalization of interest rates. The immediate response was a declining trend, which was reinforced by bank privatization. After liberalization, the intermediation spread averaged 550 basis points (excluding the year 1995, at the height of the crisis), down from an average of 1050 basis points during most of the 1980s.

Evaluation of uncovered international interest differentials shows a deviation from parity in favor of investing in foreign assets during times of financial crisis. However, during noncrisis periods, the incentives are reversed in favor of investing in local government securities. In general, the premium for investing in Mexican securities, as opposed to their foreign counterparts, has been positive. Significant increases in portfolio investments by foreign savers during the Salinas administration provide evidence for this.

Although the transition from a financially restricted to a liberalized market environment has been a critical component of the modernization of Mexico's banking system, further progress needs to be made to increase efficiency and to enhance a stronger credit and risk management culture. The banking crisis and the elimination of barriers to entry for both domestic and foreign investors have increased awareness of these issues. However, Mexico's greatest challenge ahead is to find some of the missing pieces –

---

[17] This has been achieved largely through the widespread use of brokers, whose participation in the financial markets has increased considerably since 1990.

and particularly to reduce the legal risks that now prevail – in order to strengthen the foundations of a modern financial system.

REFERENCES

Arellano, R. and M. Rojas. 1995. "Apertura y Liberalización del Sistema Financiero Mexicano". Puebla, Mexico: Universidad de las Américas. *Mimeo*.

Aspe, P. 1992. *El Camino Mexicano de la Transformacion Economica*. Mexico: Secretaria de Hacienda y Credito Publico.

Babatz, G. 1997. "Ownership Structure, Capital Structure and Investment in Emerging Markets: The Case of Mexico." Ph.D. Dissertation Harvard University.

Banco de México. 1998: "Encuesta de Tasas de Interés Activas." *Dirección General de Investigación Económica*.

Comisión Nacional Bancaria y de Valores (CNBV). *Boletín Estadístico de Banca Múltiple*. Various Dates. Mexico.

Fernández, E. 1999. Inaugural Lecture given at the 62nd Annual Mexican Banking Convention. Acapulco: México.

Ortiz Martinez, G. 1994. *La Reforma Financiera y la Desincorporacion Bancaria, Una Vision de la Modernizacion de Mexico*. Mexico: Fondo de Cultura Economica.

Ramirez-Fernandez, G. 1997. *Analisis del Nivel de Eficiencia de las Tasas de Interes en Mexico*. Unpublished Dissertation Instituto Tecnologico Autonomo de Mexico.

Tanner, E. 1998. "Deviations from Uncovered Interest Parity: A Global Guide to Where the Action Is." *International Monetary Fund Working Paper* WP/98/117.

Unal H. and M. Navarro. 1999. "The Technical Process of Bank Privatization in Mexico." *Journal of Financial Services Research* 16:61–83.

Vieira da Cunha, P. and P. Brock. 1997. "Using Interest Rate Stories for Country Analysis." Washington, D.C.: World Bank. *Mimeo*.

8

The Financial Sector in Transition: Tales of Success and Failure

Fabrizio Coricelli

INTRODUCTION

The transition economies considered here all inherited similar financial structures from the regime they succeeded. In fact, the common feature of the prereform period was the absence of financial markets, and the irrelevance of financial variables to the workings of the real economy, in particular the enterprise sector. Monetary transactions and holdings were the prerogative of the domestic sector. In the enterprise sector, money served only as an accounting unit.

Previously Centrally Planned Economies (PCPEs) were in a peculiar situation at the time reforms began. Price liberalization and market reforms certainly represented a major structural shock for these economies, and led inevitably to instability in both absolute and relative prices. In addition, soft budget constraints had to be eliminated in order to ensure that liberalized firms had a realistic incentive structure. In such a context, the functioning of a system involving banks and nonbanking intermediaries is unavoidably subject to high risks. The viability of firms that had, in the past, operated under soft budget constraints and government interference could not easily be established under the new regime. Informational problems were compounded by the lack of banking skills – indeed by the need to build a banking system from scratch. Therefore, the scope for efficient financial intermediation by banks in transition economies was bound to be limited. This may explain the low degree of financial depth (as measured for instance by the ratio of broad money to GDP) that has characterized all of the transition economies.

Some authors actually recommended that these economies start with low financial depth, in order to keep the intermediation role of banks to a minimum at the beginning of the transition period (McKinnon 1991). However, the reallocation of resources and the restructuring of firms, which are key aspects of economic transition, do require a supportive credit system. Unless private markets can substitute for the necessary credit that was previously provided through the state system, restructuring and growth of firms will be severely constrained.

Balancing the dual role of a banking system – to provide liquidity to viable firms and incentives for efficient behavior – has been a challenge for countries in transition. The response to this challenge, and the performance of financial sectors following reforms, differed sharply between countries. It is important to assess the relative role of initial conditions and subsequent policies in explaining divergent outcomes.

Within broadly similar inherited structures there were significant differences between countries in the old regime. These differences derived mainly from the process of partial decentralization and reforms implemented in some Central and Eastern European (CEE) countries, such as Hungary, Poland, and the countries of former Yugoslavia. Enterprises in those countries had been given some degree of independence in their decisions, and private firms had developed. Monetary holdings and trade credit had also been allowed. In most countries of the Commonwealth of Independent States (CIS), by contrast, firms were not permitted to hold money, and trade credit was forbidden.[1] Moreover, firms had been given much less independence in their decisions. Although the CEE strategy of implementing partial reforms failed to improve on the performance of the previous regime, it created a minimal set of market institutions that proved critical for the success of fully fledged market reforms (see Murrell 1996 and Coricelli 1998 for an elaboration of this view).

We argue in this chapter that reform policies should take initial conditions into account. Private markets may arise when there is a conducive underlying structure (a minimal set of market institutions). Otherwise, dysfunctional institutions can arise and persist. The development of well-functioning trade credit markets in countries like Hungary and Poland, in contrast with the explosion of interenterprise arrears and barter in CIS countries, is a case in point.

Reform strategies – or at least the de facto evolution of the policy environment – also differed across countries, but not in a way that that one might easily have predicted as being consistent with the differing initial conditions. Indeed, somewhat paradoxically, several of the CIS countries with weaker initial conditions began with a more rapid financial liberalization of both domestic and international transactions and investments.

---

[1] This geographic distinction is a crude shorthand used for convenience. Indeed, there are countries in CEE, such as Bulgaria and Romania, that in the present context would arguably be better grouped with CIS countries, whereas some other countries under the former Soviet Union, such as the Baltic states, would fit better with the CEE.

The more advanced CEE countries were much more cautious in this respect, taking a gradual approach to liberalization.

One interpretation might be that countries with more favorable initial conditions could afford to move more gradually (Claessens 1996). For instance, a less liberal attitude to the entry of new banks implies a recapitalization of existing banks, and therefore fiscal transfers, which were not feasible for countries with weaker fiscal accounts. However, this view is not wholly convincing, since the fiscal costs of the financial crises that took place in countries such as Russia were probably much higher than those incurred by CEE countries which invested in the recapitalization and rehabilitation of existing banks.

We also argue that financial liberalization in several CIS countries has increased their vulnerability to financial crisis. Liberal policies toward the unregulated entry of banks and the development of domestic debt markets, together with an opening of capital accounts, although not the cause of financial crises in countries like Russia or the Ukraine, sharply increased the vulnerability of these countries to crisis. Furthermore, these policies contributed to create dichotomies in the system. On the one hand, rather sophisticated financial markets developed, with the participation of banks, foreign investment banks and a few large firms; on the other hand, the bulk of the economy worked on a primitive system based on the widespread use of barter transactions. This vividly illustrates the contradiction in these countries between financial liberalization and the ultimate goal of developing financial markets that can channel funds from savers to investors.

At the same time, well-functioning private markets have failed to emerge. In fact, generalized forms of financial indiscipline, in the form of payment arrears, have flourished. In addition, the private response to the perceived high risk of payment default has pushed firms to settle a large proportion of transactions through barter.

Macroeconomic adjustment, especially in the fiscal area, together with further progress in developing an effective legal system, would help to improve the situation of several transition economies. However, a necessary condition for developing well-functioning financial markets is the establishment of credible commitments on the part of the government to honor contracts. Accumulation of payment arrears by the state, default on debt servicing, and the imposition of arbitrary taxes, all signal to the public that the government is not committed to ensuring the protection of private financial rights. In such a context, well-functioning private markets cannot emerge, and financial liberalization is likely to lead to disastrous results.

This chapter is organized as follows. In Section 1 we review some features of the financial markets in transition economies, emphasizing the low level of financial deepening and the inefficiency of the banking system throughout the area. The sharp contrast between two groups of countries is also emphasized. Section 2 isolates two distinct approaches, within the heterogeneous context of the experience of more than twenty transition countries. The first approach, associated with successful reforms in CEE countries, can be characterized as a gradual approach to financial liberalization. The other, associated with apparent failures and financial crises, especially in the countries of the CIS, displays a combination of inconsistent reform strategies, macroeconomic instability, and rapid financial liberalization. The picture that emerges from this characterization is somewhat surprising: One would have expected the less-developed and stable countries to follow a more conservative approach to financial liberalization.

While some argued in favor of a small financial sector in the early stages of transition, the demonetization that happened in Russia, described in Section 3, was quite another matter, reflecting as it did a collapse of payment discipline. Section 4 posits a possible interpretation of this collapse in a demonetized state, in terms of a model with multiple equilibria. We emphasize the interconnections between, on the one hand, the credibility of government commitment to market reforms, and, on the other hand, the development of private credit markets.

Section 5 concludes, summarizing the implications of the "rapid liberalization" approach followed in Russia and other CIS countries and emphasizing the effects of increasing systemic risk that this approach carried.

1 SOME FEATURES OF FINANCIAL MARKETS IN TRANSITION ECONOMIES

Low Level of Financial Intermediation

Almost ten years after market reforms began, perhaps the most striking feature characterizing transition economies is the extremely low level of financial depth exhibited by most of them.

With the exception of Bulgaria (where the situation is explained largely by credit to the state sector), Previously Centrally Planned Economies (PCPEs) display a much lower degree of financial deepening than market economies, at similar levels of economic development (European Bank for Reconstruction and Development [EBRD] 1998, p. 93). Such low levels of financial intermediation by the banking system appears even more striking if one takes into account that PCPEs have much less developed nonbanking financial markets (trade credit, security markets, etc.).

Although macroeconomic instability and the uncertainty associated with rapid structural change may explain the low level of financial

Table 8.1. Data on Structure of Banking System

	No. of banks	No. SOCBs	Concentration[a]	Recaps[b]	Empl[c] /mn pop	M2/GDP (%)[d]	Currency /M2 (%)[e]
Albania	8	3	100	y	83.8	45	37
Armenia	37	5	85	n	22.7	23	42
Azerbaijan	197	4	n.a.	n	14.0	26	64
Belarus	52	7	75	n	32.3	11	25
Bulgaria	34	10	90	y	62.4	65	14
China	19	7	90	n	19.9	91	15
Croatia	47	19	70	y	85.4	21	24
Czech Republic	58	1	69	y	313.6	74	10
Estonia	16	1	70	y	194.0	20	44
Georgia	203	5	90	n	21.9	3	56
Hungary	41	3	63	y	174.6	43	26
Kazakhstan	167	4	90	n	31.7	11	58
Kyrgyz Rep.	17	3	90	n	18.9	11	78
Latvia	40	3	55	y	203.7	30	43
Lithuania	27	3	70	n	89.0	17	42
FYR Macedonia	40	3	97	y	57.1	25	22
Moldova	27	4	85	n	22.3	8	51
Poland	73	5	66	y	61.4	31	26
Romania	28	7	74	y	134.9	15	30
Russia	2561	1	33	n	39.2	15	42
Slovak Republic	30	2	79	y	208.5	67	13
Slovenia	34	2	70	y	167.8	37	10
Tajikistan	14	14	90	n	11.2	42[f]	58
Turkmenistan	21	11	90	n	16.9	13[f]	47
Ukraine	217	2	70	n	25.4	16	37
Uzbekistan	35	29	95	n	12.8	79	26
Viet Nam	62	4	90	y	n.a.	22	58
Mongolia	14	1	90	n	15.8[g]	23	31
Comparator countries[h]							
United Kingdom	530		29		414.0		3
France	419		43		321.1		6
Spain	154		39		153.6		13
Greece	35		63		114.7		17
Denmark	124		77		416.1		4
Turkey	68		45		79.0		10
Venezuela	41		n.a.		223.6		9
Argentina	166		40		36.0		22

Notes: Number of banks includes the number of SOCBs (state-owned commercial banks), defined as banks where the state directly holds more than 50 percent of equity. Unless noted otherwise, data refer to the situation as of the middle of 1995 and are estimates.

deepening, this phenomenon is worrying, considering the empirical evidence to indicate the importance of financial deepening in explaining subsequent economic growth (King and Levine 1993).

There are, however, marked differences between transition economies, with CIS countries displaying by far the lowest money-to-GDP ratios. One part of the explanation is inflation: As illustrated with data representing averages over the period 1993–97, lower monetization is associated with higher inflation (Figure 8.1). Indeed, most CIS countries experienced hyperinflation as their transition began. But it should be noted that several Central and Eastern European countries also experienced hyperinflation (Poland and the countries of former Yugoslavia). What is striking is that the process of remonetization that took place in Central and Eastern Europe has not been repeated in those CIS countries that recently experienced a decline in inflation. In fact, by the end of 1997, many CIS countries had reduced inflation to rates below those of advanced reformers such as Hungary and Poland. Thus, different rates of inflation cannot fully explain the marked differences in financial depth across transition economies (Figure 8.1a).

A similar picture of an undersized banking system emerges if one looks at the magnitude of loans to nongovernment sectors as a proportion of GDP (Figure 8.2). Again, these ratios are much lower than those observed in market economies at comparable stages of development, and the differences are enormous for CIS countries (EBRD 1998).

An additional significant indicator of the lack of effective financial intermediation by banks is the ratio of currency to broad money (the inverse of the so-called "money multiplier") (Table 8.1). In many CIS

Notes to Table 8.1. *(continued)*

[a] Five-bank concentration ratio, based on assets.

[b] Refers to formal recapitalization programs; it excludes ad hoc recapitalization (such as carving out a loan for an enterprise which is privatized).

[c] Employment per million population. For all countries, except where noted, the number refers to employees in the whole financial sector, not just banking, and the real estate sector. For NIS, the source is the CIS Statistical Office Database and data are for 1994; for other countries the source is ILO and data are for 1993.

[d] Domestic currency component of Broad Money (M2) only. Data are averages of quarterly M2/GDP ratios to account for the effects of high inflation.

[e] Cash holdings as a share of domestic currency broad money (M2). End of 1994 data except where noted.

[f] 1993.

[g] Only banking sector.

[h] For comparator countries, data for the number of banks and market shares are for 1992. Except where noted, the source of the data is World Bank Staff estimates, IMF, EBRD, OECD, central bank reports, and other published sources.

Average 1993–97

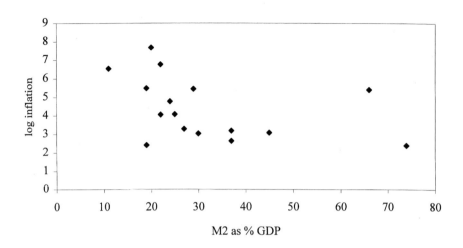

M2 as % GDP

1997

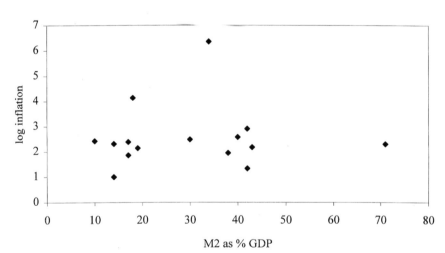

M2 as % GDP

Figure 8.1. Financial depth and inflation.

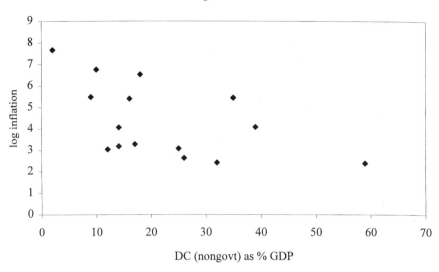

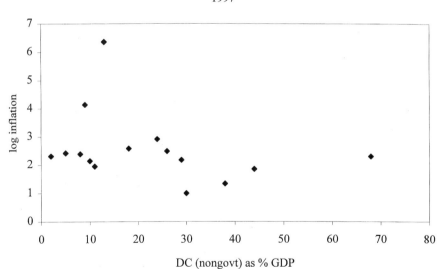

Figure 8.2. Credit to nongovernment and inflation.

countries this ratio is higher than 50 percent, compared with an average ratio of 9 percent for developed market economies, 10 percent for Turkey, and 22 percent for Argentina.

In short, within an overall picture in which most transition economies are characterized by a lack of financial depth, two radically different situations can be detected. In the group of advanced reformers of Central and Eastern Europe and the Baltic states, low levels of financial intermediation reflect the slow development of an efficient banking system, in the context of serious problems with nonperforming loans accumulated in the early stages of transition. Furthermore, as we argue as follows, hesitant privatization policies have probably limited the expansion of efficient banks. Nevertheless, the advanced CEE countries made significant progress in financial sector development and have created the institutional infrastructure to support a market-oriented financial system.

The situation in most CIS countries is markedly different, and should be judged as qualitatively different. The low level of monetization is associated with a system in which enterprise transactions are to a large extent based on nonmonetary exchanges. For instance, barter accounts for more than 50 percent of industrial sales in Russia and the Ukraine. Moreover, involuntary credit, in the form of interenterprise arrears, is a widespread phenomenon. Finally, several types of money surrogates (*veksels*) are issued by banks and enterprises. The picture that emerges is one of economies that only superficially resemble market economies: Price signals are largely irrelevant, and contracts are not honored.[2]

Reduction of inflation is not a sufficient condition for getting these economies out of what appears to be an equilibrium characterized by a low level of monetization. This equilibrium could be described as one where firms have invested in a payment and exchange technology in which money plays a marginal role. In order to replace this technology, fundamental changes in incentives and in confidence relating to contract enforcement must take place. We discuss these issues in Section 3.

The Inefficiency of the Banking System

In addition to the low level of financial intermediation in these transition economies, the activity of banks is very inefficient, as indicated by exceptionally high spreads between lending and deposit rates (EBRD 1998). Again, a sharp contrast can be found between most of the CIS countries, characterized by extremely high spreads, and the CEE and Baltic countries, characterized by more moderate spreads. High spreads are one of the

---

[2] Gaddy and Ickes (1998) used the phrase *virtual economy* to indicate a system that only formally operates as a market economy.

Table 8.2. Bank Performance Indicators, 1994–97

% of total assets	Net income before taxes	Net interest income	Nonperforming loans[a]
Belarus	3.4	7.9	12
Bulgaria	4.7	1.3	12
Croatia	0.2	5.2	12
Czech Republic	0.5	3.5	32
Estonia	2.7	5.0	3
FYR Macedonia	2.6	11.5	8
Hungary	0.0	4.1	10
Kazakhstan	2.9	7.6	14
Latvia	2.8	5.8	15
Lithuania	0.3	7.1	26
Poland	2.6	4.2	18
Romania	4.5	7.8	41
Russia	3.0	5.7	5
Slovak Republic	1.3	3.8	34
Slovenia	1.0	3.9	15
Ukraine	9.5	15.5	10
CEE	1.9	9.2	18.8
CIS	4.7	5.3	10.3
Average	2.6	6.2	16.7

[a] % of total loans.

causes of low financial deepening, and they partially reflect high rates of inflation.[3]

In the short term, high spreads permit banks to report high profits as a ratio of assets, which, for given tax rates, are in part transferred to the government. As shown in Table 8.2, measured banks' profits have been much higher in CIS countries than in CEE countries, with the exception of Bulgaria and Romania. Net interest income (a proxy for high spreads) is an important factor behind this high-measured profitability. Higher inflation partly explains this pattern. However, an analysis of individual banks carried out by the EBRD (1998) found that holdings of Treasury Bills significantly contributed to the high profitability of banks in CIS countries, especially in Russia and the Ukraine. The empirical analysis shows that losses on lending operations are more than compensated for by high yields on Treasury Bills. In these countries, the development of domestic debt markets contributed to the phenomenon of disintermedia-

---

[3] Assuming that nominal deposit rates closely follow the rate of inflation, the spread in percentage points between lending and deposit rates increases with the rate of inflation.

tion, with banks, together with foreigners, being the main beneficiaries of high-yield government bonds. In the case of Russia, as we will discuss, while temporarily boosting banks' profits, this policy ultimately pushed many banks into insolvency when the government defaulted on its debt in August 1998.

Another important finding is that banks' profitability improves significantly with privatization (EBRD 1998). Moreover, this outcome does not seem merely to reflect a sample selection bias caused by the fact that better banks are selected for privatization.

High spreads and high interest rates appear to be a central feature of bank activity in CIS countries. Access to foreign borrowing could be an effective means of reducing the cost of borrowing in countries with low levels of external debt. Indeed, for some advanced reformers (Hungary, Poland, and the Czech Republic), a significant proportion of loans to enterprises comes directly from foreign borrowing. This effectively reduces the cost of borrowing for domestic firms.

By contrast, in several CIS countries foreign borrowing is channeled to government and domestic banks; these in turn relend the funds, often in foreign currency. The example of Armenia, a low-inflation country with a reasonably stable exchange rate, is revealing in this regard. Domestic banks lend in U.S. dollars to domestic firms at rates of between 40 and 50 percent! Deposit rates in U.S. dollars are similarly remunerated at rates of between 20 and 30 percent. The picture is reminiscent of Ponzi-type schemes.

High interest rates are both a cause and a symptom of nonperforming loans. They are a cause because high interest rates induce an adverse selection process, with high-risk borrowers willing to borrow at high rates. They are also a symptom, because banks try to recover losses on bad loans by increasing their margins. Interestingly, if reported figures are to be believed, nonperforming loans seem to be more common in CEE countries than in CIS countries (Table 8.2). But this probably reflects better accounting in CEE countries as well as the continued presence of directed credit in CIS countries. Nevertheless, the large share of nonperforming loans in several CEE countries points to the need for effective bank restructuring programs, such as the one implemented in Poland, and, ultimately, to the privatization of banks as the key to avoid the recurrence of the phenomenon. The experience of Hungary is a case in point. With practically all of the banking sector privatized, bad loans have declined to levels similar to those found in advanced market economies.

The next section attempts to identify within diverse experience some common features that may be associated with different approaches to the liberalization of financial markets.

Table 8.3. **Number of Banks (Average 1993–97)**

	No. of banks 1993–97	Population 1997 (million)	No. of banks/ mn. population	GDP per capita 1997 (US$)
Armenia	35	4	9	435
Azerbaijan	156	8	21	509
Belarus	42	10	4	1314
Bulgaria	38	8	5	1227
Croatia	56	5	12	4267
Czech Republic	44	10	4	5050
Estonia	17	2	11	3230
FYR Macedonia	7	2	4	1663
Georgia	110	5	20	968
Hungary	42	10	4	4462
Kazakhstan	124	16	8	1434
Latvia	41	3	17	2211
Lithuania	14	4	4	2581
Poland	82	39	2	3512
Romania	27	23	1	1549
Russia	2007	147	14	3056
Slovak Republic	23	5	4	3624
Slovenia	39	2	19	9101
Ukraine	229	51	2591	976

2   TWO APPROACHES TO FINANCIAL LIBERALIZATION

Although countries followed different strategies, we can identify a few distinguishing features of advanced reformers in Central and Eastern Europe, which are in contrast with CIS countries. Four main points stand out.

1. In CEE countries there was a very conservative and prudent approach to the entry of new banks. To varying degrees, private banks were created through privatization of state banks, spinoffs of the central bank. By contrast, in CIS countries there was virtually free entry of new banks. The number of banks rose dramatically even before the launch of market reforms at the beginning of the 1990s. A large number of banks were created by companies. Over time, a process of consolidation and liquidation of the smaller banks took place. Nevertheless, the number of banks per head of population in many CIS countries remained higher than that in CEE countries (Table 8.3).

2. In CEE countries the problem of bad debts was tackled through comprehensive policies, while in CIS countries the problem has been generally hidden (Table 8.1, column on recapitalization).
3. Capital account liberalization has been slower in CEE countries than in several CIS countries.
4. Advanced reformers generally adopted explicit deposit insurance schemes. By contrast, explicit deposit insurance is absent from CIS countries.

The first two points indicate that CEE countries took a much more prudent approach to the banking industry, and emphasized the need to recapitalize banks through government-supported restructuring policies, rather than letting them compensate for their losses through high spreads and the purchase of Treasury Bills. Indeed, the latter strategy is self-defeating, as the asset base tends to shrink, and the composition of loan portfolios to worsen, as a result of adverse selection.

Regarding the liberalization of capital accounts, advanced reformers in Central and Eastern Europe have taken a gradual approach, retaining control especially on portfolio investments. The experience of Hungary – the country that has attracted by far the largest amount of direct foreign investment among transition economies[4] – reveals that controlling portfolio investments does not interfere with inflows of foreign direct investment (FDI) or with the activity of foreign firms and banks in the domestic economy. By contrast, since 1997, several CIS countries, such as Russia, the Ukraine, and Armenia, have fully liberalized capital accounts despite macroeconomic instability. Furthermore, many CIS countries allow residents and foreigners to hold foreign currency deposits in local banks, which – at least at the margin – is equivalent to having free international capital mobility. Among Central European countries the Czech Republic attempted full liberalization of capital accounts in 1996–97. The policy was modified after a speculative attack on the Czech currency, which resulted in a steep devaluation of the exchange rate in 1997.

Over the past few years, several CEE countries have faced the complex task of managing a rapid increase in capital inflows. In these countries, the larger share of inflows has been in the form of FDI; with the exception of the Czech Republic, more volatile short-term inflows have been contained. This contrasts with the experience in Russia and the Ukraine. In 1997, for instance, the ratio of net portfolio investments to FDI was close to 500 percent in Russia and 300 percent in the Ukraine, whereas it

[4] Per capita, cumulative FDI in Hungary during the period 1989–97 amounted to $1,667 (U.S.), compared with an average of $439 (U.S.) for CEE countries and the Baltic states, and $84 (U.S.) for CIS countries (EBRD 1998).

was well below 100 percent in Central and Eastern European countries. This is one reason why the impact of the Russian crisis of August 1998 on CEE countries was so moderate. Although the latter experienced a virtual cessation in the flow of portfolio funds, this was without major consequences for domestic financial markets and domestic economic activity.

A large share of portfolio investment took the form of investments in Treasury Bills. Thus, the opening of capital accounts occurred simultaneously with the development of domestic government debt markets.

The main elements of the strategy followed by several CIS countries sharply increased systemic risk, setting the stage for a vicious circle of high risk leading to high interest rates leading in turn to financial instability. The concern here is with volatile investment by nonresidents, rather than with capital flight by residents: Calvo (1998) stressed that the vulnerability to a run decreases when bondholders are domestic institutional investors.

3 DEMONETIZATION BY DESIGN OR ACCIDENT

One of the main concerns raised by several observers as transition began was that a fractional reserve and a decentralized banking system would imply financial instability. By its nature, transition involves a high degree of uncertainty with regard to the viability of firms, as well as absolute and relative price instability. Furthermore, newly created commercial banks, absent in the previous regime, did not possess the necessary skills to operate efficiently as screening institutions. As an alternative to reserve requirements of 100 percent, McKinnon (1991) suggested a total freeze on bank loans to firms, except for unreformed state firms, i.e., firms under full control by the state (for instance utilities). Liberalized state firms and private firms should be fully self-financing, or could access private trade credit markets where available.

Although McKinnon's proposal was nowhere adopted, it turned out, more by accident than by design, that evolving financial developments actually resembled what McKinnon had proposed. Several studies (Anderson and Kegels 1998; Coricelli 1998) found that, in advanced countries such as Hungary and Poland, many new private firms were, until recently, totally free from bank debt, even short term. Bank credit remained concentrated on state firms. However, new firms – both in Poland and in Hungary – could finance their short-term activities through trade credit. Trade credit reduces the need for holding cash balances, thus freeing resources for self-financed fixed investment. For a typical Polish or Hungarian industrial firm, trade credit was twice as large as bank credit. Therefore, difficulties and inefficiencies in the banking system could be compensated for by well-functioning private markets. However, while trade credit thus played a key role in financing firms in the advanced countries of Central and Eastern Europe, less-advanced countries, such as Romania and most CIS countries, were characterized by socially costly substitutes for bank credit, such as payment arrears (involuntary credit) and barter. One could say that, in those countries, a generalized default on payments and lack of financial discipline filled the gaps left by lack of bank credit.

In an increasingly dichotomized financial system rather sophisticated financial markets did develop, with the participation of banks, foreign investment banks, and a few large firms. But, at the same time, the bulk of the economy worked on a primitive system based on generalized default and widespread use of barter transactions.

The lesson that is to be learned from the failures, in this respect, of Russia and other transition countries relates to the preconditions for the creation of markets. Thus, a fundamental precondition for the development of financial markets is credibility of the commitment to honor contracts which entail promises to make future payments. An effective legal system ensuring the protection of private rights is one key element here. However, it is not sufficient, as default by the borrower always tends to be costly for the lender. The conviction that commitments will be honored, except in particularly bad situations, is thus an important element in credit and financial markets. Economic historians have recognized that the credibility of commitment in private markets, especially security markets, is crucially affected by the credibility of commitment by government (North and Weingast 1989). A government that defaults on its debt can hardly be trusted to protect private rights in private debt markets. This insight is clearly relevant to the experience of transition economies.

The recurrent failure of the government to honor its commitments has had a more severe adverse effect on private markets in a country like Russia than has slow progress in reforming legislation. Payment arrears by the state and default on debt servicing, together with arbitrary and often confiscatory taxation, certainly create high uncertainty with regard to private rights. This impedes the development of well-functioning private markets.[5]

Interestingly, after several years of attempted and aborted reforms, the evolving system in Russia has reproduced many features of the old regime. In particular there is again a de facto separation of monetary circuits: one linked to households, the other to the enterprise sector. In the enterprise sector, a high proportion of transactions are not monetized, in that arrears

---

[5] Thus, credible fiscal adjustment is a precondition for the creation of financial markets and the remonetization of CIS economies, not only because of its implications for macroeconomic stability, but also because of the signal it gives of a credible commitment to protect private rights.

and barter prevail. By contrast, households operate, as in the prereform period, in a cash economy. Although money prices can hardly be determined in the nonmonetized enterprise sector, inflation in the consumer-goods market is largely determined by monetary factors. In fact, inflation of the consumer-goods market anchors the rate of inflation in the enterprise sector.

So, instead of well-functioning private markets, dysfunctional payment technologies (arrears and barter) have emerged.[6] Evidently, the emergence of widespread default must imply that the cost to an individual firm of falling into arrears is lower that the opportunity cost of making the payment, i.e., the rate of return on investing the cash. The cost of falling into arrears is likely to depend not only on the number of firms involved in the chain of arrears but also on institutional factors that could be influenced by policy, such as bankruptcy procedures, the credibility of the legal system, and government commitment to enforce the rules. High inflation and expectations of bailout may make the generalized default equilibrium more likely. But, once locked into such equilibrium, macroeconomic measures may not be sufficient to pull the economy out of it.

In short, divergent outcomes of various transition economies may be thought of as a multiple equilibrium phenomenon, affected crucially by institutional factors as well as macroeconomic policies.

The next section discusses an extension of the Calvo and Coricelli (1994) model of the systemic equilibria than can occur in a model of this kind of behavior. The model captures several elements discussed in this chapter, providing an illustrative framework that summarizes the experience of Russia as a case of "bad equilibrium" arising from the interaction between financial markets (or nonmarkets), economic policies, and macroeconomic outcomes.

4 A MACROECONOMIC MODEL DISPLAYING AN ARREARS EQUILIBRIUM

The Costs and Benefits of Different Types of Nonmonetary Transaction

This section sketches a simple model which highlights the role of institutional and macroeconomic factors in determining the explosion of nonmonetary exchanges. Although, for simplicity, the model subsumes different forms of nonmonetary transactions in the same framework, Russia and several other CIS countries have seen a variety of nonmonetary transactions in practice, including interenterprise arrears, wage

---

[6] Arnott and Stiglitz (1988) discuss how dysfunctional institutions may arise in insurance markets.

arrears, and barter. Evidently, different types of nonmonetary exchange have different efficiency costs. Nevertheless, the incentives and sources for nonmonetary exchanges are similar for different payment technologies. These incentives depend on the opportunity cost of using cash – that is, on the return to alternative uses of cash, which we summarize by "the" interest rate.[7]

The share taken by each type of nonmonetary payment will depend on the specific costs and benefits of each form. For instance, barter is likely to produce large efficiency costs, but, at the same time, it provides full insurance against the risk of default by the client. In the case of trade credit or money surrogates (*veksels*), the efficiency costs are smaller, but suppliers are exposed to the risk of default by customers. In choosing one form of payment over another, firms consider the various costs associated with the different forms.

Evidently, with barter, the number of transactions necessary to achieve the desired transfer of inputs to producers increases, and this may imply a very large increase in costs; nevertheless, under some circumstances, it is apparently less costly than alternatives. In particular, the weaker the system for enforcing contracts, the more barter will happen. But that is not all. As will become evident from the discussion that follows, the higher the degree of "circularity" in the system (with firms acting as suppliers and customers for other firms) the more likely it is that generalized default (arrears) will emerge as an equilibrium phenomenon in preference to barter. This equilibrium is analogous to one involving widespread use of *veksels*, where the output cost of arrears is equivalent to the discount on *veksels*. On the other hand, if the system is characterized by significant net imbalances in enterprise positions, with firms having large net positions, either creditor or debtor, a different equilibrium output can be foreseen. In this case, net creditors have a clear incentive to resort to barter as an insurance against payment default by their customers. Moreover, net imbalances are normally associated with the presence of loss-making firms, which are the large net debtors. Therefore, the presence of loss-making firms will tend to push the system toward barter trade.

The difference in the cost of using different systems for nonmonetary transactions raises interesting questions about the relationship between these costs and the volume or frequency of each type of transaction. In the case of arrears (payment default), it is conceivable that the cost for the "offender" is a decreasing function of the aggregate level of arrears, as the potential penalties are lower. By contrast, the cost of barter is likely to increase as the overall use of barter increases. Indeed, the number of

---

[7] Discussed as follows, in a cash-in-advance model it is the nominal interest rate that is relevant.

exchanges – and thus transaction costs – necessary to obtain goods is likely to increase with the aggregate level of barter. Therefore, arrears may be characterized as a self-reinforcing process that locks the system into the high-arrears equilibrium, while barter may be characterized as an endogenous self-correcting mechanism.

A Simple Model of Nonmonetary Exchanges

We now turn to a sketch of the formal model. This model (an extension of that developed by Calvo and Coricelli 1994) posits an economy in which firms are controlled by workers. The firms can produce output on the basis of labor and material input. Each firm buys inputs from and sells output to other firms. Payments for inputs are modeled as "cash-in-advance," though arrears may arise in violation of this constraint.

With firms being controlled by workers, and in the absence of unemployment benefits, it is reasonable to model the workers as being retained by the firm so that becomes a fixed factor. The workers then maximize the discounted value of their future wage receipts over an infinite horizon. Normalizing the level of employment to one, workers choose the optimal wage path w_t to maximize

$$W = \sum_{t=0}^{\infty} \frac{w_t}{(1+r)^t}. \tag{1}$$

Output is produced through a standard production function, with labor and intermediate input x being the factors of production. For simplicity we assume that wages are paid at the end of the period, while nonlabor inputs are subject to a cash-in-advance constraint. Firms may ignore this constraint by falling into arrears, but this is costly for the firm, modelled as a loss in output. This cost of incurring arrears is assumed to be a linear function of arrears. It can be thought of as capturing such real world effects as penalties that may be imposed on offenders, for instance, or a lower quality of the inputs provided by suppliers who rationally anticipate that the buyer will default on payments. Moreover, costs for the individual firm do not depend on the behavior of arrears at aggregate level. This implies that the higher the arrears the lower the aggregate output.

(By a simple extension we could assume that an individual firm's cost increases in its own arrears but decreases in the aggregate level of arrears. This would capture the intuition that costs of default may in practice decrease when a critical mass of firms incurs arrears. For example, punishment for individual offenders is less likely to occur if most firms incur arrears. As a result, multiple states of equilibrium may arise. However, incorporating this mechanism would not add any significant new insights to the results being discussed here.)

Firms are assumed to be identical and positioned in a circle. To focus on problems of liquidity we assume that firms are viable. The decision by a firm to fall into arrears depends on whether the opportunity cost (of paying cash) exceeds the cost incurred by falling into arrears. If there were no cost to falling into arrears, firms would never pay.

Thus, we have firms maximizing expression (1) subject to the liquidity accumulation constraint:

$$M_{t+1} = f(x_t) - w_t + \kappa \left(M_t - \frac{x_t}{\theta_t} \right) \qquad (2)$$

where θ is the share of output that is paid in cash, and κ measures the cost of default.[8] In words, this equation states that next period's money holdings will equal the revenue from output less wage costs plus whatever is left from last period's money holdings after incurring the costs of acquiring inputs and paying the cost of default.

The individual benefits of arrears are the opportunity cost of the cash that would otherwise be paid out. This can be equated to the rate of return on the use of cash for purchasing financial assets rather than paying for input. In the case of Russia and other CIS countries, the return to Treasury Bills may be the relevant index for this rate of return. In the presence of inflation, the relevant rate is the nominal interest rate (see footnote 9).

As shown in Calvo and Coricelli (1994), the model we have described has a continuum of interior solutions and two corner solutions. These arise because with linear costs firms will either pay in full or pay the minimum. The continuum of interior solutions occurs when the cost of default equals the return on investing cash

$$\kappa = (1 + r).$$

Firms are indifferent to whether they fall into arrears or pay their suppliers in full, and thus there is a continuum of admissible values for θ. In principle, firms can swing from one value to another depending on their expectations. This interior solution, however, will arise only accidentally, as both κ and r are exogenous parameters.

In addition, the model yields two rather more interesting corner solutions. For lower values of the costs of arrears, specifically when $\kappa < (1 + r)$, firms will run the maximum amount of arrears, thus θ equals its minimum, $\theta = \theta_{min}$. By contrast, when the cost of arrears is higher than

---

[8] Assuming that both input and output goods are tradable, and normalizing the world price to one, in equilibrium $1/\theta$ is equal to the "effective" price of domestic goods, that is, higher than the world price, since firms have to take into account that domestic goods are only partly paid for in cash.

the return on Treasury Bills, $\kappa > (1 + r)$, arrears are zero, hence $\theta = 1$. All transactions are settled fully in cash.

An important implication of the model is that different states of equilibrium can be ranked according to their level of output. The higher the level of arrears, the lower the level of output. One can thus define the high-arrears–low-output situation as a "bad equilibrium."

The insight provided by this admittedly simple model is that arrears may reflect a multiple equilibrium phenomenon. Accordingly, once pushed toward a bad equilibrium, the economy needs a major shock to move away from it.

The model also reveals the dual role of monetary tightening. The high nominal interest rates that can push the economy toward a high-arrears equilibrium can arise either from a monetary restriction or from monetary ease. Once the economy has been locked into that "bad equilibrium," however, a monetary injection is unlikely to pull the system out of it. The multiple equilibrium structure may help to explain the apparent paradox of high arrears coexisting with periods of both high and low inflation.

That high inflation can push the economy toward a "bad equilibrium" can easily be seen in the model. With inflation, the relevant discount factor for the functional in (1) is the nominal rather than the real interest rate.[9] The nominal interest rate increased in proportion to the rate of inflation (or more precisely, the expected rate of inflation). In this way the rate of inflation becomes a key determinant for the selection mechanism of the different states of equilibrium. Indeed, if the rate of inflation is high relative to the real rate of interest, the nominal rate of return on Treasury Bills can be approximated by the inflation rate and we can therefore approximate the equilibrium conditions as depending on the relative values of κ and $(1 + \pi)$, where π denotes the rate of inflation. The higher the value of π, the more likely that the economy will be trapped in the high-arrears–low-output equilibrium, as the marginal cost of falling into arrears becomes smaller than its marginal benefits, as represented by the rate of inflation.

Bearing in mind that high *nominal* interest rates may result either from tight monetary policy (in which case they will be associated with high real interest rates) or with lax monetary policy (in which case they will be associated with low real interest rates), we argue that the experience of Russia after 1992 encompassed both situations.

The case of Russia is interesting in this respect, as arrears peaked in different periods. After 1992, arrears boomed at the same time as the

---

[9] Denoting real monetary balances by m, in a state of positive inflation the liquidity accumulation equation (2) can be rewritten with $m_{t+1}(1 + \pi)$ instead of M_{t+1}, on the left-hand side, and m_t, on the right-hand side instead of M_t.

stabilization program was collapsing and the rate of inflation was increasing. During the period 1995–98 arrears and barter boomed again, but in the context of extremely low inflation. Nominal interest rates, however, were very high, signaling persistently high expectations for the rate of inflation, which is what matters in determining the state of equilibrium in the above model.

The model also helps to rationalize the phenomenon of significant activity by large firms in arrears in the bond market, where high interest rates were available. In this respect, high nominal and real rates on domestic debts sharply raised the opportunity cost of not falling into arrears. For a while, the process was self-sustaining, as the adverse fiscal effects of arrears were compensated for by the purchase of government bonds. Of course, this was a sort of speculative bubble, and it eventually burst.

Nonmonetary Exchanges and Budget Deficits

We can augment this model adding consideration of government behavior and budget constraints and money demand by the household sector. Let us assume that real government revenues R are a decreasing function of arrears and barter (see Ickes for an analysis of the fiscal implications of the cashless economy). For a given level of real expenditure G, therefore, higher arrears and barter imply a higher budget deficit. With the deficit financed fully through the inflation tax (the receipts from which can, in equilibrium, be measured as the rate of inflation times the stock of real cash balances) we get the following budget constraint:

$$G - R(a) = \pi m(\pi), \qquad (3)$$

where m is the real demand for cash balances schedule. Assume the economy starts in a region where it is near the borderline case

$$\kappa = (1 + \pi).$$

Then a fiscal shock, by increasing the rate of inflation, may push the economy toward the high-arrears equilibrium. At that point, arrears themselves reduce budget revenues, thus increasing the budget deficit and the rate of inflation.

By extension, we might consider that part of the inflation tax is channeled to finance subsidies to firms. These subsidies could be granted in such a way as to increase the marginal cost of running arrears (the subsidy could be given only when firms pay cash, or it could be conditional on the fact that firms are not in arrears). As shown in the Appendix, higher inflation tax revenues could conceivably give the government sufficient resources to be able to subsidize firms enough to restore a low-arrears equilibrium.

To summarize, macroeconomic instability, especially in the form of a fiscal crisis, may not only be a determinant of instability in the financial sector. Indeed, instability and indiscipline in the financial sector may adversely affect fiscal accounts. Financial liberalization, and especially the creation of a domestic debt market, may in fact push the economy toward a "bad equilibrium" of low monetization and fiscal crisis.

5 CONCLUDING REMARKS

Demonetization

This chapter has stressed how the combination of weak institutions of financial discipline with high nominal interest rates contributed to demonetization in Russia and certain other CIS countries. The weak institutions – such as ineffective bankruptcy policies, uncertain protection of private rights, and weak contract enforcement – and the attendant financial indiscipline, adversely affected macroeconomic outcomes. In turn, macroeconomic instability fed back into financial markets and reinforced financial indiscipline. Demonetization is a phenomenon generally associated with high inflation, and this was certainly the case in the early 1990s. However, excessive tightening of monetary policy with its associated high interest rates can also contribute to this negative outcome. The effects of these policies through high nominal interest rates on the incentive to avoid cash payments are analogous to those of loose monetary policy and high inflation.

To illustrate the results, a simple model has been developed, with the aim of providing an interpretation of the Russian experience. One implication of the model is that monetary policy and financial liberalization should take into account the underlying strength of the institutions affecting behavior in financial markets. Weak institutional settings call for prudent liberalization strategies and a more pragmatic monetary policy. In such a context, efforts should focus on developing institutions, a precondition for successful liberalization.

The model illustrates how demonetization can come about following an attempt to tighten credit policy. Once the economy gets stuck in a low-monetization equilibrium there are endogenous forces that make the equilibrium stable, acting mainly through fiscal channels. An expansionary monetary policy would not help the economy to escape such equilibrium on nonmonetary transactions. Interestingly, the same type of equilibrium may arise with high inflation.

Other Strategic Failures

Some of the lessons to be learned from the failure of reforms in these CIS countries echo those that could already be drawn from experience elsewhere, namely that (i) financial liberalization should be implemented only after fiscal stability has been achieved, and (ii) macroeconomic stability is a necessary but not a sufficient condition for avoiding financial crises.

But in addition one can note that several other key aspects of the strategy followed in Russia (and some other CIS countries) heightened risk in financial markets.

- The huge rise in the number of loosely regulated and supervised banks, often controlled by firms, created a captive loan market for firms controlling banks. This perpetuated soft budget constraints, with attendant inefficiency and ultimately an increase in default risk.
- Lack of explicit deposit insurance, while reducing moral hazard for banks, exposed them to runs. Skyrocketing interest rates were only a partial substitute for deposit insurance.
- A liberal policy toward foreign currency deposits, despite exchange-rate instability, sharply increased foreign exchange risk in the banking system.
- The explosion of the domestic debt market increased the risk of default by the state. At the same time, major holdings of government bonds by banks, by reducing loanable funds, resulted in higher interest rates on loans and consequently tended to worsen the loan portfolios of banks. This also increased credit risk.
- Finally, the entry of foreign investors into the domestic debt market increased the instability of financial markets, as foreign investment seemed to be highly sensitive to rumors (see Calvo 1998).

Of course, overall macroeconomic instability and the weakness of the legal system contributed to the fragility of the financial sector. However, the policies described above significantly increased that fragility, and in turn adversely affected macroeconomic stability.

In general, therefore, the widely recognized notion that fiscal consolidation and macrostability are key prerequisites for financial liberalization should be complemented with the notion that the strengthening of institutions in financial markets, together with prudent and pragmatic management of financial liberalization, are preconditions for effective fiscal consolidation in transition economies.

APPENDIX: CORRECTIVE SUBSIDIES AND FISCAL RESOURCES

Here we develop the argument of Section 4 to illustrate how some counterintuitive results can arise with high inflation and high corrective subsidies coexisting with the "good" equilibrium.

Rewrite the inflation tax as:

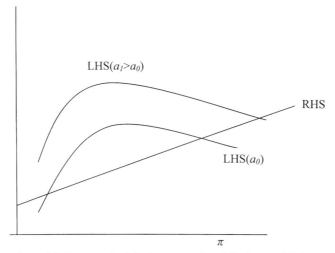

Figure 8.3. Increase in default removes low-inflation equilibrium.

$$\frac{\pi}{1+\pi} m(\pi).$$

Then let s be the amount of subsidies, and β the share of inflation tax that finances these subsidies. The key condition separating the high-arrears from the low-arrears state of equilibrium is now

$$\kappa(1+s) = (1+\pi)$$

or, substituting for s

$$\kappa\left(1 + \beta\frac{\pi}{1+\pi} m(\pi)\right) = 1 + \pi. \qquad (A1)$$

According to that condition, there is a threshold level of inflation past which the economy is pushed into a state of "bad equilibrium." The interesting point is that there is a range for which increasing inflation increases the left-hand side of equation (A1), raising the effective cost of arrears. In fact, it could happen that with a moderate increase in inflation the system moves away from the area in which the high-arrears equilibrium will occur (see Figure 8.3).

Figure 8.3 plots the left-hand side (which is a nonlinear function of inflation, because of the standard Laffer curve features of inflation tax) and the right-hand side of equation (4), as functions of the rate of inflation. Two cases may emerge. In the first case, the cost of arrears is initially higher than the benefits, and thus the economy is in the low-arrears equilibrium. If inflation rises above the rate at which the left-hand side intersects with the right-hand side, the economy can be pushed into a state of "bad equilibrium;" this would be due to inflation. By contrast, in the second case, the economy may begin in the "bad equilibrium," and a moderate increase in inflation may push it away from the high-arrears equilibrium. This case shows that an excessive concern with inflation, in the context of a weak underlying institutional structure (low cost of arrears), may in fact lead to an unfavorable outcome. However, if inflation increases above a certain rate, the economy converges on the "bad equilibrium" once again.

REFERENCES

Anderson, R.W. and C. Kegels. 1998. *Transition Banking: Financial Development of Central and Eastern Europe*. Oxford: Clarendon Press.

Arnott, R. and J. Stiglitz. 1988. "Dysfunctional Nonmarket Institutions and the Market." *National Bureau of Economic Research (NBER) Working Paper* 2666.

Calvo, G. 1998. "Understanding the Russian Virus, with Special Reference to Latin America." University of Maryland. *Mimeo*.

Calvo, G. and F. Coricelli. 1994. "Credit Market Imperfections and Output Response in Previously Centrally Planned Economies." In G. Caprio, D. Folkerts-Landau, and T. Lane (eds.), *Building Sound Finance in Emerging Market Economies*, pp. 257–294. Washington D.C.: International Monetary Fund and World Bank.

Claessens, S. 1996. "Banking Reform in Transition Countries." *World Bank Policy Research Working Paper* 1642.

Coricelli, F. 1998. *Macroeconomic Policies and the Development of Markets in Transition Economies*. Budapest: Central European University Press.

European Bank for Reconstruction and Development (EBRD). 1998. *Transition Report 1998: Financial Sector in Transition*.

Gaddy, C.G. and B.W. Ickes. 1998. "Beyond a Bail Out: Time to Face Reality about Russia's 'Virtual Economy.'" *Mimeo*.

King, R.G. and R. Levine. 1993. "Finance and Growth: Schumpeter Might Be Right." *Quarterly Journal of Economics* 108:717–37.

McKinnon, R.I. 1991. *The Order of Economic Liberalization: Financial Control in the Transition to a Market Economy*. Baltimore and London: The Johns Hopkins University Press.

Murrell, P. 1996. "How Far Has Transition Progressed?" *Journal of Economic Perspectives* 10:25–44.

North, D.C. and B.R. Weingast. 1989. "Constitutions and Commitments: The Evolution of Institutions Governing Public Choice in Seventeenth-Century England." *Journal of Economic History* 69:803–32.

9

Indonesia and India: Contrasting Approaches to Repression and Liberalization

James A. Hanson

INTRODUCTION

This chapter looks at two countries that were characterized by highly repressed interest rates and directed credit in the 1970s and 1980s. It illustrates common factors that drive financial repression and trigger liberalization, even in very different circumstances.

Indonesia and India differed, however, in their initial circumstance, the detail of their approaches to financial repression and liberalization and correspondingly, the outcomes. Indonesia, an oil exporter, emerged from hyperinflation in the 1960s and opened its capital account early, experiencing fairly rapid growth in the 1970s and 1980s. India, with less natural resources, has generally kept inflation below double digits, maintained more limited links to the international economy, and experienced rapid growth only in the 1980s. Indonesia maintained a small government budget deficit in the 1970s and 1980s and even achieved surpluses in the early 1990s, while India's Central Government deficit (consolidated public sector deficit) remains about 6 percent (10 percent) of GDP even after its stabilization of the early 1990s.

Both countries liberalized interest rate and credit allocations after they were hit by balance of payments problems. Indonesia freed rates in 1983, then, in 1988 moved to something like "free" banking, with little improvement in regulation and supervision. In contrast, India liberalized gradually and improved regulation and supervision significantly.

Section 1 discusses Indonesia: the situation leading up to interest rate liberalization, the context and characteristics of liberalization, and the results of its approach to liberalization. Section 2 considers India's financial development in the same way. Finally, Section 3 summarizes the similarities and differences in the two countries' financial repression, liberalization, and response to liberalization.

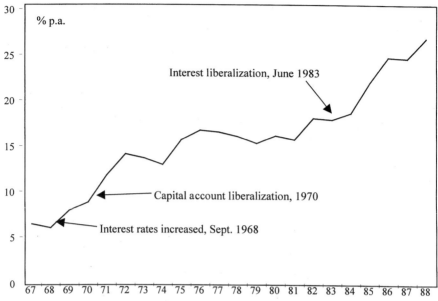

Figure 9.1. Indonesia: Money as percentage of GDP.

1 INDONESIA

Developments Prior to the 1983 Interest Rate Liberalization

Stabilization after High Inflation (1967–72)

Stabilization of hyperinflation at the end of the Sukarno Government was a major objective of Suharto's New Order Government. The government deficit was reduced sharply and state enterprises' access to bank credit was reduced. This cut nominal monetary growth sharply. Inflation fell quickly, dropping from over 500 percent in 1965 and 1966 to an average of around 15 percent in 1969 and 1970, and 10 percent in 1970 to 1972. Deposit interest rates were raised sharply in 1968 and then brought down gradually, remaining more than ten percentage points higher than inflation from 1969 to 1972. Meanwhile, economic growth remained positive in 1967 (despite a poor rice harvest), then jumped to an average of over 8 percent for the next five years. The drop in inflation, the higher real interest rates, and the other policies described as follows contributed to a more than doubling of the ratio of broad money to GDP, to over 14 percent, by 1972 (Figure 9.1). Thus, prior to 1983, a first round of interest rate liberalization brought interest rates much closer to market levels and contributed to deposit mobilization.

Two policies – the open capital account and the "Indonesian balanced budget" rule – were foundations of the Suharto Government's stabilization program that continued through the mid-1990s.[1] Indonesia opened the capital account in April 1970, a decision reflecting the practical problems of capital controls with Singapore nearby, but which represented a reversal of what later became the recommended sequence of liberalization (Cole and Slade 1996). The exchange rate was unified and pegged. Indonesia has maintained an open capital account since 1970, despite shocks that might have provided a rationale for closing the capital account, at least temporarily. Rather than the decline predicted by many theorists of the time, Indonesia's capital account opening was associated with a rise in M2/GDP.

The open capital account increased access to offshore financing for private firms. Funds came in because funds could be taken out. Domestic firms also were able to borrow offshore and they could keep balances offshore that could be used as collateral for loans. Of course, the open capital account increased the sensitivity of domestic asset holdings to monetary policy and to expectations. Funds moved onshore or offshore as monetary policy tightened or loosened relative to the international economy, in the classic pattern analyzed by Mundell (1968; *cf.* World Bank 1996, p. 19). This increasing tendency for flows of capital to offset monetary policy meant that, the central bank increasingly had to take international interest rates into account in making monetary policy.[2]

Indonesia's "balanced budget" decree, which applied to the 1967 budget and thereafter, restricted domestic borrowing. A small overall deficit was more than covered by foreign borrowing until the 1990s (Hill 1996). Although the central bank financed substantial off-budget expenditures in some years, in practice, Indonesia's rule has limited the increase in the net domestic liabilities of government by imposing a budget constraint that the finance minister can enforce easily. The rule also implies that no domestic government debt exists,[3] which is one reason why Indonesia's capital market is sometimes considered small relative to other East Asian developing economies (*cf.* World Bank 1995a).

---

[1] In addition, in 1967, Bank Negara Indonesia's operations were split up into a separate central bank (Bank Indonesia) and four state banks.

[2] Of course, this did not mean domestic interest rates were the same as, or even moved in the same direction as, international interest rates. Once market rates were established, a large and variable risk premium typically existed over international rates adjusted for ex post depreciation See for example World Bank 1996, p. 9.

[3] The central bank began selling its own debt in 1984, in order to develop an open market instrument.

*Absorption of High Petroleum Revenues and Financial
Repression (1973–82)*

Beginning in 1973, the government increased its intervention in Indonesia's financial sector. In part this reflected the process of absorbing income
from the sharp rises in world oil prices that began in 1973. As in all the
major oil exporting countries, the oil price rises provided the resources to
increase the public sector's role substantially, both directly, through government and public enterprise expansion, and indirectly, through the
financial sector (Gelb 1988). At the same time, as in other oil producing
nations, inflation control became difficult, because of increases in public
sector spending, capital inflows, and money growth.

Populist pressures to spend the oil resources were strong in Indonesia
because of the poor rice harvests and the jump in rice prices in 1972–73;
there were demonstrations in January 1974 during the visit of the
Japanese prime minister (Bresnan 1993). Nonetheless, commentators in
1988 noted that "Indonesia's economic performance since 1973 has been
unusually good" (Gelb 1988, p. 197). Compared to the other oil producers, agriculture and nonoil exports were kept up, macrostability was largely
maintained, external debt growth was limited, fewer large projects undertaken, and more public spending went to investment and agriculture (Gelb
1988). Two elements in this performance were the tight macroeconomic
policy, based on the balanced budget rule, and the Pertamina crisis discussed as follows.

In an attempt to contain inflationary pressures, while using the
increased resources and meeting the demand for redistribution, the government used a two-pronged approach. Orthodoxy was represented by an
IMF standby, contracted in 1972, and by a rise in the reserve requirement
to 30 percent. But the main approach was the introduction in April 1974
of a program of bank-by-bank credit ceilings, with subceilings by type of
loan, and a complex system of rediscounts (liquidity credits) by the central
bank that favored the state banks. This credit ceiling regime remained in
place for the next nine years. Increasingly the credit ceilings determined
banking structure and, through the subceilings by type of loan, credit allocation (Woo and Nasution 1989). Interest rates on state bank credits and
deposits continued to be controlled.[4] Nevertheless, inflation remained
in double digits, averaging over 13 percent from December 1974 to
December 1982.

The 1975 Pertamina crisis was a major shock to the economy and the
political system. As in many petroleum producing countries, Indonesia's

---

[4] Rates on deposits of less than three months' maturity were freed in January 1978 (Biro
   Pusat Statistik 1997).

state oil company, Pertamina, had become something of a government within a government, carrying out massive projects that in some cases were only peripherally related to oil and gas, such as the Krakatau steel plant and some telecommunications activities. With the oil price rise, Pertamina's activities multiplied – Pertamina's budget became half as large as the government, although it paid no taxes, and its external debt was estimated at around $10 billion (Bresnan 1993; Woo et al. 1994). Much of the debt was short term in order to skirt the IMF program and the presidential decree requiring Ministry of Finance and central bank approval of external borrowing. In 1975, when some short-term debts were not rolled over and its tanker contracts went sour, Pertamina was unable to meet debt service payments. The government and the central bank took over much of Pertamina's large external debt to maintain the country's creditworthiness. The crisis increased the public's and the political elite's skepticism regarding large public projects. It also reduced Indonesia's external borrowing capacity. Both factors probably helped Indonesia limit the excesses that characterized many oil exporting countries after 1975.

Indonesia's Repressed Financial System on the Eve of Interest Rate Deregulation

By the early 1980s, the credit policies discussed above had led to a distorted, repressed, and segmented financial system. The benefits of subsidized credit went to the state enterprises, conglomerates, and, to a small extent, agriculture and small farmers and industrialists. In 1982, the central bank still dominated the system, with about 45 percent of gross banking assets (22 percent of GDP; *cf.* Hanna 1996, p. 4). The central bank's dominance reflected the buildup of international reserves during this period, and also the central bank's privileged access to government and public enterprise deposits and the high reserve requirement (30 percent until 1977, thereafter 15 percent). Over the whole period from the late 1970s to the early 1980s, the central bank accounted for about 50 percent of banking sector credit, about 30 percent directly and another 20 percent through rediscounts of credits made by banks, with the proportion of lending through the banks rising over time (Cole and Slade 1996, p. 84; World Bank 1985, p. 8).

The central bank's involvement in lending to the banks for on-lending also entailed the central bank's supervising the use of these funds. The verification that regulations on directed credit were followed tended to "crowd out" prudential supervision of portfolio quality and capital adequacy, as well as limiting the quality of public information about banks.[5]

---

[5] Public data on the quality of the state banks' portfolio was only made available in 1993.

Five state banks dominated commercial banking, accounting for nearly 40 percent of gross bank assets.[6] Their dominance reflected their exclusive access to public sector deposits, and to most of the central bank's liquidity credits, as well as their extensive branch network. Despite deposit rate ceilings that kept rates nearly ten percentage points below the private banks and negative in real terms, state banks mobilized more resources than they could lend under the credit ceilings.[7] They used these resources to accumulate excess reserves in the central bank, as well as interbank loans and foreign assets – the latter growing almost as much as their loan portfolio during 1978–81 (Cole and Slade 1996; Woo and Nasution 1989). Aside from Bank Rakyat Indonesia's (BRI) lending to farmers and other small scale credit users, the state banks' main clients were the public enterprises and the larger conglomerates.

The private domestic banks, typically linked to a conglomerate, accounted for only about 6 percent of gross bank assets in the early 1980s. The largest were the ten domestic private foreign exchange banks, which accounted for about 4 percent of bank assets, with another 2 percent held by sixty small, nonforeign exchange, private domestic banks. Finally, the ten foreign banks and the one joint venture bank that operated in Indonesia accounted for about 4 percent of gross bank assets. Many of the foreign banks booked most of their lending offshore to avoid capital requirements and to take advantage of better legal conditions for debt recovery. No bank licenses were issued between 1971 and 1983, and the number of branches was essentially constant from the late 1970s to 1983.

Although the private banks were able to set deposit interest rates freely, and did set them higher than the state banks, the private banks mobilized only limited deposits. Their limited mobilization reflected lack of access to public sector deposits, credit ceilings that meant additional deposit resources could only be used in the money market, and their inability to open branches. The weak capital position of some small banks was also probably a factor, especially considering the closeness of more secure institutions in Singapore.

Thus, overall deposit mobilization was limited by low deposit rates, credit ceilings that limited the profitability of additional deposits, and limits on branching. From 1975 to 1981, M2/GDP was only about 16 percent, low for a country of Indonesia's per capita income. Moreover, 60 percent was currency and demand deposits, an unusually high ratio of M1

---

[6] In addition, the state-owned development banks accounted for another 4 percent.

[7] The state banks rarely met their credit targets according to Woo, Glassburner, and Nasution (1994), who hypothesize that one reason may have been due to bribes that raised the cost of their lending to the levels of the private banks. See also World Bank (1997) for evidence on bribes that raised the cost of borrowing.

to M2. The real (one year) deposit rate averaged −2.5 percent in 1975–78, −4.8 percent in 1979–82.

The complex system of directed credits at below-market rates (Appendix 1) accounted for about 50 percent of credits, as noted previously. The main beneficiaries of the subsidized credit, much of which was never repaid, were the public enterprises, the conglomerates, and, in the 1970s, agriculture and smaller farmers. The public enterprises and conglomerates accessed long-term, low-cost liquidity credits through their links to the state banks. The larger private companies also could borrow offshore, allowing them to escape the constraint of the credit ceilings. These factors contributed to the limited stock market development (see discussion in Cole and Slade 1996 and Hanna 1996). Also, the need for companies that borrowed offshore to maintain balances offshore as collateral may be a partial explanation of Indonesia's limited financial depth. Small and medium enterprises did receive some subsidized funds, but they were the main losers from the directed credit policies. Credit ceilings limited the availability of funds for their expansion, and these firms' access to offshore funds was limited. The costs of the low-interest, high-default loans were born by the government and by the depositors through low deposit rates.

Indonesia's 1983 Financial Liberalization and Other Reforms of the Mid-1980s

In March 1983, probably prompted by the pressure of falling oil revenues and a deteriorating current account deficit, the Indonesian government devalued the Rupiah by 38.5 percent and moved to a crawling peg exchange rate regime. In June 1983, it largely deregulated interest rates and credit allocation by:

- allowing state banks to set interest rates on most types of deposits[8] and on loans, except priority loans (private banks had had no restriction on setting interest rates);
- eliminating overall and subsectoral credit ceilings on individual banks; and
- reducing substantially (by an estimated 50 percent) the types and volumes of loans eligible for rediscount at the central bank in phased manner – but in fact the rate of growth of such credits increased rapidly from 1983 to 1986 and they were only really eliminated in 1990 (see Balino and Sundararajan 1986; Chant and Pangestu 1994).

---

[8] Interest rates on certificates of deposit (CDs) of less than six months' maturity had been freed in March 1983, interest rates on three month or shorter maturity CDs had been freed in 1978.

The government also implemented a thorough reform of the tax code, including imposing withholding taxes on interest collected from the payer; an exception was bank deposits, on which withholding was imposed in 1988 (Asher and Booth 1992).

In response to the measures, domestic deposit rates at the private and foreign banks rose in 1984, despite a fall in inflation and even before the tightening of credit in September 1984 and the speedup in depreciation.

A further sharp devaluation followed in 1986 and was accompanied by the start of a series of tariff cuts. In 1988, a second round of financial liberalization opened the banking sector to foreign banks and new, small, private domestic banks, a different approach to reform that is discussed in the next section.

The Response to Interest Rate Deregulation Followed McKinnon-Shaw Predictions

Following the interest rate liberalization and other measures, broad money, stagnant since 1975, started to grow rapidly (Figure 9.1).[9] Deposits increased massively at the state banks, but in the private and foreign banks as well. The state banks increased their deposit rates in response to the liberalization, by five to seven percentage points[10] – but this still left them three to five percentage points below the private banks. Nearly 60 percent of the growth in deposits came from individuals and social foundations, with 30 percent from the public sector (including public insurance firms) and 10 percent from private firms (World Bank 1985).

Much of this strong response in deposits probably came from a shift of offshore deposits to Indonesian banks. International reserves rose sharply in 1983–84, as did banks' holdings offshore. It is also possible that some of the rise in deposits reflected countervailing balances linked to the rise in loans once credit ceilings were eliminated. A temporary substitution occurred in favor of interest-bearing deposits within M2, but by 1986 cash and demand deposits had returned to their previous ratios to GDP.

Bank loans increased rapidly with the elimination of credit ceilings, by some 40 percent between 1983 and 1984. The state banks, private banks, and foreign banks all increased their loans substantially. The volume of interbank credit also increased sharply, as the state and foreign banks placed part of their increased deposits in the market and the private banks borrowed to increase their loans (Cole and Slade 1996, p. 104). Finally, as noted previously, liquidity credits continued to increase until 1990.

The increased credit went to a broader spectrum of borrowers, including small scale borrowers. According to Harris, Schiantarelli, and Siregar

---

[9] Cole and Slade (1996) show somewhat higher M2 : GDP ratios, reflecting their use of end-year money data.

[10] The subsequent decline in inflation meant a sharp increase in real interest rates.

(1994), "the economic reforms had a favorable effect on the performance of small establishments. . . . The process of shifting from an administrative allocation of credit to a market-based allocation has increased borrowing costs, particularly loans to smaller units, but, at the same time, has widened access to finance and decreased the degree of credit market segmentation. From the standpoint of investment and rates of profit, the net effect appears to have been positive" (pp. 42, 43; see also the discussion in Schiantarelli et al. 1994).

The freeing up of interest rates made it possible for BRI to set up its well-known small scale deposit and loan programs at BRI (known as *simpedes* and *kupedes* and made through the existing *unit desa* network), while increased competition encouraged them to do so. A key factor in these programs was BRI's ability to set the lending rate high enough to cover the high costs of intermediation at the village level and the credit risk. Despite the high interest rate, BRI successfully made and recovered loans to small borrowers and the program contributed substantially to BRI's profit. (For a discussion, see Cole and Slade 1996, pp. 107–09 and Soeskmono 1994, pp. 297–309.)

After liberalization, from 1984–88, banks had to cope with an increasingly unstable macroeconomic environment, reflecting the further declines in oil prices as well as lagged responses to the initial fall. Another devaluation, attempts at tightening money indirectly, and finally, a draining of reserves from the banking system in order to stabilize the deteriorating balance of payments, put substantial stress on the financial system (see Cole and Slade 1996, pp. 48–54). This external situation and policy environment obviously influenced the macroeconomic consequences of the 1983 interest rate reform discussed as follows.

For the period 1984–88, GDP growth averaged 5.1 percent p.a., which was somewhat faster than in 1980–83. The share of gross fixed investment in GDP did fall in 1984, but regained its pre-1984 level by 1988.[11] Inflation declined, despite the switch from direct to indirect monetary control and the difficulties of monetary policymaking in an open economy.[12]

---

[11] Gross investment figures (BPS 1997) are used because "inventory" figures in Indonesian GDP are actually the difference between the production- and expenditure-based estimates of GDP.

[12] The need to develop indirect monetary policy instruments was a major issue after the credit controls were dropped; see Cole and Slade 1996, pp. 47–80, and Chant and Pangestu 1994, pp. 265–68. The problem was complicated by the absence of domestic government debt because of the balanced budget rule. The central bank did create its own monetary instruments and used them to tighten money, but in the early 1990s, before the large outstanding stock was unwound, this generated a large net interest bill (quasifiscal deficit) of over 0.5 percent of GDP. Perhaps more importantly, the open economy made independent monetary policy increasingly difficult, as noted previously.

Thus, the macroeconomic productivity of investment increased after 1983. Partly this may be attributed to financial reform, partly the exchange rate adjustments and reductions in protection. Nonoil exports provided the engine of growth in this period and there can be no doubt that financial reform helped make credit available to the nascent manufacturing industry. The share of manufacturing in total credit increased by about one-third between 1982 and 1988, when it reached 33 percent (Hanna 1996, p. 7).

"There was a remarkable absence of signs of financial distress from the beginnings of the reform through 1990," according to Chant and Pangestu (1994, pp. 261–62), an assessment that corresponded with other observers' views. Partly the lack of distress reflected the strength of the economy, partly the continuation of liquidity credits until 1990. However, it should be noted that this assessment is not firmly grounded in data on non-performing assets, which became available only in 1994.

After 1990, some clear signs of financial distress appeared. It is possible that these problems reflected a carryover for many years of problems with what were nominally short-term loans. More likely, the problems relate to the sharp tightening of monetary policy in 1991 and the second round of financial reform that took place in 1988.

A full analysis of the 1988 reforms, the 1991 tightening of monetary policy, and their relation to the 1997 crisis is beyond the scope of this chapter (see Cole and Slade 1996 and Hanna 1996 for a discussion). Briefly, the aim of the 1988 reforms was different than the 1983 reforms – to introduce more competition into banking in order to lower interest rates. To that end, in October 1988, banks were allowed to set up with minimal capital. Moreover, reserve requirements were cut to a minimal 3 percent, which could be satisfied by vault cash. Regulatory and supervisory improvements were notably higher, capital ratios occurred only in the early 1990s, and regulatory forbearance remained a problem (World Bank 1995b).

The new policy led to a kind of "free banking," where banks were allowed to start up with minimal funds. The number of banks exploded, to well over 200, with a major increase in foreign banks. By 1993 the private and foreign banks accounted for a majority of assets in the commercial banking system. M2 nearly doubled in nominal terms between September 1988 and September 1989. The corresponding credit growth did increase access to credit but certainly must be questioned in terms of underlying asset quality.

The Finance Ministry's 1988 reforms neglected supervision and regulation, which were Bank Indonesia's responsibility. The low capital ratios established in the reform meant that the private banks had a limited stake in lending decisions, as was already the case in the state-owned banks. The new approach to banking also raised issues of how to manage the closure of banks when they became insolvent, how much the government would protect depositors in the absence of formal deposit insurance, and how the numerous small banks would manage in a systemic crisis; in addition, there remained the legal issues in collection of nonperforming loans (World Bank 1996, 1997). Moreover, it is likely that the political interventions in response to the crises in Bank Duta and Bank Summa in the early 1990s, and the subsequent failure to resolve them effectively (*cf.* Cole and Slade 1996), weakened both onshore and offshore banks' concerns for loan quality and collection of debt service, a weakening that magnified Indonesia's 1997 crisis.

In 1991, the government tightened credit sharply, in reaction to the earlier rise in credit growth, and, in 1992, raised capital requirements.[13] In addition to the crises in Bank Duta and Bank Summa, other banks experienced financial distress. Nonperforming loans, revealed publicly for the first time in February 1994, were estimated at 21 percent of the state banks' assets and 16 percent for the system as a whole in October 1993 (World Bank 1994). In light of the preceding financial history, it seems likely that many of these nonperforming loans reflected the rapid credit expansion after the 1988 "free banking" reforms, the weakness of regulation and supervision at the time, and then the tight money policy of 1991.

2   INDIA

Developments Prior to Interest Rate Liberalization

The Reserve Bank of India (RBI) has directly regulated interest rates on deposits since 1964.[14,15] Generally speaking, in the 1970s and 1980s, term deposit rates were kept close to inflation except when inflation rose sharply, while the savings deposit rate has typically been kept much lower than inflation (see Figure 9.2, Tables 9.1 and 9.4). Rates paid by debentures,

---

[13] The government increased the capital adequacy ratio to 5 percent in March 1992 and 8 percent by December 1993, though the minimum capital remained very low. The public banks' capital remained much below these figures, taking into account their high levels of nonperforming assets (World Bank 1995b, p. 19).

[14] Previously deposit rates were set by a voluntary agreement among the major banks (Sen and Vaidya 1997, p. 12). Deposit insurance was established in 1962. It covered a fairly large percentage of deposits in the 1980s.

[15] The Reserve Bank also controls bank openings and branching (since 1949) and regulates bank liquidation. Bank failures were a major problem in the 1930s and 1940s, in the context of India's numerous small banks. The failure of two large banks in 1960 led to legislation that permitted RBI/government to take an active role in bank mergers. By 1969, the number of banks had dropped to 85, from 566 in 1951.

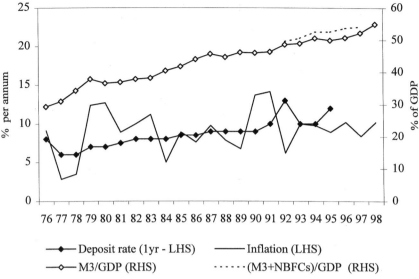

Figure 9.2. India: Monetary depth, interest rates, and inflation.

Table 9.1. Indicators of Indian Banking Policy, selected years 1968–90

Year	Deposit rate (1 year)	Loan ceiling or minimum rate[a]	Cash res. reqt. (% of deposits)	Statutory liquidity reqt[h]
1968	n.a.	n.a.	3	25[b]
1974 (Dec.)	8	16.5 Mar. 76[c]	4	32
1978 (Dec.)	6	15.0 (Mar.)[d], 18.0 (Sep. 79)	5	34
1981 (Dec.)	7.5	19.5 (Mar.)[c]	7.5	35
1983 (Nov.)	8	18.0 (Apr.)	8.5[e]	35
1984 (Sep.)	8	18.0	9.0[e]	36
1987 (Oct.)	9	16.5 (Apr.)	10	37.5
1989 (Jul.)	9	16.0 (Oct. 88)	15[f]	38
1990	9	16.0	15	38.5[g] (Sep.)

Notes: Months refer to dates when policies took effect. Interest rates are percent per annum.
[a] Refers to minimum rate effective October 1988, when ceiling rate was abolished and minimum rate imposed.
[b] Legal minimum.
[c] Includes 7 percent tax.
[d] Excludes 7 percent tax.
[e] Marginal requirement on deposit increases after November 1983 was 10 percent.
[f] Marginal requirements and special requirements on non-resident accounts removed.
[g] Legal maximum.
[h] In some cases marginal rate; percent of deposits.

convertible stock, and preference shares also were regulated, and new issues controlled, to limit competition with banks.

Despite the somewhat low "real" deposit rates, broad money (M3 as defined by RBI) was already 25 percent of GDP in the early 1970s and 45 percent of GDP in the late 1980s (Figure 9.2). The system's depth in the 1980s was similar to many middle income countries (World Bank 1989); it reflected a high national propensity to save and confidence that inflation would normally remain in single digits. Another factor was the extensive network of bank branches in rural areas, part of India's "social banking" policy that improved access of the rural population to banking services.[16]

The closed capital account was also probably a factor in financial depth. The Foreign Exchange Regulation Act of 1973 definitively closed the capital account by making it illegal for Indian residents to hold foreign currency, or engage in foreign currency transactions, including making and receiving payments with other than authorized dealers for other than specifically authorized purposes. The government controlled offshore borrowing and lending and intermediated inflows, much of which were official flows on concessional terms. Of course, there were leakages in the capital controls; not only through over- and underinvoicing of trade but also as a result of the large migrations of Indians overseas and the foreign currency deposit accounts that could be opened in the name of non-resident Indians.

Financial deepening essentially stopped in 1987–92 (Figure 9.2). Although there was no noticeable deterioration in real interest rates in 1987–89, savers may have reacted negatively to the risks arising from the deterioration of other macroeconomic indicators in this period, such as the current account, international reserves, and the government deficit. These risks materialized in the crisis of 1990–91.

Lending rates were also limited by RBI between 1962 and 1988, under its regulatory powers. For lending not subject to directed credit rules, the RBI set a ceiling rate that was generally positive in real terms compared to wholesale price inflation. However, only about 20 percent of deposits could be loaned at this rate, discussed as follows. And the ceiling rate was pushed down over the 1980s, before being converted into a floor rate in 1988 (see Table 9.1).

---

[16] Rural deposits rose from about 3 percent of deposits in 1969 to 13–15 percent in the early 1980s, after which their share leveled off. See Rosas (1973) and Fry (1988) for some evidence on the positive impact of branch office growth on money demand. Although some of the branches were not profitable and contributed to the oft-cited problems of overmaning, most Indian bankers now consider the branches as a good source of low-cost, stable deposits. However, the far flung branches, and poor telecommunications and infrastructure, made management difficult.

Rates on directed credit were also set, in increasing detail by size and type of loan – by April 1988 the list of priority lending rates covered ten pages in RBI (1998). Most of these rates were positive in real terms, except lending to agriculture. However, all the rates were below the levels that would have been set in a freer market, which would have taken into account the higher costs of priority sector lending and its higher rates of nonperformance.

Rates on the large required holdings of government debt also were held down – rates and yields typically were under 9 percent until 1986–87 when they were raised to the 10–11.5 percent range. Government debt was held, despite these low rates, because of the high liquidity requirements imposed on banks, provident funds, and insurance companies.

Regarding credit allocation, interest rates played little role before the 1990s. This was not only because rates were controlled, but because an increasing share of bank deposits was pre-empted for low-cost lending to cover public sector deficits. High reserve requirements provided the RBI with funds to buy government debt at low cost. Statutory liquidity requirements for banks and similar regulations on insurance companies forced them to place a large fraction of their assets in government debt. In addition, priority sector lending requirements were put in place after 1969 and increased over time. The large volume of priority lending and the regulations governing it in minute detail (including the specification of interest rates on loans by size and type) made income distribution an important objective in banking, and reduced the importance of allocation of credit to its most productive uses.

By 1990, about 80 percent of bank credit was subject to directed credit allocations. Cash reserves and statutory liquidity requirements had reached 53.5 percent of deposits (Table 9.1). About 55 percent of what was left was earmarked for priority and quasipriority sectors. Loan sizes, as well as interest rates, were defined by the type and sector of the loan according to predetermined coefficients (until 1997). Agriculture, especially small farmers, and "weaker" sectors were favored, as was public sector food procurement.

After political pressures led to bank nationalization of 1969, the government exerted much greater pressure to lend to priority sectors and was able to ensure that directives were carried out. However, the nationalization also had negative effects on the system. Managerial accountability was diluted not only by the extensive regulation, but by the political interference in banks' credit allocation. Pressures to meet credit targets increased, to the detriment of banks' efficiency and financial viability. Prudential standards for lending and collection, as well as for supervision, deteriorated. (See Appendix 2 and Ahluwalia 1997.)

Subsidies and Impact on the Economy of the Directed Credit System

The reserve liquidity and priority lending requirements not only allocated credit, they divided up the implicit subsidy from the repression of deposit rates and the cross-subsidy that was set up from "free" lending. Discussed as follows, this subsidy was fairly substantial.

One set of major beneficiaries of the directed credit system of the 1980s was the government through the cash reserve and statutory liquidity requirements (and the other entities eligible for the structural liquidity requirement). The cash reserve ratio, which reached 15 percent of deposits, paid at most an interest rate of 4 percent. This implied an implicit subsidy amounting to 0.5–1.0 percent of GDP, compared to the rates on loans or even the higher rates on government debt after 1986–87. The low interest rates on instruments eligible for the statutory liquidity requirement implied a further subsidy of between 0.5 percent and 1.0 percent of GDP.

The other main recipients of subsidies were farmers who received low-interest priority sector loans, bank employees (who received most of the personal loans), and those who were educated and unemployed who received loans under that program (which experienced oft-cited problems with selection of borrowers, limited impact on borrowers, and recoveries). The subsidies by sector can be estimated from Table 9.2, which shows the interest rate distribution of loans by sector, estimates the average sectoral loan rate, and thus permits an estimate of subsidies.

The estimated average interest rate on agricultural loans in 1988 averaged two percentage points less than the average interest rate on bank loans. Moreover, this figure understates the differential in favor of agriculture, because the table excludes loans under Rs. 25,000, which accounted for almost 30 percent of the total, carried low interest rate, and were heavily weighted toward agriculture. Personal loans, almost 5 percent of the table's total enjoyed an even greater interest subsidy at about 3 percent; many of these probably went to bank employees as a "perk" in a pattern of "rent-sharing" familiar in many banking systems. Average interest rates to small-scale industry were actually slightly higher than the average loan rate.

Low repayment rates also characterized priority sector loans. Firm data on loan performance is not available prior to 1992–93, when supervision was tightened, and even then data on differential performance of priority and nonpriority lending is not firm. However, recent estimates are that one-half of nonperforming loans came from the priority category, a disproportionate amount given that they represented only 40 percent of total loans (Reserve Bank of India, 1998). Assuming that eventually one-third of nonperforming asets, including lost interest, is recovered, this amounts

Table 9.2. Distribution of Scheduled Commercial Banks Lending by Sector and Interest Rate (% of Total Loans over Rs. 25,000, June 1988)

Interest rate range / Sector	<6 %	6–10 %	10–12 %	12–14 %	14–15 %	15–16 %	16–17 %	17–18 %	>18% %	Total loans to sector	Mean interest rate
Agriculture	0.11	2.17	1.11	6.74	0.38	0.28	0.76	0.12	0.02	11.69	12.11
Industry	0.22	3.40	2.07	9.26	5.08	4.50	25.76	7.69	0.45	58.44	15.08
Small-scale	0.06	0.64	0.44	4.84	1.24	2.77	4.87	1.28	0.09	16.23	14.68
Med. & large	0.16	2.76	1.63	4.42	3.83	1.74	20.89	6.41	0.36	42.21	15.24
Transport	0.03	0.03	0.32	3.38	0.75	0.07	0.38	0.26	0.01	5.23	13.54
Personal loans	2.19	1.05	0.51	1.21	0.91	0.17	1.45	0.31	0.05	7.85	11.26
Trade	0.04	0.95	0.50	2.86	0.50	0.41	4.66	1.49	0.37	11.78	14.72
Others	0.18	0.58	0.51	1.21	0.41	0.15	1.48	0.38	0.03	4.94	13.52
Total	2.77	8.20	5.01	24.70	8.02	5.58	34.53	10.25	0.92	100.00	14.24
Estimated interest paid (Rs. bn.)[a]	0.72	2.66	2.38	13.88	5.03	3.74	24.64	7.76	0.74	61.55	

[a] Estimated interest rates and interest payments are calculated using a weighted average of the midpoints of the interest ranges, and applied to the total of loans (Rs. 432 bn.) (excluding bills and foreign business). Data excludes loans under Rs. 25,000, which totaled an estimated Rs. 172 bn.
Source: RBI data.

to a further effective average subsidy of 2–3 percent p.a. on priority loans, relative to nonpriority loans. [17]

These rough estimates suggest that the total subsidy to the public sector and to the recipients of priority sector lending may have amounted to at least 2–3 percent of GDP.

In terms of access to credit, the priority sector schemes certainly increased access of agriculture and small scale industry. In 1968, these sectors accounted for only 2.9 percent and 6.9 percent of credit respectively; by 1987 they accounted for 17 percent and 15 percent respectively. This increased access was at the expense of bank credit to medium and large scale industry and wholesale trade. Medium and large scale firms' share of credit fell from 60 percent to 44 percent over the same period. But, the real losers were probably medium-scale industry; large-scale firms were able to raise funds through bonds and equity issues in the capital market and also took small amounts of deposits (in amounts limited by their capital). Some of these funds were probably used to finance the suppliers to and distributors of large firms – large scale firms' loans and advances were 20–25 percent of their assets, according to RBI surveys.

The development impact of the directed credit system on the economy and the priority sectors is unclear. The 1970s were characterized by what has often been termed the "Hindu Rate of Growth" – around 3.5 percent p.a. Growth increased dramatically in the 1980s, averaging over 5.5 percent p.a., but that growth was built upon increasing public sector deficits that were unsustainable. The crisis of 1990–91 derailed the economy, until reforms led to a rebound. The capital intensity of growth in the 1980s was much higher than in East Asia, as measured by the marginal capital to output ratio over the decade (World Bank 2000).

The priority sector lending program to agriculture and small scale industry seems to have functioned largely as a transfer program, with little impact on production. The spread of banking to the rural areas certainly did had positive effects, especially through its provision of a safe haven for savings and reduction in the power of the money lenders. However, the credits it made available seem to have had only a marginal impact on agricultural growth after the adoption of Green Revolution technology. India's overall agricultural growth in the 1970s and 1980s was about median among developing countries. Studies suggest that the directed credit had little impact on growth and was a poor substitute for the physical inputs needed for growth, rather much of the credit seems to have gone

[17] In some cases and periods, banks were able to recover part of their losses from the loan guarantee funds, as well as directly from the borrowers, but the loan guarantee funds ran substantial deficits. Legal efforts to recovery delinquent loans usually took ten years or more, and then might fail.

to increase the capital intensity of production (see, for example, Bin-swanger and Khandker 1995). Moreover, much of the commercial bank credit to agriculture went to larger farmers – for example in 1985 about one-third of the credit went to farms over five acres, and 50 percent was in credits over Rps. 25,000. Moreover, these figures understate the concentration of agricultural credit because of families taking credits under different names. The average subsidy to the farms over five acres on term loans, including arrears, amounted to an estimated Rps. 3000, roughly equivalent to the per capita GDP. These outcomes are similar to Latin American programs of directed credit to agriculture (Gonzalez-Vega 1984). The Integrated Rural Development Programme (IRDP) for low income borrowers was plagued by arrears, and seems to have had only limited impact on the borrowers in the majority of cases; there were also leakages into finders' fees and providers of livestock for the in-kind lending program (World Bank 1988, pp. 91–98). Regarding lending to small-scale industry, as with agriculture, those firms that accessed low cost credit seem to have used it to adopt more capital intensive technology, rather than expand and increase employment (Sandesara 1988). Of course, that outcome probably reflected not only the low cost credits but the incentives to remain small, which included favorable tax treatment, less strict labor regulations, and reservation of numerous products for small-scale producers.

Liberalization of Interest Rates and Credit Allocation; Tightening of Regulation and Supervision

Beginning in 1992, India gradually liberalized most interest rates. The liberalization was part of the stabilization and liberalization programs that began in response to the balance of payments crisis of 1991–92, and followed the recommendations of a number of government committees, especially the Narasimham (1991) committee.

Term deposit rates were liberalized by first setting an overall ceiling. This ceiling rate was then adjusted according to the macroeconomic situation from over the period April 1992–October 1995. Rates on various types of deposits were gradually freed, starting with the longer maturities, from October 1995–October 1997 (see Tables 9.3 and 9.4 for details).

For rates on loans, the shift from a ceiling rate to a floor rate in 1988 had allowed rates on "free" lending to be more market determined. After 1992, rates on priority lending were also gradually allowed to be set more freely, and the number of categories (and small differentials) were reduced sharply. In October 1994, rates on loans exceeding Rs. 200,000 were freed. In April 1998, rates on loans under Rs. 200,000 were freed, provided they not exceed the prime rate that the bank was now allowed to set. Finally,

Table 9.3. India: Indicators of Financial Liberalization 1990–97

Year	Deposit rate (1 year)	Loan minimum rate[a]	Cash reserve requirement[d]	Statut. liq. reqt.[d]
1990	9	16.0	15	38.5[b] Sep.
1991	10, July; 12, Oct.	19.0 Apr.	15	38.5
1992	<13, Apr.; <12, Oct.	19.0	15	30
1993	<11, Mar.; <10, Sep.	17.0 Mar.	14 May	25[c] Sep.
1994	<10	14.0 Mar., Free Oct.	15 Aug.	25
1995	<11, Feb.; <12, Apr.	Free	14 Dec.	25
1996	Free, Jul.	Free	13 May, 11 Nov.	25
1997	Free	Free	10 Jan.	25

Notes: Months refer to dates after which policies took effect.
Interest rates are percent per annum.
[a] Effective October 1988, ceiling rate abolished and minimum rate imposed.
[b] Legal maximum.
[c] Legal minimum.
[d] Percent of deposits.

interest rates on government debt were increasingly determined in auctions. However, the rules of the auction effectively allowed RBI to set the rate. And, government debt probably carries a lower rate than what would occur in a completely free market because of the Statutory Liquidity Requirement, the low-risk and the low-capital requirement associated with government debt, and the possibility of investigation of public sector banks' lending outside the public sector. Nonetheless, by mid-1998, the only interest rate controls applied were to savings deposit rates, Small Savings (postal savings) rates, Non Resident Indian foreign currency deposit rates, and the ceiling on loans under Rs. 200,000.

Additional measures over the post-1992 period liberalized credit allocation,[18] introduced more competition in banking,[19] liberalized the capital account partially through easing of restrictions on inward portfolio investment and external debt and equity issues by Indian firms. Capital market

[18] These measures included a reduction in the cash reserve and statutory liquidity requirements and broadened the eligibility for the priority sector lending requirement.
[19] Notably by the licensing of nine new private and twenty-two new foreign banks, easing of restrictions on foreign banks, and the phasing out of restrictions on forcing consortium lending led by development banks and on borrowers' switching banks. Nonbank financial corporations were also allowed to grow with less directed credit requirements and limited prudential regulation and supervision.

issues were liberalized and the regulatory agency strengthened significantly. Bank regulation was strengthened by raising capital requirements to Basel standards by 1995 and toughening standards for income recognition and provisioning; supervision was improved and CAMEL rating was introduced in 1998. (For further discussion of the reforms, see the Narasimham Committee reports 1998; Reddy 1999; World Bank 2000.)

The Impact of Interest Rate and Other Financial Liberalization in India

India's financial liberalization was accompanied by a stabilization program and liberalization of trade and investment restrictions. Furthermore, all of these measures took place over a number of years. These points must be borne in mind when considering the assessment of financial liberalization below.

After the pause in 1987–92, the growth of M3:GDP resumed. However the rate of increase was less than in the early 1980s, partly reflecting growth of nonbank financial corporations' (NBFCs), whose deposits are not in M3 (see Figure 9.2). However, following the collapse of a large NBFC in 1997 and the confirmation that NBFC deposits were not insured by the government, NBFC deposits declined. RBI set the overall parameters for the winding up of many NBFCs and imposed much tighter regulations on the remaining NBFCs.

Despite the liberalization, banks continued to hold about 40 percent of their assets in government debt.[20] This of course largely reflects the continued high government debt stock and the continued high fiscal deficit. However, the reforms made government debt an attractive investment for the banks, with a reasonable yields and minimal capital requirement (zero until the increase in risk weighting to 2.5 percent in 1998). Some foreign banks too find the government debt market, newly open to them, to be attractive. Finally, public bank managers find holdings of government debt attractive – it is free both from any risk of default and the scrutiny that nongovernment lending may receive from the Central Bureau of Investigation.

The main increases in funding for the private sector after the liberalization came from the NBFCs (including leasing and consumer finance),

---

[20] In the late 1980s, the cash reserve ratio and assets eligible for the statutory liquidity requirement represented a higher percentage of deposits than currently. However, part of the reform process was to remove nongovernment liabilities from eligibility for the statutory liquidity requirement. The decline in the rate of the statutory liquidity requirement thus affected mainly these nongovernment liabilities. Moreover, banks began to hold government debt in excess of required amounts. Hence the cash reserve requirement plus government debt holdings actually represent about the same percentage of deposits now as in the 1980s (World Bank 2000).

the growth of the stock market, and the access to foreign markets. Banks also became more active in consumer lending at the end of the 1990s. NBFCs were important in the mid-1990s, but their deposit contraction after 1997 has reduced their contribution. The stock market, which already had numerous listings, experienced a further increase in listings after liberalization, especially as foreign portfolio investors entered the market and increased the weighting of India in their portfolios. Finally, increased GDRs and foreign bond issues, though still tightly limited by the government, provided additional finance for some of the larger private and public sector firms.

As real and financial liberalization proceeded, India recovered surprisingly quickly from the 1990–91 crisis and then experienced a private investment-led boom of unprecedented proportions – growth averaged about 7.7 percent p.a. from 1994–95 to 1996–97. Investment also increased, but by less, and a fall in the ICOR suggests higher investment productivity in the aggregate (see World Bank 2000, for a discussion).

The proportion of nonperforming assets (NPAs) peaked even before interest rates were really liberalized, reaching about 12 percent of total assets in March 1993. Since 1993, the share of NPAs has declined to about 7.5 percent, and NPAs loans net of provisions were under 3 percent of assets, in March 1999.[21] Thus any financial distress in the banks after liberalization was probably more a reflection of the overhang of bad loans that had not been recognized, the tightening of regulation and supervision, and the slowdown associated with the 1991 stabilization, rather than the liberalization of interest rates.

Financial liberalization with only limited strengthening of regulation, did, however, appear to play a role in the problems in the financial sector outside commercial banking. Nonbank financial corporations took advantage of eased regulatory treatment to expand rapidly and provide credit to new areas, but then were hit by withdrawals after the collapse of a prominent corporation in 1997. Similarly, the Indian stock market which enjoyed a boom and a massive increase in initial public offerings (IPOs), then declined in 1997 and 1998. Many of the recent IPOs are failing to satisfy even the requirements to maintain listing, let alone being traded. Finally, the industrial recession that began in 1996–97, and greater competition, internally from the increased industrial capacity in some sectors and externally from East Asia and trade liberalization, limited the reduction in nonperforming assets from falling in banks and development finance institutions.

---

[21] Note that these NPA ratios are reduced substantially by the large share of government debt in bank portfolios.

3 COMPARING REPRESSION AND LIBERALIZATION
IN INDIA AND INDONESIA

Populist politics and the prevailing political and economic doctrines of development led both India in the early 1970s and Indonesia in the mid-1970s to repress interest rates and direct a substantial amount of credit to the public sector and favored groups. However, the two countries' different approach to financial repression led to a very different history of deposit mobilization.

Indonesia, as part of the stabilization of hyperinflation from 1968 to 1973, liberalized interest rates and the capital account. M2 rose relative to GDP, in contrast to the prevailing orthodox view that capital account convertibility would reduce deposits. However, from 1974 to 1983, Indonesia switched to a policy of financial repression that included holding down deposit interest rates at the state banks; tightly limiting the growth of new banks, bank branches, and nonbank institutions; and, perhaps most importantly, maintaining bank-by-bank limits on credit, thereby discouraging deposit mobilization even by private banks not subject to interest ceilings. As financial repression took hold, M2:GDP stagnated. The Indonesian central bank remained the dominant institution, doling out low-cost, directed credits. The larger private enterprises also used offshore lenders to meet their credit needs.

In India, in contrast, the deposit rate was kept close to zero in real terms in most years, the number of bank branches were expanded massively as part of the social banking policy and banks were allowed to lend what they raised. This policy combination, together with a high private propensity to save, gave India a fairly deep financial system. India's extensive rural branch network provided the rural population a safe place for their savings and an alternative to money lenders. However, India's M3 to GDP ratio stagnated in the late 1980s, as the impact of additional branches declined and the macroeconomic indicators deteriorated.

Both Indonesia and India directed credit extensively, and used high reserve requirements to obtain part of the resources for directed credit, i.e., to allow the central bank to purchase government bonds in India and to discount loans in Indonesia. The other sources of funding for the countries' low-interest, directed credit programs were different. In Indonesia (as for other oil exporters) petroleum revenues were channeled through the banking system. Lacking such natural resource rents, India funded its directed credits with official external borrowing and cross subsidies through a complicated, central bank-run system of required reserves, priority lending, and interest rate regulations.

In both India and Indonesia the public sector was a major beneficiary of the interest rate repression and directed credit allocation. In Indonesia it was mainly the public enterprises, because the Indonesian "balanced budget rule" prohibited Government domestic borrowing. Much of the directed credit appears to have been related to the state oil company's external default in 1975 and the company's investments. In India, both the public enterprises and government benefited; the government preempted an increasing share of loanable funds in order to fund a large and growing deficit.

Another beneficiary in both countries was agriculture and government-run price support schemes, particularly in the early years of directed credit. Small-scale firms also received directed credit in both countries. In India, the increasing demands of the public sector for funding eventually even reduced the share of priority sectors in the deposits. In both countries, the main losers in credit access were middle-sized firms; large firms had access to the capital market in the case of India and to offshore financing in Indonesia.

In India, rough estimates suggest that the subsidy going to public sector borrowing through the cash reserve requirement and the statutory liquidity requirement may have been 1–2 percent of GDP. The cross subsidy to the priority sector was roughly equivalent to a further 1 percent of GDP annually, mostly in much higher rates of default on debt service. These figures probably reflect the limits imposed by political pressures from those paying the cross subsidy and the need to keep banks solvent. Though the subsidy is large compared to India's fiscal deficit, it is much smaller than in Latin America, for example, where high inflation often wiped out the real value of loans with controlled rates.

The development benefits of repressed interest rates and directed credit appear limited. Initially, agriculture benefited from the allocation of more credit, which helped the Green Revolution get started in both countries. However, later analyses suggest no further major effects on agricultural growth. The programs became more of a transfer mechanism through bank loans with low repayment rates rather than a credit program. Concerns also have been expressed about "leakages" into finders' fees and so on. Studies of both agriculture and small-scale industry in India suggest that low-cost credits did not lead to much of an increase in size or employment, but rather to the adoption of more capital-intensive production methods.

The directed credit allocation mechanism also hampered the two countries' financial system in a number of other ways. Public banks dominated the system in the two countries, in Indonesia as a heritage of independence and limits on new banks (until 1988) and in India as a result of nationalization. Channeling of directed credit through the public banks left the credit allocation mechanism more open to political interference and increasingly turned it into a transfer program. Moreover, civil servant bankers had little incentive to evaluate loans carefully or collect on them, their main objective became meeting targets of credit programs.

In both countries, the central bank became involved in the minutiae of loan decisions by issuing detailed regulations fixing rates and volumes of credits, including, in India, ratios of credit for various types of activities. In an effort to enforce these regulations, banking supervision in the two countries increasingly focused on checking the implementation of the allocative regulations, to the detriment of prudential analysis of the quality of lending or public bank capitalization or profitability.

Interest rate and financial liberalization followed balance of payments problems in both countries, and formed part of wider macroeconomic stabilization and structural reform programs. In Indonesia the crisis followed the drop of oil prices in the mid-1980s. In India the crisis followed the excesses of the late 1980s and early 1990s. Broadly speaking the rationale for liberalization in both cases seems to have been to increase resource mobilization and credit going to the private sector. In both cases devaluation, reduction in public sector spending and in public deficits, as well as deregulation of trade and domestic investment accompanied the financial sector liberalization.

The two countries' approach to financial sector liberalization was, however, quite different. India liberalized interest rates gradually from 1992–98, and lowered reserve requirements and liquidity requirements. Priority sector lending was liberalized only to the extent that interest rates were liberalized and additional types of credit were made eligible. India also strengthened prudential regulation and supervision of banks at the same time. Indonesia freed interest rates (at the state banks) "overnight" in mid-1983, and announced that about 50 percent of directed credit would not be renewed (though de facto renewals continued until 1990). Regulation and supervision only began to improve in the 1990s.

Following interest rate liberalization, deposit mobilization grew rapidly in Indonesia and resumed its stalled growth in India. The realignment of the exchange rate and the general deregulation probably also played a part in stimulating deposit mobilization. By the mid-1990s, Indonesia's ratio of M2:GDP was similar to India, despite Indonesia's open capital account, although India's capital market was still far larger.

In both countries, credit allocation changed after liberalization, but not always in the ways that fit standard theory.

- In Indonesia, despite the announcement that directed credit would be cut, low-cost liquidity credits continued until 1990, maintaining the old beneficiaries of directed credit. Nonetheless, expansion of the private banks increased credit access to a wider group of borrowers who used the resources more efficiently. The liberalization allowed

Indonesia's BRI to develop its well-known small-scale lending program.

* In India, despite the drop in the liquidity requirement, banks continued to invest nearly the same percentage of their portfolio in public sector debt, because of the exigencies of funding the large outstanding public debt stock and a large continuing public sector deficit. However, these purchases were now more voluntary and reflected the higher, auction-set interest rates on government debt. Increased funding for the private sector came from growth in nonbanks, capital markets, and external flows through the capital market and overseas issues. Priority sector lending remained about the same percent of credit but carried higher interest rates, it also included more export lending as a result of growth of foreign banks.

Growth picked up in both countries after interest liberalization and there is some indication that investment productivity increased. It is worth noting again that this occurred twice in Indonesia in the context of an open capital account, which reversed the recommended sequence of liberalization with no apparent effects (as was the case in Uruguay).[22] However, it is difficult to separate the impact of financial liberalization from the other elements of reform, especially in India. Identification of the results of liberalization are also clouded by the impact of stabilization programs, developments in the international macroeconomic environment, and the length of the liberalization process in India.

While insufficient regulation and supervision of new entrants caused problems in banks in Indonesia, in NBFCs in India, the relation between financial liberalization and financial distress was otherwise fairly tenuous.

* Indonesia's 1983 interest rate liberalization probably had little to do with either the financial sector problems of the early 1990s or the 1997 crisis; other developments in the intervening years probably played a much greater role. The 1988 bank liberalization allowed numerous small banks, some owned by well-connected parties, to open with little capital and under minimal regulation. Regulations did not begin to be tightened until 1991 and enforcement remained limited. While some weak loans may have been rolled over for years, the real land mines in bank balance sheets probably developed from the sharp tightening of credit in the early 1990s. Another factor in the poor quality of lending probably was the process by which the failures of Bank Summa and Bank Duta in the early 1990s were handled, which suggested that depositors and external lenders would be covered and political

---

[22] See Cole and Slade (1996) for Indonesia, and De Melo and Hanson (1983) for Uruguay.

Table 9.4. India: Liberalization of Deposit Interest Rates 1989–98

Effective Date	Savings deposits	45 days to 1 year[a]	1–2 years	2–3 years	≥3 years
Oct. 11, 1989	5.0	8.0	9.0	10.0	10.0
Oct. 10, 1990	5.0	8.0	9.0	10.0	11.0
Apr. 13, 1991	5.0	8.0	9.0	10.0	12.0
Jul. 4, 1991	5.0	9.0	10.0	11.0	13.0
Oct. 9, 1991	5.0	11.0	12.0	12.0	13.0
Apr. 22, 1992	6.0	———————— ≤13.0 ————————			
Oct. 9, 1992	6.0	———————— ≤12.0 ————————			
Mar. 1, 1993	6.0	———————— ≤11.0 ————————			
July 1, 1993	5.0	———————— ≤11.0 ————————			
Sep. 2, 1993	5.0	———————— ≤10.0 ————————			
Nov. 1, 1994	4.5	———————— ≤10.0 ————————			
Feb. 10, 1995	4.5	———————— ≤11.0 ————————			
Apr. 18, 1995	4.5	———————— ≤12.0 ————————			
Oct. 1, 1995	4.5	——— ≤12.0 ———		——— Free ———	
Jul. 2, 1996	4.5	≤11.0	——————— Free ———————		
Oct. 21, 1996	4.5	≤10.0	——————— Free ———————		
Apr. 16, 1997	4.5	≤9.0%[b]	——————— Free ———————		
Jun. 26, 1997	4.5	≤8.0%[b]	——————— Free ———————		
Oct. 22, 1997	4.5	———————————— Free ————————————			
Mar./Apr., 1998	4.5	Banks allowed to set different rates for same maturity deposits and set penalties for early withdrawal.			

Notes: Excludes nonresident deposits. Rates in percent per annum.
[a] After July 2, 1996 applies to term deposits of 30 days and up to 1 year.
[b] Bank rate minus 2.0 percent.
Source: *Reserve Bank of India*.

connections, not lending quality, were important. Finally, it is important to note that a large part of Indonesia's financial crisis reflected direct offshore lending to Indonesian corporates by international banks. These banks chose not to book their loans through their Indonesian offices and their lending decisions reflected their own internal decisions, uninfluenced by weak regulation and supervision in Indonesia and in full knowledge of the extent of corruption in the country. Indonesian borrowers encountered severe difficulties in repaying these foreign currency loans when the rupiah depreciated sharply after the collapse of the Thai baht in mid-1997, in the context of the attempts to keep interest rates in Indonesia down, the runs on the banks and the currency that intensified after banks were closed under the IMF program, the deterioration of the president's health and political status, the limited compliance with the IMF program, and investors negative reactions to the 1998–99 budget speech. The companies that were bankrupted by the rising local currency value of their dollar debt also began defaulting on local currency debt. It is also worth noting that Indonesian banks' direct exposure to dollar liabilities was relatively less than in Thailand or Korea, partly because of limits on foreign currency borrowing by the state banks and the limits on foreign currency exposure linked to capital requirements.

- In India, tightening of regulation and supervision led to large measured nonperforming assets, even though interest rate liberalization had barely begun. Over the next few years, both nonperforming assets were reduced relative to bank assets and provisions were increased, while interest rates were liberalized. Problems did develop among the nonbank financial corporations in 1997–98, but this seems related to the limited regulation and supervision of that sector of the financial market. The government appropriately denied any ex post guarantee of NBFC deposits, so the sector's problems did not result in any direct cost to the government. Problems also have developed with some of the industrial loans of the banks and the development of finance institutions, but this seems related to the shakeout after liberalization and the industrial slowdown, rather than interest rate liberalization per se.

APPENDIX 1: INDONESIA'S DIRECTED CREDIT PROGRAMS IN THE 1970s AND EARLY 1980s

Indonesia's complex directed programs included the following (*cf.* Cole and Slade 1996, pp. 83–88):

- Credits to Bulog, the public procurement agency charged with stabilization of food prices, particularly rice prices, both directly from the central bank and from BRI (refinanced by the central bank), during the years when Bulog built up its network.
- The Bimas program was established in 1969 to supply inputs to farmers, mainly rice farmers, to encourage adoption of the new rice technology. Initially it involved direct payments from the central bank to foreign suppliers, then distribution to farmers of preset packages of inputs and cash that were to be repaid after the harvest at local units (*unit desai*) of BRI at 12 percent interest. However, the preset packages often did not match the farmers' preferences and were subject to leakages from excessive purchases and poor quality. Observers also consider that the low-cost loans also were used for many nonagricultural purposes. Repayments were weak, particularly in years of bad harvests, and defaults reached 60 percent in the 1980s

(Soeksmono 1994, p. 294). To meet targets and because eligibility
was limited to those who repaid loans, the distributions of inputs
increasingly went to larger farmers, who in turn often resold them,
which led to further charges of corruption. Inmas replaced Bimas
in the late 1970s; it allowed flexible input packages and credit was
separately approved by the *unit desa*. The program contributed
to Indonesia's Green Revolution, which eliminated the country's
chronic rice imports. But, "BRI was continuously plagued by financial manipulation by dishonest staff in collusion with borrowers or
government officials" (Soeksmono 1994, p. 295). BRI required con-
tinuous injections of funds from the government, and was bankrupt
in 1984.

• Investment credits were begun in the late 1960s, as part of Indonesia's first development plan, to support investment. The program
channeled low-interest loans through the state commercial banks,
Bapindo, and in the latter stages of the program, private banks
to some degree. The loans involved various terms; in 1982 the
typical rate was 12 percent, with rediscounts typically available at
3–4 percent. Rediscount proportions varied widely, over time and
between loans; the average for all loans was 43 percent in 1982 (Balino
and Sundararajan 1986). The loans could go to public and private
enterprises; a large percentage went to conglomerates. Since the rates
were well below deposit rates in the private banks, substantial profits
could be made on access to these credits and this undoubtedly led to
corruption. Recovery rates were poor. The banks had little incentive
to either evaluate the borrowers or pursue collections since a) much
of the loan had been rediscounted with the central bank, which probably could be made to share in the loss, and b) a large percentage
of the loan was covered by a government credit insurance scheme
(Askrindo) for a one-time fee of 3 percent, half of which was paid
by the central bank. (Askrindo was reported to have paid out Rps.
23.5 trillion between 1971 and 1992, equivalent to over $10 billion at
the 1992 exchange rate and thus much more over the period. "Light
at the end of Askrindo's Tunnel," *Indonesia Business Weekly*, cited in
Cole and Slade 1996, p. 96.) Despite these possibilities of avoiding
losses on the loans, Bapindo went bankrupt in the 1980s. In the aftermath of the pressures to distribute the oil revenues, two small programs solely for nonethnic Chinese businessmen were set up in 1974
to fund small-scale firms' investment and working capital, KIK and
KMKP. Their terms were similar to investment credits – 12 percent,
with rediscount of 80 percent at 3 percent, and insurance of 75
percent for a 3 percent up-front fee; recoveries on these loans were
also low (see Soeksmono 1994).

• Credits to public enterprises direct from the central bank were another type of low-cost credits. Credit extended to Pertamina following the 1975 bailout was a major element in these credits (some of which covered obligations related to the Krakatau Steel Company) accounting for as much as half of directed credit in some years (Cole and Slade 1996, p. 84).

APPENDIX 2: THE CAUSES AND IMPACT OF BANK NATIONALIZATION IN INDIA

In 1955, the State Bank of India was created by the nationalization of the Imperial Bank; eight major state banks were added to it in 1959, to form the State Bank Group. In 1969, nationalization of the fourteen largest private banks increased the share of public sector banks in total deposits from 31 percent to 86 percent. In 1980, six more banks were nationalized, raising the public banks' share of deposits to 92 percent.

The nationalization of 1969 was the culmination of political pressures to use the banks as public instruments of development and reflected the statist development philosophy of the times – the preamble to the Banking Companies (Acquisition and Transfer of Undertakings) Act of 1969 justifies the nationalization in terms of the "need to control the commanding heights of the economy and to meet progressively . . . the needs of development of the economy in conformity with national policy and objectives." The Fourth Plan (1969) emphasized the need to finance the Green Revolution. It also called for massive deposit mobilization through branching and for increased lending to small-scale industry and the creditworthy poor. It was thought that national output would increase as a result of such lending to sectors that had been neglected by traditional banking, foreshadowing concerns of the more recent credit rationing literature.

Nationalization also reflected a populist attack on the banks' links to conglomerates, their lending to related parties, their neglect of the "weaker" sectors, and, in general, what was considered a diversion of the community's saving to increase profits and economic power while neglecting economic and social objectives set out in the plans (Business India 1997; Sen and Vaidya 1997).

The priority sector lending policy was a manifestation of the state-directed philosophy of development then prevalent; nationalization increased the ability of the government to carry it out. In addition, nationalization increased the role of political interference in individual loans. In the late 1980s, these pressures culminated in loan "fairs" at which loans were given to masses of individuals at the behest of local politicians, and in debt forgiveness programs.

An important goal of the nationalized bank's management became meeting priority credit targets. Less attention was paid to collection, or to the usual measures of bank performance such as exposures, maturity mismatches, efficiency profits, and so on, than would be typical of private banks. Selection of management reflected the civil service hierarchy and rules, rather than contribution to the bank's performance. High-level appointments also were affected by political interference and appointees remained in office only a short time. Overmaning developed and unionization of the sector contributed to slow improvements in technology – there was even an industrial action against calculators in the late 1980s – and deterioration of service.

Another aspect of the directed credit system was that RBI increasingly focused supervisory resources on trying to ensure that the banks' funds were allocated according to the priority sector requirements and to the numerous regulations defining the allowable volume of lending in relation to various parameters. The "civil servant bankers" felt obliged to comply in order to avoid legal action, which stripped them of initiative to vary lending in response to individual circumstances of the borrower. Larger loans had to be approved fairly high up the managerial ladder, increasing the possibility of political interference. Finally, RBI also initiated a system in which it had to approve loans to large borrowers; until 1988 this approval was required prior to lending; from then until 1997 these loans were subject to ex post approval.

REFERENCES

Ahluwalia, M. 1997. "Governance Issues in India's Economic Reforms." Workshop on Governance Issues in South Asia, Yale University. *Mimeo.*

Asher, M. and A. Booth. 1992. " Fiscal Policy." In A. Booth (ed.), *The Oil Boom and After: Indonesian Economic Policy and Performance in the Soeharto Era*, pp. 42–76. New York: Oxford University Press.

Balino, T. and V. Sundararajan. 1986. "Financial Reforms in Indonesia." In H.S. Cheng (ed.), *Financial Policy and Reform in the Pacific Basin Countries*, pp. 191–220. Lexington University Press.

Binswanger, H. and S. Khandakar. 1995. "The Impact of Formal Finance on the Rural Economy of India." *Journal of Development Studies* 32(2):234–65.

Biro Pusat Statistik. 1997. *Statistics During 50 Years of Indonesian Independence.* Jakarta.

Bresnan, J. 1993. *Managing Indonesia: The Modern Political Economy.* New York: Columbia University Press.

Business India. 1997. "Coming Full Circle." August 11–24.

Chant, J. and M. Pangestu. 1994. "An Assessment of Financial Reform in Indonesia 1983–90." In G. Caprio, I. Atiyas, and J. Hanson (eds.), *Financial Reform, Theory and Experience*, pp. 223–275. New York: Cambridge University Press.

Cole, D. and B. Slade. 1996. *Building a Modern Financial System: The Indonesian Experience*. New York: Cambridge University Press.

De Melo, J. and J. Hanson. 1983. "The Uruguayan Experience with Liberalization and Stabilization, 1974–1981." *Journal of Interamerican Studies and World Affairs* 25(4): 477–508.

Fry, M. 1988. *Money, Interest, and Banking in Economic Development*. Baltimore: Johns Hopkins University Press.

Gelb, A. ed. 1988. *Oil Windfalls: Blessing or Curse*. Oxford: Oxford University Press.

Gonzalez-Vega, C. 1984. "The Credit Rationing Behavior of Agricultural Lenders: The Iron Law of Interest Rate Restrictions." In D. Adams, D.H. Graham, and J.D. von Pischke (eds.), *Undermining Rural Development with Cheap Credit*, pp. 78–95. Boulder, CO: Westview Press.

Hanna, D. 1996. "Indonesian Experience with Financial Sector Reform." *World Bank Discussion Paper* No. 237.

Harris, J., F. Schiantarelli, and M. Siregar. 1994. "The Effect of Financial Liberalization on the Capital Structure and Investment Decisions of Indonesian Manufacturing Establishments." *The World Bank Economic Review* 8:17–47.

Hill, H. 1996. *The Indonesian Economy Since 1966*. New York: Cambridge University Press.

Martokoesoemo, Soeksmono B. 1994. "Small Scale Finance: Lessons from Indonesia." In R. McLeod, *Indonesia Assessment 1994: Finance as a Key Sector in Indonesia's Development*, pp. 292–313. Singapore: Australian National University and Institute of Southeast Asian Studies.

Mundell, R. 1968. *International Economics*. London: Macmillan.

Narasimham, M. (Chairman). 1991. *Report of the Committee on Financial System*. New Delhi: Reserve Bank of India.

Narasimham, M. (Chairman). 1998. *Report of the Committee on Banking Sector Reforms*. New Delhi: Reserve Bank of India.

Reddy, Y.V. 1999. "Financial Reform: Review and Prospects." *Reserve Bank of India Bulletin* LII(1): 33–94.

Reserve Bank of India (RBI). 1998. *Report on Trend and Progress in Banking*. New Delhi.

Rosas, L.E. 1973. "Inflation and Financial Development." Unpublished Ph.D. dissertation. Brown University.

Sandesara, J.C. 1988. "Small Industry Development Programmes in India – Efficiency Explanations and Lessons: Some Field Studies." In K.B. Suri (ed.), *Small Scale Enterprises in Industrial Development: The Indian Experience*. New Delhi: Sage Publications.

Schiantarelli, F., I. Atiyas, G. Caprio, J. Harris, and A. Weiss. 1994. "Credit Where It Is Due? A Review of the Macro and Micro Evidence on the Real Effects of Financial Reform." In G. Caprio, I Atiyas, and J. Hanson (eds.), *Financial Reform: Theory and Experience*, pp. 64–81. New York: Cambridge University Press.

Sen, K. and R.R. Vaidya. 1997. *The Process of Financial Liberalization in India*. New Delhi: Oxford University Press.

Woo, W.T., B. Glassburner, and A. Nasution. 1994. *Macroeconomic Policies, Crises, and Long-Term Economic Growth in Indonesia, 1965–1990*. Washington, DC: World Bank.

Woo, W.T. and A. Nasution. 1989. "Indonesian Economic Policies and Their Relation to External Debt Management." In J. Sachs and S. Collins (eds.) *Developing Country Debt and Economic Performance, Vol. 3*, pp. 17–149. Chicago: University of Chicago Press.

World Bank. 1985. *Indonesia: Policies and Prospects for Long Term Financial Development*. Report No. 5501-IND.

World Bank. 1988. *India: Poverty Employment and Social Services*. Report No. 7617-IN.

World Bank. 1989. *Financial Systems and Development*. World Development Report. New York: Oxford University Press.

World Bank. 1994. *Indonesia: Stability, Growth and Equity in Repelita VI*. Report No. 12857-IND.

World Bank. 1995a. *The Emerging Asian Bond Market*.

World Bank. 1995b. *Indonesia: Improving Efficiency and Equity: Changes in the Public Sector's Role*. Report No. 14006-IN.

World Bank. 1996. *Indonesia: Dimensions of Growth*. Report No. 15383-IND.

World Bank. 1997. *Indonesia: Sustaining Growth with Equity*. Report No. 16433-IND.

World Bank. 2000. *India: Reducing Poverty, Accelerating Development*. New Delhi: Oxford University Press.

10

Reforming Finance in a Low Income Country: Uganda

Irfan Aleem and Louis Kasekende[1]

INTRODUCTION

In 1992, the government of Uganda embarked on an ambitious program of financial system liberalization as a means of consolidating the gains achieved during the economic recovery program (ERP) it had initiated in 1987. The reforms had two main objectives: to facilitate macroeconomic stability and to promote GDP growth by enhancing the efficiency of the financial system. The liberalization process involved policy and institutional reforms aimed at reducing the role of the government in the financial sector and allowing the market to play a greater role in the allocation of resources. The measures introduced centered around the removal of interest rate controls, restructuring financial institutions to enhance competition and efficiency, and improving the legal and regulatory framework for the financial sector.

The first eight years of Uganda's far reaching and relatively successful liberalization can throw light on the question posed by the title of this volume. We evaluate this experience at both macro- and microlevels. At the macrolevel, we look at trends in interest rates, resource mobilization, investment, and growth. At the microlevel, we test whether the rationale behind financial liberalization – improving competition and hence efficiency in allocation of resources – has been realized under the imperfect, heavily segmented market conditions that characterize the Ugandan financial system. We describe the segmentation in banking and document the contrasting performance of different groups of banks: state-owned, excolonial, prudent, and aggressive. We also allude to the political economy of financial liberalization by assessing who are the winners and losers in the process.

---

[1] The chapter should not be interpreted as reflecting the views of the Bank of Uganda. The authors wish to acknowledge the excellent research assistance of Mrs. Rachel Ssebudde.

Section 1 provides a description of the context, the initial conditions, and the design phasing of the liberalization program. Sections 2 and 3 examine the impact at the macro- and microeconomic levels respectively. Section 4 provides some information about quasifiscal subsidies flowing through the financial system. The chapter concludes with an assessment of the lessons that can be drawn from the Uganda experience and their policy implications.

1   THE APPROACH TO LIBERALIZATION

Macroeconomic Context

When the National Resistance Movement (NRM) government came to power in Uganda in early 1986, it inherited an economy that had been shattered by almost two decades of economic mismanagement, political instability, and civil war, reversing the gains from robust growth that had been witnessed in the first eight years of independence.[2] Much of the country's economic and social infrastructure had been destroyed, production had stagnated, inflation was in three digits (300 percent in 1986), and the domestic currency was highly overvalued.

In May 1987, Uganda embarked upon an economic recovery program (ERP) with the objective of alleviating poverty and improving the standard of living for its population. The program was supported by credits from the World Bank, IMF, and various donors. The program's main objectives focused on macroeconomic stability, liberalization of dealing in foreign exchange, trade, price, and marketing systems, improving the incentive structure and business climate to promote savings mobilization and investment, and rehabilitating the country's economic, social, and institutional infrastructure. By the end of 1992, the government had achieved considerable progress in implementing the ERP. Real GDP was growing at an annual average rate of 5.9 percent, the exchange and trade regime was almost fully liberalized, price controls were eliminated (except for utilities and petroleum products), and annual inflation was down to 30 percent from 240 percent in 1987. The foreign exchange system had been significantly liberalized with the introduction of foreign exchange bureaus to allocate noncoffee foreign exchange receipts to a variety of uses according to market demand and introduction of a weekly

---

[2] During the period 1971–79, the government expatriated foreigners and expropriated their property. The period between 1979 and 1985 was one of both political and social, and hence economic, chaos. Although President Obote returned to power in 1980, efforts to return to proper economic management were not successful. Even the IMF/World Bank-supported program initiated in 1981 was cancelled in 1984.

foreign exchange auction to supplement the import requirements above and beyond those catered for by the bureaus.

In spite of the progress since 1987, Uganda's economy in 1992 was still fragile and highly vulnerable to external shocks. Savings and investment remained very low (1 percent and 11 percent of GDP respectively), and inflation was still too high and uncertain to encourage long-term business and other initiatives needed for sustained economic development. More importantly, the financial sector had major weaknesses and the inefficiencies associated with it contributed significantly to macroeconomic instability.

The State of the Financial System before Liberalization

For the early period after independence in the late 1960s, the financial system had expanded rapidly beyond the provision of crop financing to support internal trade and the growing manufacturing sector. By the early 1970s the economy had a reasonably well-developed financial network complete with commercial banks, nonbank savings, and housing finance institutions. A typical indicator of the system's robust performance at this time is financial depth, as measured by M2/GDP, which rose to a peak of 24 percent in 1974 (Figure 10.1), close to the values obtained by neighboring Kenya (28 percent) and Tanzania (27 percent).

The sector suffered serious dislocation following the civil disturbances of the 1970s and 1980s. There was a rapid decline in the size of the monetary economy and the level of financial intermediation.[3] The financial system lost both the depth and breadth that it had achieved in the early 1970s and financial services became concentrated in a few commercial banks situated in the capital city, Kampala. Nonprofessional management and fraud became common within financial institutions and normal business discipline collapsed. Parallel markets in foreign exchange, trade, and credit developed. The use of credit instruments such as checks and hire purchase declined. Financial repression in the form of controls on interest rates and directed credit contributed to the disintermediation of the financial system. On top of negative real interest rates, a one-off currency conversion scheme involving a 30 percent tax on shilling holdings further eroded confidence in the financial system.

By 1991 Uganda's financial system was fragile, with M2 down to around 6 percent of GDP – or less than half a billion U.S. dollars – and about 70 percent of bank credit going to the public sector. The ratio of credit to GDP had declined to four percent (compared to a peak of 18

---

[3] For further discussion, refer to Kasekende and Malik (1996).

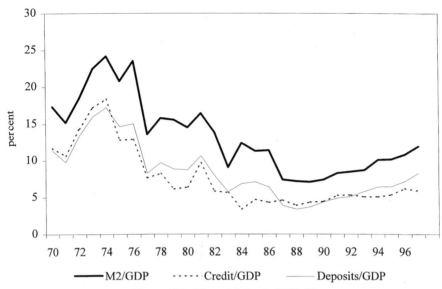

Figure 10.1. Financial depth, 1970–98.

percent in 1974) and cash in circulation as a proportion of money stock had risen to 53 percent (from 28 percent in 1974).

At the macrolevel, the government was caught in a vicious circle. Negative real interest rates, high inflation, and associated expectations of devaluation had undermined confidence in the financial sector, resulting in a low savings rate and a lack of monetary depth. In turn, the lack of monetary depth and other inefficiencies in the financial system had contributed to macroeconomic instability. Monetary discipline had been difficult to enforce and even relatively small fiscal deficits were generating large monetary and inflationary pressures because of the small monetary holdings in the economy (monetary financing of a deficit equal to 4 percent of GDP results in a monetary expansion of almost 70 percent if the ratio of M2 to GDP is only 6 percent). Although the government appeared to be coming to grips with stabilization, the damage done in earlier unstable periods, in terms of the effect of instability on the financial sector, continued to make fiscal deficits unusually dangerous.

Another avenue through which the financial system contributed to macroinstability was through the government's policy of accommodating excessive lending by distressed "public sector" banks combined with little effort to recover loans. This policy, combined with excessive operating costs (attributable to rapid expansion of the branch network), and other losses hidden in a mushrooming "items in transit" account, led the two dominant banks, Uganda Commercial Bank (UCB) and Cooperative Bank (COOP) – accounting for about two-thirds of the commercial banking system – into insolvency and an acute shortage of liquidity.[4] Their combined overdrawn position with the Bank of Uganda (BOU) – without which they would have ceased to operate – deteriorated from USh 287 million at the end of 1987 to USh 6034 million by the end of August 1989 at which point it was equivalent to more than 30 percent of their total deposits.

In spite of the wide range of financial institutions, the system lacked instruments for the mobilization of savings, diversification of risks, and management of liquidity. There was lack of confidence in the existing, but limited, financial instruments (checks) as reflected by a high reluctance by the public to use checks as a system of domestic payments. The problem was emanating, not from the checks being stolen in transit, but rather in their misuse by the holders, who would issue these instruments for payments with little or no surety of funds on account. The number of monthly checks being cleared at the BOU in 1989 was only 12,305 compared to a peak in December 1970 of 135,502. In effect, Uganda had, by 1992, largely reverted to a cash economy. Capital markets and merchant banks were nonexistent and the money market was in an embryonic state. There was no formal interbank market and interbank lending was being conducted on an infrequent bilateral basis.

There was a fundamental problem of lack of financial discipline, which was exacerbated by a weak legal and regulatory system and lack of capacity of the central bank to supervise the financial system. In addition to the banking insolvency, the government was in large arrears with respect to payment to its contractors. The legal and regulatory framework was also inadequate. Responsibility for the formulation and implementation of monetary policy and in the enforcement of bank regulation was split between the BOU and Ministry of Finance (MOF) and the power of the BOU to enforce directives was limited. Even if it had the capacity and skills necessary to effectively regulate and supervise the banking system, the BOU's role of prudential supervision was undermined by the obligation to give precedence to government objectives, at times, at the expense of strict regulation and prudent banking.

---

[4] Both banks were government controlled: the UCB directly state owned, and COOP owned by government-dependent cooperatives. In addition, the government held a 49 percent equity holding in all five foreign banks. It also owned two development banks, the Post Office Savings Bank (POSB), National Social Security Fund (NSSF), and two-thirds of the insurance business. The commercial banks dominated the financial sector and held 90 percent of the assets of the system. The UCB accounted for half of the banking business in terms of both assets and deposits. It also accounted for 85 percent of the total national branch network.

In the aftermath of the political and economic crises, transparency about the financial health of local banks and their clients was conspicuous by its absence. There were few good accounting and auditing firms and this made it difficult to rely on the quality of financial information produced by most of the local banks and firms. There was no regulatory body to oversee prudent accounting standards, and standardized accounting principles did not exist in Uganda at the time. At the same time, there were no commercial laws governing accounting requirements by private firms.

The effectiveness of the limited amount of private credit that could be extended was diminished by official pressure to prefer agriculture and industry over trade and commerce. Furthermore, the creditworthiness of firms and individuals was compromised by such factors as lack of ownership titles (especially for the firms representing assets confiscated from departed Asians), overindebtedness and insolvency, and the absence or outdated nature of financial accounts kept by the firms. Politicians contributed to the problems of loan delinquency by encouraging a culture of nonrepayment, especially of loans from government banks. There were cases of politicians taking loans on their own account and failing to pay while some encouraged their constituents to do likewise.

The Elements, Timing, and Phasing of Liberalization

The process of financial liberalization in Uganda included the removal of interest rate controls, reduced barriers for the entry of new private banks into the system, restricting the direct role of government in the allocation of financial resources including crop financing and divestiture of the government's ownership in commercial banks. This process was complemented by parallel measures to strengthen bank supervision and foster financial discipline through new legislation and regulations, and policies to improve the efficiency and profitability of financial institutions. It is important to note that this liberalization did not include the capital account of the balance of payments.

Phasing and Sequencing of the Reforms

The liberalization process of the Ugandan financial system has been gradual and it is useful to distinguish the process among three major phrases.

- Phase I – 1987–91: In this phase the focus was on macroeconomic measures to stabilize the economy, but the measures also included some steps to lay the groundwork for financial sector liberalization. The financial sector also benefited indirectly through reduction in inflation which saw a shift toward positive real interest rates required to stimulate financial savings. The first significant steps toward financial liberalization were taken in July 1988 when the interest rates were raised by ten percentage points. During 1989, authorities decided to adjust nominal interest rates in line with inflation to maintain positive real interest rates. Related reforms pertaining to the foreign exchange market were also instituted simultaneously to improve financial intermediation.

- Phase II – 1992–94: The key liberalization measures were introduced in 1992, but controls on both interest rates and credit allocation were removed in several steps over a two-year period. In 1992, the removal of interest rate controls affected Treasury Bill (TB) rates as the government switched from ad hoc issues to a market-based auction for determination of interest rates. From then, the key bank interest rates were linked to the weighted average of the TB rate as determined in the four preceding TB auctions. This move affected bank lending rates, bank deposit rates, and was also accompanied by a removal in credit ceilings, directed credit, and a reduction in compulsory reserves at the Central Bank. The rates that were payable on time deposits remained subject to minimum limits while rates applicable to agricultural and development lending were subject to a ceiling. All the other rates were left to market forces. In 1994, the BOU fully liberalized interest rates and began to manage these rates through indirect monetary policy instruments with the TB rate as the anchor. In summary, while 1992 represented a liberalization of the wholesale interest rates with other rates still pegged to TB rates, the moves in 1994 decontrolled all the remaining retail interest rates. The main focus was on the removal of controls on interest rates, but institutional reforms were also initiated. In particular, many of the legislative changes mentioned in Table 10.1 were enacted by parliament.
- Phase III – 1995–97: This phase focused on the development and strengthening of institutions to complement the policy and legal reforms made by the government in the second phase. While full liberalization of interest rates had been completed in July 1994, the government realized that the weak financial system had constrained the gains from the economic reform program. The financial system was still characterized by a high level of nonperforming loans (over 50 percent of the total loan portfolio), high intermediation margins, violation of capital adequacy and/or insider lending limits by more than half of the commercial banks, and a lack of adequate provision of financial services outside the capital city. In order to address these weaknesses, the government shifted focus to institution-building measures. These included: strengthening of the Central Bank to enable it

Table 10.1. Uganda: Liberalization of the Financial Sector

Action	Started	Completed	Comments
Auction-based TB market	4.92		Used as an anchor.
Decontrol of interest rates	11.92	7.94	And removal of directed credit.
Interbank market	1993	Evolving	Improved check clearing; curtailed bank access to BOU overdraft; rediscount facilities; banks allowed to hold T-Bills.
Entry of banks	1991–92		No. of banks jumps from 9 in 1991 to 20 in 1996. Two-year moratorium on banking licenses imposed in 1996.
Exit of banks	1992		One exit only (in 1993). Two banks taken over, restructured and sold to strategic investors in 1996 by BOU. Two others taken over by BOU in 1998
Direct lending by BOU to govt.	1988	1991–92	BOU assumes role of coffee financing (1988). Policy was reversed in 1991.
Phasing out of subsidies and directed lending	1992	Ongoing	Directed and subsidized lending gradually reduced.
Divestiture of equity holdings in foreign banks	1994	1998	Government sold its shares in 3 other foreign banks domiciled in Uganda.
Privatization of UCB	1996	Ongoing	Govt. sold 49 percent of UCB in October 1997.
Reforms to complement liberalization			
Removal of foreign exchange controls	7.90	1993	
Legal and regulatory framework	1992	1996	Five major new or revised laws.
Strengthening, reorganization & recapitalization of BOU	1993	Ongoing	
Strengthening bank supervision and enforcement of prudential guidelines	1992	Ongoing	Significant investment of resources by govt. (especially after 1996) to enhance BOU's onsite and offsite supervision capacity.
Setting up Nonperforming Asset Recovery Trust (NPART)	1995	Ongoing	NPART created as an agency to recover nonperforming loans (totaling $69 million) transferred to it from UCB.
Institutional reforms to enhance liquidity management by commercial banks and BOU.	1997	Ongoing	Central Depository System to facilitate efficient transfer of government securities, secondary trading and the interbank market in final stages of installation.

to enforce the regulatory framework developed in the previous phases, an expedited program of divestiture of government holdings in commercial banks, and a mechanism for the resolution of bad debt (with the creation of the Nonperforming Asset Recovery Trust (NPART) to recover UCB's bad loans).

To complement the interest rate liberalization, several other measures were introduced to increase the competition and efficiency in the financial sector. These measures were aimed at facilitating the entry of new domestic and foreign banks, exit of nonviable banks, and to reduce the role of the state in the allocation of credit (Table 10.1). The government also took active measures to reduce its equity ownership in banks. It has over several years sold its shares in privately owned foreign banks. In 1997, after attempting to restructure UCB for about three years, the government put UCB up for sale on an "as is" basis and sold 49 percent of its shareholding to a private strategic partner who was also given management control. Other measures included a major program to upgrade a legal and regulatory framework to enhance market discipline and competition among the private sector banks.

2 IMPACT AND CONSEQUENCES OF LIBERALIZATION AT THE MACRO LEVEL

Given the objectives of the reform program, the two most important questions at the macrolevel concern the impact that financial sector liberalization has had, firstly on the government's efforts to maintain macroeconomic stability and secondly on Uganda's growth prospects. There are two methodological difficulties in addressing these questions directly. Firstly, as shown in Table 10.1, the program has been introduced gradually over a number of years and some of the measures such as the divestiture of state ownership in banks were only completed a year ago. In that sense, it may be a bit early to have a full assessment of the impact of the liberalization at the macroeconomic level. In essence, this poses limitations on the use of time series and econometric analysis. Secondly, it is difficult to distinguish between the impact of financial sector liberalization and the effects of other fundamental reforms that the government has instituted since 1987, as part of the ERP. These reforms, which included measures to contain the fiscal deficit and trade policy reforms, also made a major contribution toward attaining macroeconomic stability and improving the environment for investment and growth.

In these circumstances, we take a more modest approach and also assess the main channels, suggested by economic theory, through which financial sector liberalization is likely to impact on stabilization and growth. These channels include interest rates, domestic savings, and in particular, financial savings (time and savings deposits), financial deepening (M2/GDP), and investment.

Behavior of Interest Rates in the Postliberalization Era

On an ex ante basis, one would expect interest rates in a postliberalization period to be higher and more volatile than when they were controlled. The experience in Uganda has been consistent with this hypothesis in real terms but not in nominal terms.

Figure 10.2 plots the movement of nominal interest rates since 1988. As can be seen, following the partial liberalization of interest rates in November 1992, there was a sharp decline in the entire structure of interest rates including both treasury and bank rates. This, in part, reflects liquidity conditions in the market. The replacement of ceilings based on nonmarket TB rates to rates based on a more competitive TB market was mainly responsible for this development. The pictorial representation is indicative of the two regime changes mentioned previously – the wholesale interest rates in 1992 and latter liberalization of all the interest rates in 1994. Since the market was not fully liberalized until July 1994, interest rates in the fully liberalized environment are only observable from that point of time onward. Again they show a larger downward trend apart from the significant margin that opened up between lending and deposit rates. The rates since then have been relatively stable.

Figure 10.3 outlines the movement in real rates since January 1990. Real rates, which were largely negative prior to 1992 (apart from 1991–92, when the decline in regulated interest rates lagged behind the decline in inflation) increased sharply in 1993 before coming down to more stable levels in 1994. It is clear from the figure that interest rates have since remained largely positive in real terms.

Between 1995 and 1998, while the rates seem to follow a similar trend, significant margins between the lending and the other rates have persisted. This thus raises the question as to whether there have been any efficiency gains derived from liberalization of the interest rates.

Savings Mobilization and Volume of Investment

Total savings in the banking system have maintained an upward trend over the last ten years. As a share of GDP, deposits increased from 3.4 percent to 8.3 percent between 1988 and 1997. There has also been a shift toward interest earning medium- and long-term deposits. The share of savings and time deposits in total deposits has increased from 17 percent recorded in 1988 to the current level of 49 percent. This is all consistent with the hypothesis that the emergence of positive real interest rates has pulled some savings into the formal financial sector (Shaw 1973).

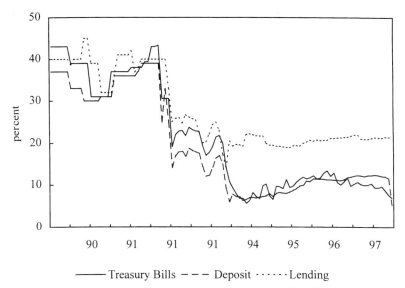

Figure 10.2. Trend in nominal interest rates pre- and postliberalization (*Source*: Bank of Uganda: Research Department Records).

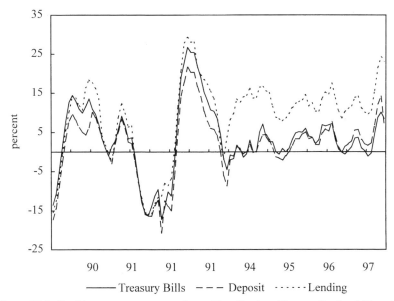

Figure 10.3. Real interest rates pre- and postliberalization (*Source*: Bank of Uganda, Research Department Data Base).

However, the level of financial savings remains low and compares poorly with those of other countries at a similar level of development. (In Kenya and Tanzania for instance, financial savings in 1997 were recorded at 39 percent and 14 percent of GDP respectively.) Urban households still siphon some of their savings into real estate and foreign exchange following the liberalization of the current account. Moreover, because of the limited access to financial services, the asset composition of the rural households is to a large extent determined by local economic activities in their area of residence; savings are in the form of commodity stocks, livestock, and land. This in turn is reflected in the magnitude of the nonmonetary sector which contributes to a loss of efficiency in the economy (Areeyetey and Nissanke 1998; Kasekende and Ating-Ego 1999).

Econometrics

Econometric techniques can be employed to attempt to identify the impact of financial liberalization on Uganda's financial savings and monetary depth. But for the present, such attempts must remain preliminary in that the liberalization process has been gradual and the postliberalization period has spanned only four years. Nevertheless, as observed by Khan and Aftab (1994), historical data can be used to establish the direction of the relationship between variables of interest to appreciate the need for such reforms. Despite data limitations and the short sample, the results may help throw light on the postliberalization experience.

From a theoretical perspective, one would expect higher interest rates to generate higher savings with the banking system. At the same time, the level of savings is also expected to be influenced by the level of income and the rate of return on such savings relative to the return on alternatives. For Uganda, we focused on the level of bank deposits as a measure of financial savings and the real rate of interest on those deposits as the own rate of return. We experimented with the CPI inflation rate as the opportunity cost. Using quarterly data from 1981–97,[5] we successfully identified a long-run cointegrating relationship between financial savings, the own rate of return, and GDP. (Inflation was significant in the associated dynamic equation, but with a counterintuitive sign.)

An alternative specification was also employed, with financial depth (log of M2/GDP) as a dependent variable, and the rate of depreciation of the Uganda shilling was employed as opportunity cost. (M2 excludes foreign currency deposits, and Ugandan residents can easily substitute between domestic and foreign currency deposits.) Here again we found a

---

[5] Details of the time series cointegration techniques employed, together with detailed results, are contained in the working paper version of this chapter.

cointegrating relationship this time with both own return and opportunity cost significant and with the expected sign.

On the strength of these results, in the long run, financial savings in Uganda are sensitive to changes in the real interest rates and income. For that matter, the financial sector policies that have seen Uganda achieve positive real interest rates have contributed positively to the increase in financial savings in the system.

Investment

Increased financial saving (or financial deepening) is not viewed as an end in and of itself: The hope and expectation is that financial saving inter- mediated by the banking sector contribute to efficient investment with beneficial effects for the economy.

The direct evidence on investment and the role of intermediation is mixed. However, this is based on an assessment of data on investment levels from 1988 to 1994 – a period which covers only the early phases of liberalization. This data reveals that Uganda achieved a high rate of eco- nomic growth with relatively little investment in productive enterprises; in the absence of sufficient national savings the bulk of the investment that took place was funded by resources mobilized from abroad. Total invest- ment expenditures over this period averaged 12 percent of GDP, of which estimated private investment was about half that level. Public investment was largely financed by donors' grants and loans. Private investment has been assisted by the emergence, in the 1990s, of a strong inflow of private transfers from abroad which was estimated to exceed $300 million per annum in 1994.

Impact on Growth

Uganda has now displayed robust economic growth for more than a decade. For an economy in the state that Uganda had reached since 1988, it is relatively easy to achieve short-term gains in output even with an unstable macroeconomic environment and a seriously impaired financial sector. However, these gains were largely based on existing capacity and emphasized traditional forms of economic activity rather than the diver- sification and modernization associated with a more robust economy. Such a basis could not have sustained growth beyond the period 1988–92: The fact that the pace of growth has been sustained naturally raises the ques- tion as to what role that financial sector reforms have played in this success.

A "supply-leading" hypothesis would suggest that financial sector reforms have had a beneficial impact on Uganda's growth prospects by mobilizing financial savings and intermediating them toward productive investment. In fact, there has been a substantial shift in the sectoral shares of formal sector credit: Agriculture's share dropped from 34 percent in

1991 to 19 percent in 1997, largely a reflection of the government's previous efforts to direct credit to this sector (and to a shift of the lucrative prefinancing of coffee exports to offshore financing sources). Taking up the slack was trade and commerce (whose share increased from 39 to 50 percent) and manufacturing (from 12 to 23 percent).

In an attempt to provide an econometric assessment of the macrorole of credit in growth, Kasekende and Ating-Ego (1999)[6] estimated a long-run log-linear cointegrating relationship between industrial output in Uganda and four determinants: bank lending to the industrial sector (positive effect), the bank lending rate, the foreign exchange premium (a proxy for the degree of foreign exchange market regulation), and CPI inflation (all with negative effects).

The positive significance of bank lending and the negative effect of the cost of credit are interpreted as capturing the role of the financial sector in allocating mobilized resources to generating industrial output. This is evidenced by the positive relationship between growth and availability of credit and the negative relationship between growth and cost of credit.

Our conclusion is that the supply-leading hypothesis is supported in the Ugandan macrodata, and that the reforms that are geared toward improving the efficiency of the sector can promote growth.

Impact on Stabilization

With GDP growth averaging 7 percent per annum in the past decade while inflation has fallen from 250 percent per annum to single digits, Uganda has been successful at achieving and sustaining macroeconomic stability. There has also been a reduction in the external disequilibrium: The current account deficit has declined from 16.5 percent of GDP in 1993–94 to 8.8 percent in 1997–98. Uganda has also remained largely unaffected by the contagion effects of the recent global financial crisis.

Taken together, the above developments suggest that, at the very least, liberalization has been achieved without a major disturbance to macrostability. In part, this is because the capital account was not fully liberalized until 1997 and this has insulated Uganda from rapid capital movements in and out of the country.

The maintenance of macro and, in particular, monetary stability has also been facilitated by the skillful use of fiscal policy to overcome weaknesses in financial markets. A good example is provided by the response

---

[6] The authors further test for causality using the weak exogeneity test and find that all financial sector variables explain growth while growth does not explain the financial sector variables. The conclusion is hence that the causation runs from the financial sector to growth in the industrial sector. Further details are in the working paper version of this chapter.

of the economy to terms of trade shocks, such as in early 1994 when the prices of coffee, Uganda's major export earner, tripled. The shock was absorbed by the economy without a reemergence of excess demand and inflation. A significant factor underlying the economy's ability to absorb the terms of trade shock was the use of fiscal policies to sterilize the expansionary effect of large inflows of private capital. Taxes on coffee exports were temporarily increased but the increase in revenues was not translated into expenditures and the government ran up credit balances with the BOU. The use of fiscal policy instruments to manage liquidity reflected the government's realization that the effectiveness of indirect monetary policy instruments (such as the use of open-market operations) was, at least in the short term, circumscribed by the embryonic state of money markets – the main channel for transmitting the effects of monetary policy to the rest of the economy.

In addition to the increase in monetary depth, the reforms have had a positive effect on macroeconomic stability through:

- restricting the earlier practice of BOU lending to public sector banks (financed largely by printing money) and encouraging instead the use of the interbank market. Following their recapitalization,[7] the combined liquid asset ratio of UCB and COOP averaged 46 percent during 1996–98 (compared with a negative ratio in 1988–92). This illustrates the profound effect of the change in the rules of the game for the public sector banks.
- reforms in the crop financing system. As shown in the flow of funds table (Table 10.2), the BOU, formerly an apex lending organization for development and crop finance, is no longer actively involved in crop finance, since coffee exporters have been able to obtain prefinancing from abroad. And domestic credit creation by the BOU is no longer the prime source of base money growth as used to be the case prior to 1991 (Figure 10.4).

It goes without saying that the impact of investment on growth is determined not only by the quantity of its investment but also by its quality. The next section focuses on the microlevel factors driving the efficiency with which the financial sector allocates resources for productive activities.

3 IMPACT OF LIBERALIZATION AT THE MICRO LEVEL

Turning to microaspects, this section shows that, occurring as it did while effective regulation was still being developed, financial liberalization

---

[7] UCB was recapitalized by issue of government bonds worth UShs 72.billion to write off certain liabilities to government. By definition, these are liquid assets.

Table 10.2. Flow of Funds in the Ugandan Economy

Ush billions Sources	Govt	BOU	Users Banks	Other	Foreign	Year
Government		−14	10			1992
		44	4			1993
		274	21			1994
		210	43			1995
		137	−10			1996
		119	−7			1997
		221	−4			1998
Bank of Uganda	36		−4	−0	50	1992
	−24		1	−11	50	1993
	227		0	4	75	1994
	148		−1	3	162	1995
	69		−3	−3	135	1996
	28		7	−0	154	1997
	112		2	−4	261	1998
Commercial banks	6	31		26	35	1992
	4	15		46	46	1993
	17	20		40	8	1994
	8			42	14	1995
	27			80	12	1996
	84			16	31	1997
	35			65	74	1998
Private nonbank sector	5		70			1992
	−6		86			1993
	10		75			1994
	9		89			1995
	−31		72			1996
	25		114			1997
	−20		178			1998
Foreign	196	191	7	131		1992
	177	15	16	290		1993
	218	−54	8	208		1994
		52	−17	243		1995
		25	9	407		1996
		−6	−8	308		1997
		16	22	539		1998

Source: *Background to the Budget 1997/98*; BOU Staff Estimates.

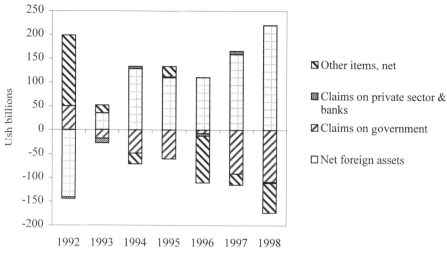

Figure 10.4. Factors contributing to base money growth, end-June 1992–98.

did not result in a fully competitive outcome, but instead saw market segmentation, exit constraints, and gaps in the provision of services by the formal financial sector (over 95 percent of whose assets are accounted for by the banks). Furthermore, despite the limitations on competition posed by the environment, the liberalization of the internal market has improved economic efficiency overall both through an improvement in the allocation of resources and with a reduction in the cost of intermediation.

Market Segmentation and Noncompetitive Behavior in a Liberalized Environment

Market Segmentation

The preliberalization banking system was oligopolistic, with just eight banks falling into groups: (1) the publicly controlled ("state-owned") banks and (2) the subsidiaries of foreign banks (the "excolonial" banks) which though in the majority of cases were partially owned by government had to follow guidelines defined by their head offices abroad. Group 1 (the state-owned) banks had deficient capital, suffered from liquidity and management problems, and were, at the time the sector was liberalized, undergoing restructuring programs at the behest of the government. The excolonial (Group 2) banks, on the other hand, did not face these difficulties, and were subject to internal regulations and strict management controls from their head offices.

Following the liberalization of 1992 the number of banks increased and, with it, the level of competition in the market for banking services – at least in the major cities (Table 10.3). One indicator of this is the loss of market shares by both Group 1 and Group 2 banks to new entrants: Groups 3 and 4 (Table 10.4). Group 3 ("prudent") represents new entrants (domestic and foreign) that were generally conservative in their pricing and expansion plans. Group 4 ("aggressive"), on the other hand, represents a set of competitive banks that were aggressive in their policies to capture market share.[8]

A comparison of Tables 10.4 and 10.5 reveals that banks were able to compete with each other more effectively for deposits. As shown in Figure 10.5, the losses and gains in the share of deposits broadly corresponds to their pricing: The lower the interest rate paid, relative to the market, the greater the loss in share and vice versa.

As usual, competition appears to be less effective on the lending side where information problems are more acute. The excolonial banks had the lowest (or close to the lowest) rates on loans yet did not see an increase in market share. The state-owned group banks maintained the lowest lending rates throughout the period but still lost market shares to Group 3 and 4 banks. Finally, the aggressive Group 4 banks maintained the highest interest rates in the market during the 1996–98 period, yet gained the largest market shares. On the lending side, market share seems to be insensitive to interest rates changes. The lending data suggests a perverse upward-sloping demand for credit. The higher interest rates are charged by banks increasing market shares indicating that their average portfolio risk is also increasing as shown later in the section analyzing nonperforming assets. The figures reflect the well-known selectivity and risk aversion of excolonial banks who leave the lower end of the credit market, where default rates are higher, to the Group 3 and Group 4 banks.

This behavior of the excolonial banks (Group 2) in the postliberalization period lends further support to the hypothesis that the environment constrained effective competition. Thus in the period 1994–96, it could be argued that these banks took advantage of the high interest rates charged by more inefficient banks in the market to increase profitability and rebuild their capital base. The fact they were able to do so without concerns about losing their customer base also reflects an element of

---

[8] This latter group also included two institutions that could be said to represent elements of "crony capitalism"; they were owned by politically influential individuals not averse to insider lending. These banks failed and were taken over by the central bank after a few years of operation and resold to a new ownership structure.

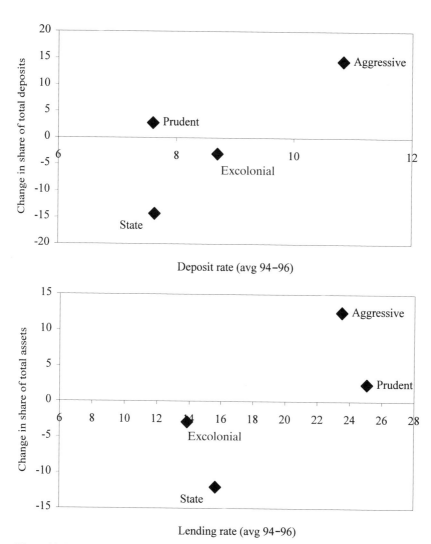

Figure 10.5. Competition for deposits in the postliberalization period (*Note*: Groups 1 and 2 banks both lost market shares to Group 4 banks which paid higher rates on deposits. Deposit rates were in the range of 9–13 percent for Group 4 banks compared to about 7 percent and 10 percent respectively for Group 1 and 2 banks. The latter two groups also lost significant market share to Group 3 in the 1996–98 period when the latter moved to higher interest rate on deposits. The loss of market share was much greater for Group 1 than for Group 2 banks, which is again consistent with their ranking on the deposit rates paid.)

Table 10.3. Evolution of the Institutional Architecture of the Financial System

No./Ush billions	1988–92		1993–94		1995		1997		1998	
	#	Assets	#	Assets	#	Assets	#	Assets	#	Assets
Commercial banks	11	351	15	567	15	703	20	1021	20	1175
State-owned	1	173	1	185	1	288	1	281	0	82
Majority	5	125	5	239	5	260	6	383	6	489
foreign-owned	2	...	3	...	5	...	6	43	7	57
Credit institutions										
Insurance companies	...	...	...	...	...	...	...	...	22	...
Building societies	...	...	7	...	...	...	...	...	1	...
Development banks	3	...	3	...	3	...	3	...	3	...
Microfinance institutions[a]	14	...	19	...	32	...	47	...	48	...

[a] MFIs: based on 1998 survey by PRESTO, pertaining to microfinance institutions existing at end-1997.
Source: Bank of Uganda.

Table 10.4. Evolution of Market Shares in the Pre- and Postliberalization Periods

	June 88–June 92		July 92–June 96		July 96–June 98	
	Deposits	Assets	Deposits	Assets	Deposits	Assets
Group 1 (state-owned)	54.0	56.4	49.6	43.4	35.3	31.4
Group 2 (excolonial)	39.8	38.4	36.0	41.3	33.0	38.4
Group 3 (prudent)	1.4	1.5	2.8	2.9	5.6	5.3
Group 4 (aggressive)	4.8	3.7	11.6	12.4	26.1	24.9

Source: Bank of Uganda, Research Department Records.

Table 10.5. Group Analysis of Interest Rates in the Postliberalization Period

	Time deposit rates			Lending rates			Spreads		
	1994	1996	1998	1994	1996	1998	1994	1996	1998
Group 1	9.9	6.0	7.0	15.2	15.6	16.2	5.3	9.6	9.2
Group 2	6.8	9.5	9.8	12.7	16.4	12.6	5.9	6.9	2.8
Group 3	4.1	6.8	11.9	33.0	25.0	17.2	28.2	17.1	5.3
Group 4	9.6	9.6	13.3	20.5	24.9	25.1	10.9	14.6	11.8
Bankwide	8.60	8.03	9.96	15.19	18.24	17.22	6.60	10.20	7.26

Note: As at June of each year.

monopoly power that lenders have over their borrowers in the presence of imperfect information.[9]

Insolvent Banks and the Problem of Exit

Another structural weakness that constrained the functioning of a competitive market in Uganda was the presence of insolvent banks that did not exit the system and were allowed to stay in the market. To put matters in perspective, more than half the commercial banks in the financial system experienced losses in 1994 and seven out of the fifteen banks were insolvent. At different points in time, over the period 1996–98, a number of banks were found to be again experiencing liquidity and solvency problems and were in violation of prudential guidelines. As shown in Table 10.1, since the initiation of interest rate liberalization measures in 1992,

---

[9] Alternatively, one could argue that Group 4 banks threatened the market share of Group 2 banks, thus forcing them to respond by raising deposit rates. The high cost of deposit mobilization was in turn translated into higher lending rates. However this argument loses its appeal as it is not valid for the 1996–98 period when Group 2 banks did not follow the Group 4 banks in raising deposit rates further.

only one bank has been closed and liquidated in the conventional sense, in 1992, and that was also in special circumstances which predate the liberalization.

Between 1995–98, the BOU has intervened in four other banks – all from Group 4 – and restructured two of them under a new ownership structure, but the extent to which this can be seen as an exit of the distressed banks is questionable, as the BOU allowed the original owners to retain a residual value in the restructured banks and has provided loans to restore the banks to positive net worth. This arrangement has helped to avoid any run on the banking system as depositors have not lost any money and in effect have been insulated from the problem of the distressed banks. In addition to concerns about systemic stability, the actions of the BOU have also been influenced by the law which does not allow the central bank to extinguish the share ownership in banks that it has taken over. So while in a sense the original banking entity does not exist, exit in the conventional sense has not taken place – the bank was not liquidated, the owners did not lose their holdings entirely, and depositors have been absolved of their responsibility in their choice of bank.

Market forces have clearly tolerated the emergence of high-risk banks, and regulators have had difficulty in closing distressed institutions. Concerns about the impact on systemic stability, combined with the legal restrictions mentioned above and political considerations, have been important factors in constraining BOU from the option of outright closure and liquidation.

Gaps in the Provision of Services

The informal sector for financial services has grown rapidly in the post-liberalization period and this is largely attributed to the structural deficiencies in the formal financial system. Official surveys carried out in the period 1995–96 suggest the emergence of an increasing gap in the provision of financial services by the formal financial system, in particular to small enterprises and in rural areas. It is not entirely clear from the data whether the gap was increasing because of liberalization measures or whether this problem was becoming more clearly identified. However, it is very likely that the rationalization in UCB's branch network and limitations on its ability to extend credit generally, as part of its restructuring program, did restrict access to financial services to small indigenous firms (its main customers) and in some rural areas. Moreover, the low level of monetization in these areas represses credit activity limiting profitable financial intermediation business.

This gap in the provision of financial services is now being filled by informal and semiformal institutions. The informal sector, which in the preliberalization period existed due to severe restrictions and controls on the formal sector, exists today for different reasons. These include provision of financial services to agents that do not have access to the formal sector, and a means of efficiently distributing externally mobilized resources to credit-deficient sectors of the economy. In the preliberalization period, the informal and semiformal sector comprised of institutions whose main purpose was to mobilize savings and included community savings cooperatives and building societies. The postliberalization informal sector, however, comprises institutions with little intention or success in mobilization of deposits. These institutions rely heavily on their own resources and/or grants especially those originating from external sources (donor disbursements). The postliberalization sector is however much larger and comprises a range of participants including local money lenders, rotating credit cooperatives, community savings cooperatives, and loans associations.

Information asymmetries with respect to the small and medium enterprises bias the banking system risk assessment for credit allocation. This, combined with high transaction cost and lack of collateral has limited access of small borrowers to bank credit. Credit extension from the banking system is therefore concentrated to the large firms that include export marketing, oil companies, and the big manufacturers. Kasekende and Ating-Ego (1999) elaborate the variation in access to credit in the informal money markets and in the formal financial system.

Comparison of the banking system to the informal money market indicates existence of large premiums of up to fifty percentage points between the rates charged in the two segments of the financial system for similar projects. Could this imply that intermediation in the informal sector, where rates are higher, is economically more inefficient and hence costly to the economy? The way of doing business in the informal market tends to lower credit risks and the cost of screening and monitoring relative to the formal sector. Whereas the informal sector devotes the bigger proportion of their loan administration costs in prescreening the clients' ability to pay, and not the use of funds, banks devote a considerable amount of resources to project evaluation.[10] This is consistent with the experience in other developing countries (see Aleem 1990). Loan recovery rates are consequently higher in the informal sector than is the case for the formal sector. The degree of inefficiency in intermediation in the informal financial sector (as reflected by the high cost of credit) implies that the extent to which the informal sector can substitute for the banking system is limited. The current development can therefore be

---

[10] It has been estimated that the informal institutions allocate less than 5 percent of loan amounts to administer loans (*cf.* Musinguzi, Obwona, and Stryker 2000).

interpreted as an exploitation of the deficiencies that still exist in the banking and other institutions of the formal financial sector.

Efficiency of Liberalized Financial Markets

Some indications suggestive of a deterioration in the efficiency in parts of the banking system can be obtained from analysis of the incidence of nonperforming loans and of interest rate spreads.

Nonperforming Assets as a Measure of the (In)efficiency of Resource Allocation

The extent of the bad debts in the commercial banks balance sheets (see Table 10.6), even after the restructuring of UCB[11] and several other banks, suggests significant misallocation of credit, which is detrimental to the real sector performance.

With the removal of credit ceiling favoring certain sectors of the economy and reduction of political intervention in the banking system, the banks of Group 2 and Group 3 largely base their lending decision on commercial viability. The incidence of nonperforming assets, as a percentage of the loan portfolio, has declined for Groups 1, 2, and 3 and for the sector as a whole. This is an improvement, if we can interpret it as meaning that loans are being allocated to more productive uses that allow the borrower to repay.

But a loan that has not been repaid does not necessarily mean that the resources were wasted. The increasing share of performing loans may partly reflect cultural improvement in repayment or recoverability of loans. The willingness could have been a cultural change so far as repayment of bank loans was concerned, and partly a shift in loans to lower-risk projects or sectors, following the reduction in directed lending.

Group 4 (the aggressive) banks provide an exception to the trend of a reduction in the incidence of nonperforming loans. They are characterized by a high incidence of insider lending and granting credit to more speculative ventures which are prepared to pay high interest charges, but the risk of default is disproportionately greater. Group 4 banks have therefore seen a fast growth in deposits accompanied by similar growth in the non-

---

[11] Prior to the 1994 divestiture program, Uganda Commercial Bank (UCB) was a state-owned enterprise and accounted for 40.6 percent of the banking system assets. It had however, accumulated losses over the years and nonperforming assets accounted for 55.55 percent of its total assets. In preparation for the divestiture, the bulk of its total NPAs worth Shs 26 billion and Shs 55 billion were waived off by government and transferred to an independent debt collecting body NPART. The bank was recapitalized with a total of Shs 72 billion. By end June 1998, 49 percent of the shares in the bank had been sold to a foreign merchant bank based in Malaysia. An account of the complex sequence of subsequent events is beyond the scope of this chapter.

Table 10.6. Asset Quality in the Pre- and Postliberalization Periods

	1993	1994	1995	1996	1997	1998
Group 1	54.2	39.5	32.6	35.3	16.0	12.2
Group 2	10.3	10.5	9.7	10.2	9.8	5.3
Group 3	11.7	10.7	8.8	3.2	4.6	4.3
Group 4	8.6	4.3	9.7	24.2	10.2	7.0
Total system	21.2	16.2	15.5	18.3	10.1	7.2

Notes: Table shows nonperforming assets as percentage of total assets. Data for 1993 refers to end-December; otherwise average of June and December.
Source: Bank of Uganda, Research Department Records.

performing assets (NPAs; see Table 10.5). As shown in Table 10.6, Group 4 banks, which have been aggressive in their conduct of banking business, have high levels of NPAs averaging over 15 percent for the two-year period to June 1998, compared with under 9 percent for the 1992–96 period. This is why higher rates they are charging on their loans are not translating into profits and they are barely able to keep afloat. In fact the high interest rates could be making matters worse for them by attracting more risky customers.

Bank Margins and the Efficiency of Intermediation

Another indicator of the efficiency of bank intermediation is the movement in interest rate spreads. Ex ante spreads (Table 10.5) are calculated from the contractual rates charged on loans and rates paid on deposits and embody an allowance for expected loan losses. The ex post net interest margins, calculated as the actual difference between a bank's interest revenues and their actual interest expenses, and the net income margins (net interest *plus* net noninterest income *less* loan-loss provisions) are potentially more free of this deficiency.[12] The ex post margins may be more easily interpreted if expressed as a percentage of performing assets (shown in Table 10.7 as adjusted intermediation margin).

Table 10.5 reveals that the Ugandan banking system has high and increasing intermediation margins, rising from 3.84 percent to 5.75 percent

[12] There are some difficulties with the data. In particular the absence of an uniform accounting system is reflected in the fact that some banks record interest income on accrual basis, others do it on cash basis. Tax treatment also differs, some banks reporting profits without deduction of tax (some banks enjoy a tax exemption under the Ugandan Investment Code). On the other hand, the year-to-year trend here is not much affected by changes in reserve requirements: These were only changed once during the period (in 1996) and only by one percentage point to the current level of 8 percent and 9 percent for demand and, time and savings deposits respectively.

Table 10.7. Group Analysis of Ex Post Intermediation Margins and Net Profit in the Postliberalization Period

	Intermediation margin[a]			Adjusted intermediation margin[b]			Net profit ratio		
	1994	1996	1998	1994	1996	1998	1994	1996	1998
Group 1	2.58	4.89	6.45	3.97	7.29	8.33	−15.8	−1.52	−3.61
Group 2	5.27	6.31	6.41	5.74	6.86	6.62	−0.30	2.79	5.60
Group 3	4.58	6.19	9.66	5.09	6.33	10.91	0.00	0.41	2.69
Group 4	3.79	2.08	3.17	3.95	2.30	3.69	−0.22	−0.80	−1.21
Bankwide	3.84	4.88	5.75	4.79	5.88	6.49	−7.30	0.36	1.32

Notes: Intermediation margin (a) = Net interest income as a percentage of total assets.
Intermediation margin (b) = Net interest income as a percentage of (total assets less non-performing assets).
Net profit ratio = net income as percentage of total assets.
Net income = net interest income + noninterest income − overheads − loan-loss provisioning.
Source: Bank of Uganda, Research Department Records.

during the postliberalization period, 1994–98. This intermediation margin is high compared with levels estimated at 3.5 percent for the global banking system or 4.8 percent for Africa (Demirgúç-Kunt and Huizinga 1999). The sustained increase cannot be attributed exclusively to the reduction in nonperforming assets. It suggests that the Ugandan economy has yet to benefit fully from liberalization of the banking system.

A group-by-group analysis of the banking system portrays some interesting patterns in ex post intermediation margins and ex ante interest spreads (Figure 10.6). First, the intermediation margins have been on an upward trend across all banks with the prudent Group 3 banks recording the fastest increase and aggressive Group 4 banks suffering a decline in margins in 1996.

Second, a comparison of Tables 10.7 and 10.5 reveals that as ex ante interest rate spreads narrowed for Group 2 and 3 banks, the ex post intermediation margins were widening and their profits were also increasing. On the contrary, the aggressive Group 4 banks, which have throughout the period maintained high ex ante spreads, have barely improved on their ex post intermediation margin and as a group have experienced negative before tax profits. Similarly, the state-owned Group 1 banks, raised their interest rate spreads by lowering deposit rates and maintaining high lending rates, and the ex ante spreads rose (from 5.3 percent to a peak of 9.6 percent in 1996) as did their ex post margins banks but this was not sufficient to make up for the substantive loss in customers and market share, and they remained unprofitable for the period under review.

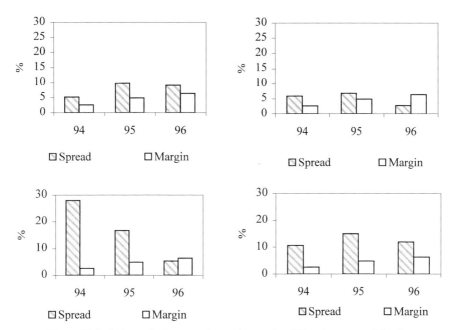

Figure 10.6. Intermediation margins and spreads: different groups of banks.

The factors underlying the profitability of Group 2 and 3 banks is worth reviewing. The excolonial Group 2 banks are much more efficient in liquidity and risk management. Moreover, in addition to being subjected to additional surveillance by their head offices abroad, they can also import management skills. Not surprisingly, it seems the interest rate adjustments (on both deposits and loans) were designed to ensure consistent net intermediation margins. Although the prudent Group 3 banks gradually increased deposit rates over the postliberalization era, their lending rates have been gradually reduced. This resulted in declining interest spreads over the postliberalization era. However, ex post intermediation margins have been increasing, despite the interest rate adjustment. This increase reflects both a halving of the rate of loan default and a substantive increase in their market share (gained at the expense of Group 1 and 2 banks) with a resulting spreading of costs.

Indeed the public sector banks, formerly publicly owned and commanding the biggest share of the market proved too big to fail in spite of their inefficiencies. While the solution has been to restructure and recapitalize these banks as explained previously, the implicit protection enjoyed by these banks, allowed inefficiencies to persist and promoted noncompetitive behavior. Indeed it could be argued that some banks (Groups 1 and 4) have kept interest rates and ex ante high just to remain afloat and cover their high costs, while the other banks (in Groups 2 and 3) have benefited from the atmosphere of relatively high lending rates – they have not reduced their lending rates as much as they could have and the resulting high margins have allowed them to earn profits which are very high by international standards.[13] Unlike a competitive market, prices (lending rates) are being determined not by the most efficient suppliers but are being driven by the needs of the most inefficient ones. Inefficiencies persist and the banks' customers are paying for them.[14]

4 SUBSIDIES THROUGH THE FINANCIAL SYSTEM

This final section provides some partial information as to the size and trends in quasifiscal subsidization of the public enterprises (SOEs) through the financial system. It represents a partial approach to the wider question of who gained and who lost from the process of financial sector liberalization in Uganda.

Table 10.8 provides annual snapshot estimates of direct and indirect subsidies provided to the state-owned enterprises sector over the period 1991–97. Total state subsidies to the SOE sector averaged Ush 154 billion per year at 1993 prices, (that is about $180 million at the 1993 exchange rate). The rest was accounted for by indirect subsidies. The figures for 1995 and 1996 suggest that the overall level of subsidies remained largely unchanged at the 1993 level before declining significantly in 1997 to Ush 123 billion (estimated at current prices).

The largest amount of subsidies in the 1991–93 period was related to the terms on which SOEs borrowed funds from the banking system or the Central Bank. There have been two broad types of such subsidies. The first involves the price at which funds have been made available. Thus SOEs have benefited from subsidized, below market, interest rates on loans made available to them through the treasury, the state-owned commercial banks, or development banks. Financial institutions have also benefited from funds made available to them at low or zero rates. For example, UCB, the

---

[13] Net profits as a percentage of total assets for Group 2 and Group 3 banks were 5.6 and 2.7 percent respectively in 1998. This compares with a figure of 0.8 percent for the global banking system, and 1.5 percent for Africa (Demirguc-Kunt and Huizinga 1999).

[14] Data for nonperfoming assets (NPAs) and bank profitability are hard to interpret in an environment of poor accounting, auditing, and a weak regulatory authority, as banks will tend to withhold information, improperly classify loans and as a result, make inappropriate provisions. Hence, the NPAs are understated and earnings overstated. Reduced profitability may simply reflect the imposition of stricter loan classification and provisioning requirements. Furthermore, in the case of Group 1, a substantial portfolio of NPAs of UCB were removed from its books and replaced with government bonds which have greatly increased its earning capacity.

Table 10.8. Subsidy Estimates for the Public Enterprise Sector, 1991–97

Ush billions	SOE sector 1991–93	Sample 1995	Sample 1996	Sample 1997	SOE sector 1996	SOE sector 1997
Direct subsidies	15.2	48.1	44.0	15.2	52.3	17.5
Equity support	55.1	47.3	12.4	0.0	14.8	0.0
Financing terms	27.3	55.9	49.0	49.2	58.4	56.6
Fiscal terms	43.0	15.9	8.6	7.5	8.9	7.7
Other	14.0	7.4	20.3	27.0	20.3	27.0
Total	154.6	174.6	146.6	111.9	169.3	123.9

preferred bank for government transactions, had access to large deposits from the state and other SOEs on which it was not obliged to pay interest. Similarly, UCB and other state-owned development banks benefited from donor loans provided to them at highly concessional terms with the government bearing the exchange risk and providing guarantees at zero cost.

The second source of quasirents derived by SOEs from borrowed funds involved arrears on loan payments. In the past, SOEs benefited extensively by going into arrears on loan repayments without facing interest or late payment charges on these arrears. In many cases the government took over debt servicing and converted the debt into equity. In the case of financial institutions, a common practice involved the government taking over bad loans these institutions had made even though no government guarantees were involved and the bad loans had been fully provisioned for in their accounts.

As shown in Table 10.8, indirect equity support, including the writeoff of bad loans which were already provided for, or conversion of debt to equity, amounted in the 1991–93 period to an annual average of Ush 55 billion. This was equivalent to 35 percent of total estimated subsidies to the SOE sector. At the same time the benefits from loans provided on soft terms by the government were estimated at Ush 27 billion. These two categories together accounted for 52 percent of total subsidies, or in value terms approximately $90 million.

The size of the estimated subsidies in the above sample of SOEs gives an indication of the quasirents that the SOE sector stood to lose in 1991–93 as a result of financial sector liberalization. A large part of these quasirents derived from soft terms on which loans were provided and government intervention to rescue firms and banks in financial difficulty by writing off bad loans or by converting debt to equity.

A comparison of the subsidies in the 1991–93 period with the estimates made for the postliberalization period – the years 1995 through 1997 – raises the possibility of an underlying resistance by those who lost out in the process of liberalization. The size of subsidies to SOEs given by the state in the form of debt to equity conversion of loans or unloading of nonperforming assets (in the case of financial institutions) has declined steadily. However subsidies in the form of loans provided on soft terms have increased substantially from Ush 27 billion in the 1991–93 period to Ush 71 billion in 1997. One possible reason for this development may be that some of the mechanisms for providing quasirents, and which also distort the market allocation process, may still be in place some seven years after the government initiated the liberalization of the financial sector. However one cannot exclude the possibility that the rise in (real) interest rates following deregulation may well have badly hit those SOEs which were not prepared for the increases and have been slow to adjust. They have built up arrears which they are still struggling to remove.

5 CONCLUDING REMARKS

In the wake of financial sector liberalization and the complementary reform measures introduced by the government of Uganda, there has been a major transformation in the structure and performance of the financial system and a significant strengthening of confidence in domestic financial instruments.

While monetary depth remains low by African and developing country standards, it has almost doubled, whether measured by the ratio of money supply (M2) or of bank deposits to GDP. The share of time and savings deposits in total deposits has jumped from 17 percent to almost 50 percent. Available econometric is also supportive of the view that financial sector liberalization has contributed to macroeconomic stability and the high rate of economic growth by increasing financial savings and monetary depth, enhancing financial discipline, and shifting the responsibility for crop financing from the government to the commercial banks.

At the sector level, there has been a significant decline in the incidence of nonperforming assets. Associated with this improvement in the culture of honoring financial contracts, there has been a substantial reduction in the role of the state in allocating and intermediating financial savings and in its equity holding in commercial banks. The competitive environment has also improved – while UCB remains a major player, the level of concentration in the banking system has fallen substantially, a large number of new private banks has entered the market, and there has been a leveling of the playing field between state-owned and private-sector banks. Standards of bank supervision and transparency in the banking system have improved substantially, as has the confidence of the authorities to intervene and expeditiously address the incidence of insolvent or illiquid banks.

At the same time liberalization has imposed certain costs on the economy. First of all the initial conditions and the sequencing of the reforms have resulted in a costly adjustment process. The financial sector was liberalized before prudential supervision and regulations had been adequately strengthened. As a consequence, unsound banks were allowed to enter the financial system and their shortcomings were not expeditiously addressed. Their presence increased the cost of intermediation and led eventually to costly bailouts by the central bank.

Second, the presence of asymmetric information and the absence of institutions (adequate accounting standards, credit information agencies, etc.) which could help alleviate this problem constrained effective competition, resulting in higher margins and interest rates with attendant economic costs (including the adverse impact on growth). Interest rates, in this environment, appeared to be determined not by the costs facing the most efficient supplier but instead by the most inefficient ones, which had not exited. An environment with greater information flows, stronger enforcement of regulations, better trained bankers and regulators, and healthier banks to start with, would have provided better initial conditions for liberalizing interest rates.

The greater emphasis being placed since 1995 on institutional development, including enhancing BOU's capacity to supervise and regulate banks and ensuring greater transparency about the health of the banking sector, seems therefore appropriate. During this phase a lot of resources have been devoted to training bankers in both the public and private sectors to operate more effectively in a liberalized environment.

There is some evidence that, in the postliberalization period, microenterprises and farmers in small rural communities found it more difficult to access services provided by the formal financial system. The gap in the provision of financial services is being filled increasingly by the informal sector.

Finally, liberalization in Uganda has involved the transfer of quasirents from the government (including SOEs) and well-heeled borrowers (who have often been able to avoid repayment) to depositors and banks. This transfer has been facilitated by the availability of foreign aid to the government to cover its budget deficit.

* * *

Among the policy implications of the Ugandan experience the following are worth highlighting:

- As illustrated by the successful fiscal sterilization of the 1994–95 coffee boom, skillful coordination of monetary and fiscal policy can help retain macrostability even in the face of financial structure weaknesses in a liberalizing economy.
- There is a tradeoff between the gains from early liberalization (which can improve resource allocation and facilitate macrostabilization) and the advantages of waiting for effective regulatory framework and macrostability to be in place to avoid risks of excessive credit expansion, imprudent behavior, and associated bank distress.
- To reduce the costs of liberalization, more attention needs to be paid to improve the flow of information in the financial market, the exit of distressed banks, and to avoid overbanking by ensuring quality at entry (perhaps through higher capital requirements).

There will be resistance from those who may be adversely affected by the process. Thus, while they must remain publicly accountable, regulators need to be given sufficient powers through modern legislation.

APPENDIX: INTEREST RATES AND MARKET SHARES – COMPARATIVE DATA FROM PAKISTAN

Confirmation of some of the broad trends identified in Uganda comes from the experience of another liberalizing low-income country: Pakistan. Pakistan's reforms came in two stages. The first stage, in 1990–91, included privatization of state-owned banks (in effect reversing the 1974 nationalizations), free entry of private banks, auctioning of public debt, and the replacement of credit ceilings with an open market approach to liquidity management. The structure of interest rates was rationalized, with banks being allowed to set rates within a range determined by the central bank. Complete liberalization, including removal of a cap on interest rates, took place in 1995, at the start of the second stage of reforms.

As a result of privatization and more liberalized entry, the number of banks increased from thirty-six in 1990 to forty-six in 1998, and the market of state-owned banks fell below 50 percent. As well as the business captured by newly established private banks, foreign banks almost doubled their market share in ten years to about 20 percent (Table 10.9).

Much as in postliberalization Uganda, average deposit interest rates changed little, while average lending rates increased substantially. Within a decade, the ex ante spread had jumped fivefold (Table 10.10). Rationalization of the structure of interest rates also had a significant positive impact on intermediation margins (which jumped to over 4 percent for foreign banks). The systemwide average intermediation margin increased from 2.2 percent in 1986 to 2.8 percent in 1992–94 (and to about 4 percent in 1996–97). The data for 1998 suggests that systemwide margins have

Table 10.9. Changing Market Shares in Pakistan Banking

	June 86–June 88		June 96–June 98	
	by deposits	by assets	by deposits	by assets
Nationalized banks	87.7	76.0	46.9	46.0
Privatized banks	0.0	0.0	18.9	15.4
Private banks	0.0	0.0	12.6	10.8
Specialized banks	0.7	11.8	1.0	7.6
Foreign banks	11.6	12.3	20.5	20.2

Source: State Bank of Pakistan; Aleem and Janjua 2000.

Table 10.10. Pakistan: Bank Interest Rate Spreads and Intermediation Margins

	1986–88	1992–94	1998
Quoted rates[a]			
Average deposit rate	9.13	9.67	
Average lending rate	10.87	14.85	
Spread	1.74	5.18	
Intermediation margins			
Nationalized banks	2.09	2.48	2.15
Privatized banks	2.63	2.58	2.89
New private banks		2.78	2.35
Foreign banks	3.39	4.08	2.54
Systemwide	2.20	2.78	2.65

[a] Weighted average of June figures.
Source: State Bank of Pakistan; Aleem and Janjua 2000.

remained largely unchanged following the initial increase but the data needs careful interpretation given other reforms that were introduced after 1995 including the provisioning policy on loans.

REFERENCES

Aleem, I. 1990. "Imperfect Information, Screening and the Costs of Informal Lending: A Study of a Rural Credit Market in Pakistan." *World Bank Economic Review* 4(3):329–49.
Aleem, I. and A. Janjua. 2000. "Interest Rates and Market Shares in Pakistan Banking." World Bank. *Mimeo.*
Aryeetey, E. and M. Nissanke. 1998. *Financial Integration and Development: Liberalization and Reform in Sub-Saharan Africa*. London and New York: Routledge.

Demirgüç-Kunt, A. and H. Huizinga. 1999. "Determination of Commercial Bank Interest Margins and Profitability: Some International Evidence." *World Bank Economic Review* 13(2):379–408.

Khan, S.R. and S. Aftab. 1994. "Impact of Financial Reforms on Pakistan's Economy." *Pakistan Journal of Applied Economics* 10:1–2.

Kasekende, L. and M. Atingi-Ego. 1999. "Impact of Liberalization on Key Markets in Sub-Saharan Africa: The Case of Uganda." *Journal of International Development* 11(3):411–36.

Kasekende, L. and M. Malik. 1996. "The Financial Systems, Savings and Investment in Uganda." Paper presented at the Ad hoc Expert Group Meeting of UNECA and published in ECA Monograph Series on African Issues and Policies.

Musinguzi, P. with M.B. Obwona and J.D. Stryker. 2000. "Monetary and Exchange Rate Policy in Uganda," *Eager Discussion Paper* 23.

Shaw E.S. 1973. *Financial Deepening in Economic Development*. Oxford: Oxford University Press.

Index